Diaspora and Belief

Creative Multiverse: New Explorations in Transformative Learning and Research

There is an epochal challenge of learning from multiple experiments in self and social transformations now. *Creative Multiverse* seeks to explore and present different pathways of transformations in societies and histories around the world. It builds upon engagements in learning in different disciplines of life and academy and seeks to create a transdisciplinary space of research, dialogues and transformations.

A Series from Shipra Publications, Delhi
Email: info@shiprapublications.com

Editor: Ananta Kumar Giri,
Madras Institute of Development Studies, Chennai, India.
Email: aumkrishna@yahoo.com; Website: www.mids.ac.in/ananta.htm

Diaspora and Belief

Globalisation, Religion and Identity in Postcolonial Asia

John Clammer

SHIPRA

ISBN : 978-81-7541-435-8

First Published in India in 2009

Diaspora and Belief: Globalisation, Religion and Identity in Postcolonial Asia

Published by:
SHIPRA PUBLICATIONS
115-A, Vikas Marg, Shakarpur, Delhi-110092, INDIA
Phone: 91-11-65277210, 22500954 Fax: 91-11-22458662
E-mail: info@shiprapublications.com
www.shiprapublications.com

Foreword

Towards Rainbows of Identities and Planetary Realizations

My heart leaps up when I behold
A Rainbow in the sky;
So was it when my life began
So is it now I am a man
So be it when I grow old
Or let me die!

The child is the father of Man;
And I could wish my days to be
Bound each to each by natural piety.

—William Wordsworth

Indeed, there are times when the work of contemporary sociologists is characterized by such depth and seriousness that one is inclined to think that they are the true inheritors of the ancient prophetic traditions working in the world today.

—David Smith (2007), *Moving Towards Emmaus: Hope in a Time of Uncertainty*, p. 83.

We also need to consider how a deliberate engagement with the twentieth century's histories of suffering might furnish resources for the peaceful accommodation of otherness in relation to fundamental commonalty. In particular, we need to ask how an increased familiarity with the blood stained working of racism [..] might be made to yield lessons that could be applied more generally, in the demanding contemporary settlings of multicultural social relations. This possibly should not imply the exaltation of victimage or the world-historic ranking of injustices that always seem to remain the unique property of their victims. Instead of these easy choices, I will suggest that multi-cultural ethics and politics could be premised upon an agonistic, planetary humanism capable of understanding the universality of our elementary vulnerability to the wrongs we visit upon each other.

—Paul Gilroy (2004), *After Empire: Melancholia or Convivial Culture*?, pp. 3-4.

> The historian Arnold Toynbee goes to remark that for a true and lasting peace, a religious revolution is an indispensable condition. By religion he means the overcoming of self-centredness, in the life of individuals as well as of communities. Martin Buber has in one of his writings appealed to us to meet the world with the fullness of our being and in this way only will we meet God. The expressions denote that the familiar meanings man has traditionally given to God and religion are fast changing. Religions with the entire world of their paraphernalia are gradually receding giving place to a new spiritual consciousness which we can describe as religious, but which may not be exclusively Hindu, Buddhistic or Christian. Temples, churches, synagogues and mosques are receding making room for a spiritual living as if God were right up here before us. [..] Half-Gods have to recede if God is to be very much visible here. Paul Tillich, the theologian, perhaps suggests something like that when he talks of the God above God.
>
> As our consciousness grows and expands, our concept of God has also to grow and expand. We are soon approaching an encounter where everybody's heritage will become also everyone else's heritage.
>
> —Chitta Ranjan Das (2008),
> "*Jesus Christ: White, Black or Yellow*?"

Creative Multiverse seeks to explore new paths of self-transformation and collective realizations and the present book, *Diaspora and Belief: Globalization, Religion and Identity in Postcolonial Asia*, by John Clammer, a deep and heart-touching scholar of our times, is a significant contribution to our contemporary strivings in transformative learning and research. Our first book in the series, *Kristen Kold: A Revolutionary in Education and Pioneer of the Danish Folk High School Movement* by Chitta Ranjan Das had presented us glimpses of creative multiverse of education, human development and social transformation in Europe, particularly in Denmark. In the present book, John Clammer presents us insightful narratives and deep analyses of transformation in religion, identity, postcoloniality and globality in Asia, particularly Japan and South East Asia. Born in England to parents who met in a camp in Southern England having been displaced from Vienna because of Nazism, Clammer had studied at Oxford and has lived and worked in East Asia and Japan for the last three decades. Clammer has striven to be a friend of the world with personal friendship with seekers, scholars and social movements across the globe—in India, Europe, and Latin America.

In *Diaspora and Belief* Clammer raises profound questions about identity and universality and presents us new landscapes of learning and socio-cultural reflections. It questions available understanding of globalization as the author writes: "The abstract globalization as seen from Wall Street looks a little different seen from a Calcutta slum." For Clammer, identity in any simple sense is "shattered by the cultural impact of globalization." But even before the present intensification of cultural globalization, identities were always multidimensional and it is to a creative nuturance of the multidimensionality of our identities that Clammer urges us to move forward.

Clammer urges us to rethink not only identity but also universality realizing both as rainbows and going beyond an abstract, one-dimensional conceptualization and categorical fixation. Religion plays an important role in these unfolding rainbows, particularly in the Asian context. Clammer laments lack of profound engagement with religion in secularized Euro-American sociology and cultural studies and in the works of their uncritical followers in Asia. For Clammer, "The possibility that the social semiotics of many Asian societies could still be rooted not in 'information' but in religion, is something entirely beyond the conception of myopic Western postmodernists." Furthermore, "The shying away on the part of both postcolonial theorists and cultural studies specialists in and of Asia from the subject of religion is very revealing here, not only for its suppression of what is a vital element of life in many Asian societies, but because taking religion seriously would expose the really alternative cosmologies upon which differing civilizations have built themselves. A Buddhist epistemology is a much greater challenge to the philosophical assumptions of the West than any amount of political posturing by Asian Marxists who in reality share a Western ideology." *Diaspora and Belief* presents us empirically rich and theoretically nuanced understanding the work of religion, especially new religious movements such as Soka Gakkai from Japan, and postcolonial reconstruction of religion in countries such as Singapore and Thailand. Describing the work of Thai social critic and religious reformer Sulak Sivaraksa Clammer tells us how Sivaraksha helps us realize that transindividuality is an important part of self and society. Western sociology is locked in a cult of individuality and in order to understand new ways of self-conceptualization and social imagination we need to open up our cultural and religious presuppositions and be engaged in cross-cultural, transcultural and planetary conversations. Inviting us to be engaged simultaneously with dialogues with thinkers such as Louis Dumont and Sulak Sivaraksa together Clammer writes: "In much the same way that Louis Dumont has argued that Western individualism has its roots in Christianity and that the consequences of this individualism are profound for the arrangement of society and assumptions about how relationships within it work, so Sulak is arguing for a 'trans-individualism' that arises from Buddhist roots, and which has profound implications for the ordering of society."

Diaspora and Belief not only presents us glimpse of transindividuality but also transculturality. Both these are part of Clammer's continued inspiring strivings to go beyond closures of many kinds—both nativistic as well as universalistic. Clammer pleads for a new planetary sociology and anthropology involving mutual learning rather than being a prisoner of facile dualism such as East and West. He also asks probing questions in the field of comparative sociology. Taking the case of Japan, Clammer writes: "For comparative analysis then Japan poses a number of interesting questions: can a society be modern but non-Western? How are rights and duties rooted in a Buddhist / Shinto religious environment rather than a Judeo-Christian one? What forms might cultural citizenship take in a society in which identity has always been framed in cultural as much as political terms? Can one be cosmopolitan in a society with a strong sense of its own homogeneity?"

Clammer helps us not only to reconstitute identity and universality but also postcoloniality moving beyond both anti-colonial rejection and colonialist domination and urging us to realize what he calls historical polycentrism. In his insightful essay in the volume, "After Orientalism: Postcolonialism, Culture and Globalization," Clammer tells us how Europeans are struggling to move beyond "Eurocentrism of the superior variety in both its practical manifestations (e.g. racialism) and in academic discourse (vestigial Orientalism) just as Asians are hopefully moving beyond [..] 'counter-othering' and vacuous claims about "Asian values' to alternative and more open relations with the West and with more realistic and less triumphalistic or subordinated searches for viable new identities." In such emergent moves we can find glimpses of a post-colonial cosmopolis.

Diaspora and Belief also embodies Clammer's passionate concerns such as exploring ways out of anthropocentrism which is part of his inspiring multi-dimensional struggle to go beyond dualism of various kinds, Eurocentrism and nation-state centered rationality. These concerns overflow into Clammer's recent work on deep sociology; art, spirituality and human development; and ecological self as a companion of a new rooted cosmopolitanism. Clammer's work inspires us to realize that we are not only members of the human family but also children of Mother Earth and at the contemporary juncture our fixed identities need to be part of multidimensional strivings and struggles of planetary realizations. Clammer himself continues to strive towards creating and nurturing new spaces of cross-cultural communication and planetary realizations such as nurturing an innovative dialogical project called Meeting Rivers at Fireflies Asrham, Bangalore, and we are grateful to him for this significant contribution of him to our unfolding *Creative Multiverse* series. We hope that this gift of Clammer would add new momentum to our creativity and inspire all of us to renew our commitment towards transformative learning and research and making this fragile of ours a rainbow of creative identity formation and planetary realizations.

Guru Divas — **Ananta Kumar Giri**
September 5, 2008 — Madras Institute of Development Studies
Chennai

Acknowledgements

As with all books, many influences have gone into the formulation of ideas presented here. I would especially like to acknowledge the input of colleagues who commented on earlier versions of many of the chapters when they were first presented as seminar papers or lectures at the University of East Anglia, the University of Birmingham, Oxford University and at the Korean UNESCO Centre. An earlier version of chapter four appeared in P.W. Preston and J. Gilson (eds.) The European Union and East Asia (Edward Elgar 2001), and of chapter six in Eyal Ben-Ari and John Clammer (eds.) Japan in Singapore: Cultural Occurances and Cultural Flows (Richmond: Curzon Press 2000). My special thanks go to Ho Swee Lin whose meticulous editing turned a messy manuscript into a presentable book and whose cheerful efficiency and friendship made the stages of final preparation a pleasure.

Contents

Part One
Religion and Globalisation in Postcolonial Asia: Globalisation, Secularisation and Identity

Part Two
Japan and the Globalisation of Religion in Southeast Asia

Part Three
Postcolonial Reconstruction of Religion

Part Four
Religion and Popular Culture

Part One

Religion and Globalisation in Postcolonial Asia: Globalisation, Secularisation and Identity

1

The Culture(s) of Globalisation

Religion, Identity and Citizenship

One of the major cultural effects of globalisation has been to stimulate intense debates about identity, both on the part of individuals and communities experiencing the massive social and cultural shifts that are accompanying and signalling the new economic and political configurations of international society, and on the part of scholars intent on mapping, describing and theorising the new understandings of self, society and belonging—the new subjectivities and concepts of community—that inevitably mirror social transformations.

The body of work that exists that attempts to chart the nature of globalisation is now immense, but yet is marked by silences and absences that render it incomplete as a general theory of contemporary social transformations. Amongst these spaces of absence are three significant ones. First, that much of the literature on globalisation is written from or takes as its primary evidence the experience of Western and in particular the most developed North Atlantic societies. While substantial comment has come from Latin America both from older forms of what was then called dependency theory and latterly from the pens of such contemporary commentators as Enrique Dussel (e.g. Dussel 1996), much less (known at least to the wider world) has emerged from Africa or Asia. One aim of this book is to redress this imbalance by presenting perspectives from Asia, a region that has experienced the effects of globalisation, which has itself generated many of those effects itself through the power of regional economies (Japan, as the world's second biggest economy preminently, but with China, Taiwan and South Korea not so far behind) and through culture (Hong Kong and "Bollywood" film, Japanese popular culture in the form of comics and animated movies and so on). Furthermore, Asia has produced its own social theories of social transformation, including indigenous theories of modernity, globalisation and postmodernity (Clammer 2001c; Dirlik and Zhang 2000), and, very significantly, postcolonial theory. Although the latter has not billed itself as a theory of globalisation, in effect it is via its critiques of imperialism and neo-colonialism, and like Japanese theories of alternative modernities, its opposition to colonialism is not based only on the economic consequences of dependency, but very much on its cultural consequences. Asian approaches to globalisation and postcolonial theory however are rarely brought together, something that in this book we will endeavour to do.

Second amongst the silences of globalisation theory has been serious consideration of culture. For although globalisation may rightly be understood as a process driven largely by economic forces and in particular the massive impact of the universalisation of neo-liberal capitalist practices, at the local level in particular it penetrates the life-worlds of individuals and communities through cultural mechanisms including consumption practices, the media, converging expectations about the correct nature of "modern" institutions, legal systems and education, center-periphery relationships in publishing and the recognition of scientific and literary achievements, and the erosion of local languages (Hamm and Smandych 2005). On the occasions on which scholarly debate has attempted to confront the issue directly (e.g. Tomlinson 2000), the discussion proceeds at a highly theoretical level as essentially an internal debate amongst Western sociologists with virtually no examples of actual culture or cultural practices, and with a strong Eurocentrism pervading the implied relationship between globalisation and culture.

The third great silence is religion. Whereas classical sociological studies of secularisation (e.g. Martin 1978) seen as intimately tied up with modernisation and the broader process of modernity, with a few notable exceptions (e.g. Beyer 1997; Marfleet 1998; Camilleri and Muzaffar 1998) religion has not been explored in relation to globalisation in any great detail. This is surprising in view of contemporary interest in "fundamentalisms" and the centrality that religion has been given in such formulations as the "clash of civilisations" hypothesis. It is even more surprising when a very strong case can be made that it is impossible to understand Asian societies without reference to the strong and continuing religious element in their socio-cultural make-up (Ghosh and Muecke 2004; Hamilton 2004). This being so, it is necessary to re-examine the role of religion in defining identity in Asia, and in reincorporating this element into discussions of the relationship between culture and globalisation (and a range of other issues including development) when Asian (and undoubtedly African and Latin American) societies are the subject of debate. The exclusion of religion from cultural studies, whether or not it is valid in the West (itself a doubtful proposition), has seriously negative effects on the attempt to understand Asian cultures and their relationship to world transforming processes. A major objective of this book is to address this absence and to redress it, not mainly through a purely theoretical discussion, but through the medium of case studies and the voices of exemplary individuals that actually provide evidence of the nature of culture in actual modernising and globalising Asian societies—a necessary move to redress the lack of substantial cultural reference even in literature that does nominally discuss culture in relationship to either or both of globalisation or development (for example, Schech and Haggis 2000).

The result is a multiple absence—the absence of the religious dimension of culture from globalisation theory, from cultural theory and from postcolonial theory. In the context of Asia in particular, this is a glaring absence, since not only has religion historically pervaded and shaped, or even constituted, Asian cultures, but within almost any culture conceptions of personhood and the self, of social hierarchy, of the balance between individualism and collectivism, of the body, gender roles, nature, diet cultural memory and political order are all fundamentally shaped by the religious heritage and environment (for example on nature, see Callicott and Ames 1989; Bruun and Lalland 1995). In the emerging global order, or disorder, notions of identity at both the personal and collective levels and hence the associated concepts of citizenship available to people caught between the competing demands of authoritarianism/militarism and democratisation, the expectations of their traditional culture and social mores and the new social configurations imposed by the economic restructurings of neo-liberal capitalism and consumerism, are frequently shaped by their historical religious allegiances or by adherence to new religions that offer more coherent senses of meaning under the chaotic conditions of what Zygmunt Bauman has called "liquid modernity" (Bauman 2000).

The contribution of this book is to weave together two levels of complex debate—the potentially fruitful dialogue between globalisation theory, cultural theory and postcolonial theory at one level, and the relationship between religion, individual and collective identities and conceptions of citizenship at the other. It will suggest that in Southeast and East Asia the formulation of the relationship between these elements is rather different from that of European and North American experience and that the theoretical tools employed to discuss these dimensions, especially cultural studies and globalisation theory, still both suffer from a strong Eurocentric bias.

From this two levels of analysis emerge. On the one hand, social theory is deepened both by a comparative perspective and by the reincorporation of the dimensions of meaning systems and values excluded from it by the so-called postmodern turn (Fekete 1987), and on the other East and Southeast Asian social experience is brought much more fully into mainstream sociology. The current division, especially in North America, between area specialists and theoreticians is unnecessary and counterproductive to sound sociological and anthropological understanding. This book challenges that distinction by showing how it is precisely through their integration that social science progresses and that far better tools for addressing the actual social problems of much if not most of humankind are advanced. For Asian social experience addresses squarely many of the central concerns of sociology—class and other forms of social inequality, social movements, identity politics, to name but a few. And in Asia it turns out that most of these issues are directly related to religion—many social movements in the region taking the form of new religious movements or revivalism amongst older ones for example, and identity politics taking not the form of the "multiculturalism" debates prevalent in North America, but debate between religious communities or ethno-religious ones about their position within national polities—the "plural societies" of Malaysia or Singapore for example, ethnic separatism in the borderlands of Myanmar, Muslim-Buddhist conflict in southern Thailand or Muslim-Christian conflict in eastern Indonesia.

Religion and the Narratives of Identity

Sociologically speaking, religion has acted in a number of conflicting ways as a marker of identity—as a conservative force legitimating Rightist and nationalist visions of a purist order (as in India with the role of Hindu fundamentalism and its political expressions), as an ideological force for radical social transformations (Liberation Theology in the Philippines, and some forms of "Engaged" or activist Buddhism in Thailand and Sri Lanka), or as a Statist tool of national identity construction (Islam in Malaysia and Indonesia). This variety of faces gives the lie to attempts to reduce religion to one set of "functions." The failure to grasp this has led to either shallow theories of secularisation on the one hand, assuming the general diminution of some one essentialist category named "religion", or on the other the tendency to see religious conservatism with its many tradition-preserving and continuity-creating aspects, as "fundamentalism."

What is certain, whichever form of religion is evoked, is that throughout Asia, with the exception of relentlessly atheistic North Korea, religion continues to function as a primary narrative of identity creation. This is why religion appears both as a celebration of or at least accommodation to modernity, as a counter-narrative to modernity, or, through its evocations of a spiritualised form of utopianism, radically different forms of modernity in which the enchantment of the world is enhanced rather than lost and in which mysteries are not replaced by problems and in which the dominance of instrumental rationality is kept at bay by the continual placing of existential questions (and the religious answers to them) at the heart of culture. For this reason the perception of the abandonment of religion's transcendental role in favour of the mirroring of the authoritarian and patriarchal characteristics of many Asian polities, ensures that the critique of religion becomes part of the critique of culture.

Cultural memory itself throughout much of Asia is to a great extent embodied in religion as are the sources of notions of time, space, cycles of events and the deep grammar of cultural myths—the organising principles around which cultures are framed and the well from which cultural imagination bubbles up. As some culturally oriented postcolonial theorists have demonstrated, even as language, and the literatures and myths expressed in particular languages, code the ethos of particular communities (Tripathy 2005) so too religion. Just as the destruction of local languages destroys the organic web of indigenous life, so too does the imposition of alien religions, which is why they are so fiercely resisted and still prove to be the site of conflict in communities in which contending religions have existed side by side for generations as has happened so recently in eastern Indonesia and in southern Thailand. For religion is not only a system of beliefs, but is fundamentally linked to cultural practices, strategies and ontologies and deeply implicated in cultural understandings of suffering, disappointment and distress, the relationship between the natural world and that of humans, the structuring and expression of emotions and the cultural understanding of embodiment. Social experience is embodied—felt and experienced not just cogitated. All religions reflect, create and structure states of being-in-the body and generate somatic regimes and notions of harmony or disharmony with nature, landscape, climate and other living creatures that collectively comprise the biosphere. Hence notions of self and of the body are intertwined. While Arthur Kleinman argues that "In the fragmented, pluralistic modern world, anxiety is increasingly free floating and requires personal processes of creating idiosyncratic meaning to supplement the shared moral and religious significance that guided our ancestors on how to suffer" (Kleinman 1988), this remains even today only partially true of Asia where it is precisely religiously based social movements that are attempting to create a politics of meaning against the alienating tendencies of the modernity and globalisation that encroach on the lives of ordinary people throughout the region. It has to be said that much postmodern cultural and globalisation theory is very classist, reflecting not only the class position of its authors as well-heeled academics, but which also frequently fails to reflect the actual life experiences of those living in rural or urban poverty, in the teeming postcolonial cities of Asia and still very much within the boundaries of ancient cultural traditions.

From this perspective, religious practice and belief, rather than a form of false-consciousness, represents one of the most authentic quests for self-knowledge, knowledge of the Other and knowledge about the relationship between the self and the cosmos—an essential cultural resource available to and utilised by far more people in practice than any political ideologies or "scientific" explanations of the social and physical universes. But what is also important is the recognition that the modes of structuring the constant dialogue between the individual and the larger environment vary substantially from one religious tradition to another, and the inner logic of any culture cannot be grasped without elucidating this logic. Suffering in Buddhism for example (and perhaps in some traditional forms of Catholicism), while clearly a "negative" experience, is something to be accepted and transcended through that acceptance, rather than struggled against as a "problem" with a technical (medical, political, sociological, economic) "solution." If such a technical vocabulary can be applied at all, it is in the seeing of religions as in a sense spiritual technologies for the generation of meaning and values, the management of suffering and the creation of identity. As such, their "success" has much to do with their ability to successfully impart such techniques to their followers and thereby to create a shared cultural frame in or through which suffering, struggle and social and personal transformation ("salvation," "redemption") are to be achieved.

So while it is common, particularly from within the framework of any specific religion, to see its particular framework of explanation as the "truth", sociologically and anthropologically it is actually better to situate religion within the realm of the imagination. The creation of a common sense of belonging and shared histories is in a very real sense a myth-making activity, and any given religion is as much (to use Benedict Anderson's celebrated phrase) an "imagined community," as its secular political counterpart, the nation-state.

So while there can be little doubt that at the local level religions act as profound identity-creating agents, the situation is made complex by the fact that at the macro-level religions "migrate"—Buddhism from East Asia to the West, Japanese "New Religions" to the West, Southeast Asia, Africa and Latin America, Greek Orthodoxy from the Mediterranean to Australia, Charismatic forms of Christianity from the United States to Africa and South Korea and so forth, and at the micro-level individuals move—convert in other words—between these possibilities, many of which have become real options for them because of the globalisation of the religions themselves, or because of the migration of peoples. "White" Russians who fled to Japan from Shanghai, where they had previously fled from Russia to escape the Bolshevik revolution, introduced both Judaism and Russian Orthodox Christianity into their new country of sojourn, but today the local Jewish and Orthodox communities are not only highly multi-national, but also contain many converts from the Japanese host society. Under these circumstances of multi-layered globalisation, the relationship between religion and identity formation becomes complex and interesting. In the chapters that follow some facets of that interplay will be exposed to scrutiny, the different cases revealing some of the strategic identity forming or maintaining options available across much of contemporary Asia. Listening to religion means hearing some of these voices, and furthermore means listening in many cases to the voices of those marginalised by modernity, not only in some cases marginalised socially (by exclusion from the supposed benefits of "development"), but also epistemologically as their systems of indigenous knowledge have been eroded or threatened and by the erasure of the sacred in modernism itself.

The world in fact is an untidy place, and whereas many sociologists and historians of religion have attempted to characterise their subject matter as "systems,", actual religions are a tissue of textual and oral knowledges, of practices rather than strictly defendable beliefs, of the intersection between the canonical doctrines of a faith and its innumerable local variants, many of which derive from "folk" beliefs (such as practices of magic or sorcery) not officially part of the formal religion at all (e.g. Lambek 1993). So while at one level of analysis, most religions prove actually to be syncretic amalgams of many elements, some derived from the past, some from interaction with the local cultural environment, others the result of new flows of ideas and influences, at another they themselves clearly play a major sociological and cultural role. They constitute social movements of a kind rarely studied by social movements theorists, but which dovetail very closely with values based secular movements (for example Jasper 1997), constitute one of the major sources of ideas about alternative development, embody images of the future and comprise one of the main forms of contemporary utopian thinking and experiment and are important sources of conceptions of social justice and responses to ecological problems, gender issues and questions of human rights. In the context of globalisation and postcolonial societies, religions are on the one hand vital sources of cultural innovation, resistance, conservatism and the preservation or creation of what is thought to be tradition, and on the other are not only themselves examples of hybridity, but actively contribute to the cultural complexity of the contemporary world system by forming one of the main channels of cultural flow (together with such factors as media and popular culture) through which contemporary forms of cultural diffusion are taking place.

Religion and identity politics are consequently intimately related, or in some cases are the same thing, Western debates about multiculturalism, race, gender and sexualities by no means exhaust this field, although reviewing Western literature on the subject certainly gives the impression that religion is irrelevant (e.g. Jordan and Weedon 1995). In fact reviving and revisiting the sociology of Asian religions suggests a very different picture of the cultural role of religions, which prove to have a rich and complex relationship to modernity, globalisation, postcolonialism, social movements, identity politics and a host of other practical and philosophical issues. Thus not only have postcolonial scholars demonstrated the colonial construction of local religions and "traditions" (Balagangadhara 1994, Clammer 1975a), but within colonised societies religious resources, including those introduced by the colonisers themselves, have been used in unexpected ways, as forms of resistance and as the basis for anti-colonial re-readings of local cultures by the indigenes themselves (Sugirtharajah 1998).

Religion and the Cultural Politics of Identity in Globalising Asia

Drawing on the work of Max Weber, Abbas Manoochehri suggests that colonialism can be represented as a process of disenchantment:

> Applying such a method to the written discourse of postcolonialism, it can be said that it opens up a world of *double disenchantment.* Postcolonial discourse is a discourse emanating and exteriorizing *the pathos of double disenchantment*...... This is a *pathos* resulting from the colonial experience which in the first instance is similar to what Max Weber has referred to as disenchantment (*Entzauberung*) in the modern era as the sense of intellectual and cultural disassociation with what had formed and saturated the way of living and thinking in the pre-modern era. Weber argued that such intellectual and cultural reorientation has had an essential association with 'calculative rationality' (*Zweekrationnalitat*) through which the modern European's conception of the world has changed. Economy, politics and culture were recreated through the rationalization of life and the life-world. Capitalist economy, the bureaucratic system, and secular culture were the three fundamental dimensions of the new 'disenchanted world.'"
>
> (Manoochehri 2005: 291)

The notion of disenchantment remains a valuable one for understanding the tenacity of religion in Asia and elsewhere, and is a means of relating religious dynamics as much to globalisation with its own intensified rationalisation of the life-world, as it is with its precursor, colonialism. The ideas of Durkheim also prove to be of continuing relevance here: "Indeed, his discussion of the powerful emotional bonding between people and the resilience of the sacred in the modern world, would seem to have continuing relevance for the understanding of the contemporary resurgence of nationalism, new religious movements and even aspects of consumer culture" (Featherstone 1997: 133). Oddly though, even in Featherstone's own account of the relations between globalisation, culture and identity, any extended discussion of religion is absent, an absence that we are here attempting to fill, not by utilising some essentialist definitions of religion, but through the recognition of the very varied forms that relationships to the sacred can take, in some cases not directly expressing themselves as "religion" at all, but as ritual and performativity (Balaganangadhara 1994), forms of local knowledge pertaining to the environment (Posey 2002), as systems of magic, witchcraft or sorcery (Lambek 1993) or as theories of embodiment and emotion (Law 1995). When linked to issues of identity and globalisation it should be immediately apparent that a much subtler model is required than that so often used by sociologists of religion to connect religion and society.

In fact such a model—"religion" and "society"—understood as two entities that have to be somehow related to each other, is itself inadequate. As Martin Fuchs has argued, religion has as much to do with transcending society as with integrating oneself into it. As such it may not only be emancipatory in the sense of liberation theology's attempt to situate religion within society as a critique of that society, but also as an attempt to relativise the whole ontological status of society by posing an alternative conception of reality altogether. It is for this reason that the study of spiritually-based social movements is an essential for such "movements express the self-defining subjectivity—identification and distanciation, (self) reflexivity and (self) transformation—in an exemplary way and as *social* act. Social movements are the place of articulation of difference and of the search for latent possibilities" (Fuchs 2004). Implicit here is the fundamentally important notion of the non-identity of society with itself. The naturalism and positivism of much contemporary sociology and anthropology in fact reifies its subject—"society." The study of religion, rather than locating the often equally reified notion of religion within this problematic conception of society, actually radicalises the entire discourse of the social sciences by posing the question of its whole ontological status.

Religion is certainly tied to identity, but often to identities that are posited to lie outside of society in a transcendent realm from which the radical critique of culture takes place and thereby challenging an overly constructionist conception of society itself.

In discussing the relationships between religion, identity, globalisation and postcolonialism, these nuances must be taken centrally into account, for they constitute the very medium through which these interfaces and interpenetrations take place. Similarly, religious expressions intersect with directly sociological factors such as class. It is well known from Western sociology that religion itself is stratified along class lines with, in Christian contexts, denominational choice being strongly influenced by social background. This too is true in Asia, with the additional complications of ethnicity and caste. The revival of Buddhism in its Indian homeland is largely due for instance to the migration of low caste Hindus into a religion that does not recognise caste distinctions (and the same is true to some extent for Christianity in the Sub-Continent). Muslim communities are not only divided along Sunni/Shiite lines, but by ethnic variations too, with Indian Muslims, Malays, Arabs, Sufis and converts constituting rather different strata within what purports to be a highly egalitarian religion. Similarly politics strongly shapes religion every bit as much as it is shaped by it and state elites frequently utilise or manipulate religion as a "nation-building" tool as can be seen variously in Thailand, Malaysia, Indonesia, Sri Lanka, in pre-war State Shinto in Japan, and in many other instances across the region (Vohra and Dixit 1998). The politicisation of cultural differences, within and between societies, not the existence of those differences per se (often encoded as religion) is consequently the danger in identity formation social processes (Meyer 2001).

The notion of identity in Asia coalesces around such cultural differences—expressed as ethnicity, cultural nationalism, religion, memory, or more usually some conflation of these elements depending on political context (Kahn 1998). What is significant about these (hardly new) processes is their encapsulation in the contemporary world in an environment of postcolonialism and globalisation. This has not only had the effect of creating new religions, many of them international in scope (Hexham and Poewe 1997), and encouraging new forms of expressive and performative identity construction in which older concepts of liminality, rites of passage, pilgrimage and communitarianism are reinvented and reshaped, often again in the context of new religions or New Age movements (Hetherington 1998), but also of reconfiguring the relationships between religion and identity in a pluralistic and globalising situation.

This is especially true when viewed from within Asia. Western theories of postmodernity for example neglect the extent to which in much of Asia the struggle is both for and with modernity. The religious trajectories of Asia have been very different from those of the West, not only for reasons of theological difference (if such a word can be used at all in relation to Buddhism for instance), but equally because imposed on what might have otherwise been their indigenous histories and development have been colonialism, migrations of peoples (Chinese and Indians to Southeast Asia for example), inter-Asian religious and cultural flows (the penetration of first Hinduism and later Islam into the southern zone of Southeast Asia, and of Buddhism from its Indian birthplace south to Sri Lanka, onwards to the northern zone of Southeast Asia and as far east as China, Japan, Korea and Mongolia. The latter day re-export of Asian religions to the West, the dialogue that this has created with the local cultures in those places to which they have spread (e.g. Yoo 1999), and the feed back effects to the places or origin have generated new patterns of flows, new cultural hybridities, and with them new possibilities for identity construction. The argument of some postmodernists for example is that culture has become less organised, less authoritative and more deregulated or unpoliced (Heelas 1998), creating more possibilities for individualism, freedom of religious choice and cultural identity in the past two decades or so. While there is some evidence for this, these new possibilities are also in fact delimited by other kinds of boundaries—the difficulties for a Malaysian or Singapore Malay to leave Islam, a Japanese to embrace Islam, a Sunni to become a Shiite or a Jew to become a Christian. Other boundaries are easier to cross—some Japanese do convert to Judaism, not a few Chinese in Southeast Asia to Islam and many people find a new socio-religious identity in a new religion.

Citizenship—the formal membership of a polity and with the rights and duties that accompany such membership—is frequently linked to debates about the necessity of adherence to a particular religion—as in Thailand, Malaysia or Indonesia—and the problems that secularisation raises in such contexts where the difficulty of detaching purely civil citizenship from a religious identity can be acute (Hefner 1998). This is especially so in the context of debates about "postmodern" society where claims are made that the notion of citizenship is dead because it is predicated on the existence of the autonomous individual, a species that has allegedly been "dissolved" in the commodified regime of signs that has supposedly replaced "society" which is now only the play of simulcra (Wexler 1990). The assumption that the world is now post-industrial or based on an economy of informationalism, is in fact now a "society of signs" is not only to extend a (false) model of reality from a tiny privileged sector of the West to Asia and elsewhere, but equally to assume that all signs are equal. The possibility that the social semiotics of many Asian societies could still be rooted not in "information" but in religion, is something entirely beyond the conception of myopic Western postmodernists. In fact as Wexler for example recognises, the real question is "What is the path from such a semiotic society towards a new model of citizenship that takes account of class psychology and identity work?"—the situation in which social and economic differences still deeply exist and in which the "problem" of identity is not solved by its being "dissolved" in the free play of signs—and suggests that "The simplest solution, but one that underestimates…the tenacity of antagonistic class difference, proposes the restoration of collective memory as part of a project of collective emancipation. Narration does not serve individual self-order, but the realization of new collective identities" (Wexler 1990; 173). This memory work is to a great extent rooted in religious models of self and collective understanding.

In fact at work here is a complex interaction of ethnicity, cultural identity, geography, formal political identity and religion. In the context of globalisation the older model of citizenship as a political category encompassing rights, duties and privileges is at least in part superseded by the alternative notion of "cultural citizenship" in which cultural rights are paramount and through which new forms of inclusion can be crafted. But at the same time, by stressing the legitimacy of difference, it can also be a point of friction between communities sharing the same geopolitical space when notions of multiculturalism clash with older conservative notions of the identity of ethnicity and nationality. "At stake in this clash of different kinds of citizenship is the role of cultural parameters associated with diasporas—ethnicity, cultural difference, plural social identities and affiliations—within the existing tolerances even of modern immigrant nations like Australia" (Goh 2004: 10). Amongst the "cultural rights" that can be added to the classical list of citizenship rights is that of toleration of religious differences, a factor which complicates the older notion of passive rights conferred by a nation-state as in a globalised situation, membership in an internationally dispersed religion is very likely to coincide with particularistic citizenship in a specific nation. This new model of citizenship radically transcends the prior concept of cultural citizenship being the ability to contribute to the reproduction of a specific national culture, now that such cultures themselves are in fact hybridised, open to globalisation and ethnically and religiously plural, suggesting to some commentators the question indeed of whether or not "Is it possible for notions of cultural citizenship to be extended to even wider imagined communities, to post-national, post-ethnic, or global formations? Are diaspora populations and their hybridized cultures…the very models for the postmodern ethnicities and identities of a future globalized world?" (Ommundsen 2004: 93). If they are, then the role of religious identity must clearly be factored into this equation in a central and essential way.

While no abstract model can be built that encompasses all these possible mappings of identity, citizenship, religion, globalisation and post-colonialism across Asia, in the light of this broad theoretical framework case studies illustrating the variety and complexity of these interplays illuminate the many possible configurations that exist, and it is to these that we will now turn.

The Structure of the Book

In its attempt to map these themes, the book is divided into four sections. The first consists of this introduction and three chapters that set out to rethink the relationships between religion, identity, cultural studies, postcolonial studies and globalisation in the context of contemporary Asia. In this setting it is still necessary to re-examine the older problem of Orientalism and its place in the intellectual configurations that have shaped readings of both religion and Asian societies. The second part, which takes the impact of Japan on the religious cultures of Southeast Asia and of transformations within Japanese religion within that country, as its empirical core, deals specifically with the issue of conversion as paradigmatic and the impact of changes in religious allegiance on self-identity, conceptions of cultural membership and social roles and the agency of actors in the process of renegotiating their relationship to former religious affiliations, given that those affiliations are embedded in cultural, political and sociological considerations much more powerful in their restraining character than those encountered by the average Westerner contemplating a change of religious membership in a situation in which the New Age and new spiritualities have already eroded boundaries between belief systems. Japan's attempt to resite itself as a global center of spiritual influence and not only of economic influence, has significant implications both for its impact on the surrounding Asian societies and beyond, and also for its own internal identity politics. The third part addresses the linkages between religion, globalisation, regionalism, citizenship and cultural memory and explores an example of what Fred Dallmayr has called "exemplary voices" (Dallmayr 2002) long concerned with understanding the relationships between culture, modernity and post-colonialism, and the book concludes with a postscript that attempts to relocate identity issues in relation to studies of popular culture, the intellectual space in Asia that has been most concerned with cultural flows, cultural contact and the globalisation of cultural forms. When such an analysis is placed in relation to the exploration of religion, fruitful new possibilities for understanding emerge.

Taken as a whole the intention of the book is to reconfigure the understanding of the relationships between religion, identity and wider social (global) processes. The study of religion has occupied an important but limited place in East and Southeast Asian sociological studies. For while there are many monographs starting from a history of religions approach, concerned with such specific issues as iconography in Asian religious art, and many anthropological studies of local religions, ritual practices, pilgrimage and regional cults, there are few studies of the larger scale dynamics of religious interaction and religious change across this complex and vibrant area, and their connections to emerging regional politics of identity and belonging.

As suggested above and as illustrated in the case studies that follow, this is a major gap in our understanding of contemporary Asia given the perennial significance of religion in the social dynamics of the region. Not only does religion continue to be a major aspect of the fabric of everyday life, but the rise of varieties of "fundamentalisms," the widespread emergence of social movements and civil society organisations basing themselves explicitly on religious premises, the role of religion in political discourses (for example the attempt to create a Confucian-based national ideology in Singapore or the role of Islam in Malaysia and Indonesia), the existence of widespread religious networks (such as the Japanese "new religions" with their extensive memberships in Southeast Asia) place religion in the forefront of the issues to be addressed in understanding the region and its contemporary social and cultural dynamics.

In the following this understanding is pursued through several levels of analysis interwoven with each other. The first of these concerns the empirical place of religion in contemporary Asian societies and the roles of religion in relation to new social movements and identity politics across the region and in the flows of cultural influence between the sub-regions of the entire area. The second is to relate the study of Asian religious cultures to developments in cultural studies along two lines—on the one hand to utilise the tools of cultural studies (amongst which have been its emphasis on popular cultures, the body and the structures of everyday life) to examine Asian socio-cultural dynamics, and on the other to reinstate the study of religion within cultural studies, from which at the moment it is largely absent. An important theoretical subtext of the book is to attempt to overcome the Western bias of a great deal of cultural theory and to bring it into dialogue with other civilisations in the expectation that this will greatly enrich its range and depth and contribute thereby to its potential genuine universality as a mode of analysis.

The third objective is to explore some of the significant shifts in social theories of religion and to relate these specifically to the exploration of important facets of contemporary Asian religion. Discussions of postmodernity in relation to religion in the West (for example King 1998, Berry and Wernick 1992), still shaped by essentially Christian models of religion and of religion/society interactions, have had little impact on the serious study of Asian religions with the possible exception of Islam, the religion of Asia formally and historically closest to Christianity (Ahmed and Hastings 1994). Another sub-text of this volume is the attempt to revitalise interest in the sociology of Asian religions by showing how such a dialogue with social theory can be achieved and how fruitful the theoretical and empirical outcomes can be.

The final objective of the book is to relate issues of religion in Asia to broader questions of modernity, globalisation, postcoloniality, popular culture and social and cultural change. This will inevitably involve consideration of the impact of the media, the export of Asian religions westward to Europe and the Americas, and the classical sociological question of secularisation. Western theories of secularisation have assumed a basically Christian world view that are of doubtful utility in Asia where patterns of sectarianism, of the links between religion and ethnicity, of conceptions of nature and human agency and of the taking over (or not) of the functions traditionally associated with religion by secular agencies in fields such as education and welfare differ radically from the European and North American experiences (Clammer 1984).

The book in short will suggest a fresh perspective on the sociology of Asian religions and of contemporary Asian societies seen from this perspective of the continuing central role of religion in their sociological and cultural life. It will attempt to represent back to Western sociology the value and relevance of studying Asia, not only through the application of Western tools of analysis, but also reciprocally through the application to the social analysis of Western religion of models developed out of the study of Asia (Clammer 1995). Central to the analysis is the nature of globalisation and its complex relationship to postcoloniality and it contributes to contemporary debates about globalisation by showing how cultural globalisation and regionalisation flows along unexpected channels, not only those of economics, media and popular culture, but equally through the route of mutual religious influence and in the interplay between religion and those other categories of social analysis.

The book then in part is a study of Asian religions in a globalised world, and is also a study of the integration of religious and cultural studies in the Asian context through attention to the nature of religious flows and the issues of identity that arise when these new choices and new relationships between religious identity and traditional modes of cultural affiliation are challenged by the globalisation of religious options. It is a paradoxical fact that postcoloniality likewise, while it may spark attempts at the recovery of indigenous expressions of spirituality suppressed by colonialism and its religious imports, may weaken those very local traditional possibilities not by intensifying the postcolonial impact of the religion of the dominators, but by flooding the newly freed political environment with a plethora of new choices—Japanese new religions, Baha'i, Subud, Sai Baba, new expressions of Sufism, syncretic religions, New Age spirituality, few of which may have any roots at in the pre-colonial culture. The consequence is the emergence of a complex new religious sociology based less on local rootings than on new networks, the globalisation of flows of religious information and local adaptions resulting in new syncretisms, patterns of assimilation of these imported forms and ever proliferating forms of hybridity as a form of religious creativity.

This new patterning is not of course simply a matter of individual choices and predilictions—it is profoundly shaped by states, local political cultures, discoures of nation-building and presumptive conflation of religious and political identity, nationalist ideologies and concepts of modernity. But not only is passive ways, for religious communities themselves respond to these challenges or opportunities in a variety of ways, ranging from the rejection of modernity, through political opposition, to the creation of new forms of civil society organisation to withdrawal into privatised religion. The result is a rich environment for the study of contemporary socio-cultural dynamics and an equally rich field for exploring the classical issues of the sociology of religion, including secularisation, political religion, conversion, missionary activity and a host of other questions. The resiting of Asian religions both within the framework of cultural studies, and in relation to the complexity of globalisation processes, illustrates modes of understanding contemporary socio-religious relationships that might not only enhance scholarly insight, but which more importantly helps to provide the tools for grasping the contemporary salience of religion in the politics of terrorism and counter-terrorism, the growing ecological crisis, the search for roots in the emerging "risk society" and its fundamentally identity-conferring qualities for millions of people across the globe. If cultural studies is to break out of its all too frequent narcissism, this latter task offers it a significant public role, provided that it retains both a critical perspective on the many and often contradictory roles of religion, and a vivid awareness of its profound significance that has extended and perhaps even deepened in the opening decades of the new Millennium.

2

Cultural Studies and the Cultural Politics of Asian Religion

The social sciences in Asia face a peculiar theoretical challenge. Heirs to ancient civilisations and traditions of thought and cradles to all of the great world religions, they nevertheless perceive themselves as suffering from a "theoretical deficit." This deficit arises from the fact that despite their cultural specificities and their corresponding status as objects of study by foreign scholars, the societies of Asia have not for the most part produced what might be called "high theory" of their own. High theory—universally quoted perspectives on social life which are the points of reference and departure, sources of paradigms and required professional knowledge for social science practitioners and which are widely translated from their languages of origin—are, let us face it, almost entirely Western and in fact largely European in provenance. The litany of required readings—Lacan, Derrida, Foucault and their host of derivatives, followers and critics—rarely contains an Asian name and the endless scholarly debates that they have spawned rarely contain any Asian themes, except those generated by acolytes (often Western trained and reading or speaking European languages often better than they do their mother tongues) of Asian origin or working in Asia.

This perceived (and in many ways real) hegemony of European social theory (despite the polycentrality of the modern world system and the actual economic, cultural and demographic power of Asia) has naturally triggered attempts to redress the balance of theory-power in the world intellectual economy. These attempts have taken a number of forms—critiques of Orientalism (Said 1978), of falsely Eurocentric visions of the world system and its origins (e.g. Chaudhuri 1990, Ikeda 1996), of dependency theory and of the concept of "development" in general (Chng 1977), of postcolonialism (Chakrabarty 1992) from the critical side, and of attempts from the constructive side to develop indigenous alternatives often based on religion—usually Buddhism, Islam or Confucianism or of some system of "Asian values" derivative from them (e.g. Sivaraksa 1992; Jomo 1993).

The latest attempt in this list is one that purports to bring together in a single package both the critical and the constructive and which is having a substantial impact on the contemporary practice of the social sciences in Asia and of approaches to the study of Asia by non-Asian scholars—notably the approach which despite its internal diversity is generically referred to as "Cultural Studies." It is to the possibility of constructing an Asian variety of cultural studies and of the likely influences of such a possibility on the international study of Asia that this chapter is directed, together with the corresponding raising of the necessary critical question that the simple assertion that there is an "Asian cultural studies" does not guarantee that such an approach is in fact appropriate to the study of really existing Asian societies or that it is not simply another form of Eurocentric theory heavily disguised in rather operatic Asian make-up.

Clearly on the surface a cultural studies approach offers certain advantages. By placing culture at the centre of debate it potentially allows the specific characteristics of individual Asian societies to be theorised from within. Its concerns with issues of multiculturalism, gender and race allow it to address primary issues in those same societies. And its tendency to treat the idea of "culture" itself critically and reflexively and to pursue its goals through processural procedures (rather than through artefacts) and in the context of global forces (rather than as wholly localised) gives it an analytical edge that avoids the seductions of culturalism while permitting a critical and historical mode of thinking, a methodology which also transforms rather than displaces other disciplines which have attempted to put culture at their centre, such as anthropology (Friedman 1996). But in order to make these gains effective a specifically Asian cultural studies must also define more clearly both its own subject matter (the cultural specificity of Asian societies) and its own (non-Eurocentric) theoretical posture.

To understand how this double-barrelled project might proceed, a useful starting point is to examine initially some of the approaches that have been offered. Here I will select a small number of such options, but ones that I would argue are both representative and important, for what they miss out as much as for what they include. But before I do this it is necessary to briefly note that they are all framed by certain common considerations. These include a common language of postcolonialism and anti-Eurocentrism, an elevation of the particularly indigenous over the possibility of universalism, their embeddedness regardless of specific political leanings in the international capitalist economy of late modernity and the globalising forces that this entails. At the same time there is the attempt to develop a local critical theory aware of those forces, educated about Western social theory yet attempting to develop a vocabulary and methodological sensitivity that is not simply "nativist," but which, in common with Latin American and African initiatives (e.g. Esteva 1992) attempts to transcend a hegemonic language of "development" in favour of a "listening" to the actual voices and practices that make up the "culture" which cultural studies purports to explore. Whether it actually does this in its rush from one form of theory ("European") to another ("Asian") is moot. "Indigenous" cannot mean simply practiced by indigenes: it must mean a true representation of the voices of those it claims to speak for.

So far there have been several main attempts to define an Asian cultural studies, and these fall into four main categories. The first is that represented by Chen Kuan-Hsing and his collaborators in a recent volume (Chen 1998) either noteworthy for its inconsistencies or praiseworthy for its anarchy, depending on how one wants to read it. In his editor's introduction Chen makes a strong case for the thesis that Asian cultural studies should be identified with the analysis of neo-colonialism, a case that he makes without specifically invoking the language of postcolonial studies. Apart from the six contributors (out of nineteen) who specifically devote themselves to "Refiguring the Colonial" however the remainder deal with questions as diverse as multiculturalism, Chinese nationalism, the cultural politics of Thai pop music, Indonesian short stories, AIDS and gay sub-cultures. Two of the essays are actually on Australia and one is on African-American cultural studies and another on Europe. What is positive (other than the intrinsic quality of the individual papers, which is of a high standard) is not the putative concern with postcoloniality, but the emphasis on new social movements both as cultural phenomena in their own right and as generators of new values and of cultural alternatives. As such the collection is really post-postcolonial. This is important since postcolonial studies, by defining itself in relation to that which it wishes to critique, never really transcends that object but must remain forever in its fatal embrace. This is not to decry the achievements of postcolonial studies in naming and struggling with the demons of domination with which colonialism (Asian as well as Western) has imposed inauthenticity on its subject cultures, merely to point out that the logic of postcoloniality is that it can never transcend its object. The way out of this impasse must necessarily lie outside of postcolonial studies itself.

A second possibility, even though again it derives from a Western innovation, is postmodernism. Postmodernism as an intellectual (or anti-intellectual) movement in its denial of metanarratives radically undermines the grand tropes of Eurocentric domination ("development," progress, universalism, scientific rationality etc.) in favour of local, negotiated identities.

It is for this reason that it has found its followers in Asia where it is popular partly because it reinstates emotions over reason, but also because if interpreted in certain ways it allows the argument that some Asian societies (Japan in particular), already possessing the appropriate characteristics, have achieved postmodernity without ever passing through the stage of modernity. This places them outside of the frame of Western universalistic history and makes possible the claim of cultural exceptionalism—societies not "without history," but "outside of history" (Miyoshi and Harootunian 1989) while also having specific cultural features—for example being "relational" or "interpersonal" rather than individualistic (Hamaguchi 1982). The postmodern option however, while apparently making possible this resistance to (Western) universalism, does so within the language of an intensely Western theory which, while effectively deconstructing Western metanarratives, also deconstructs Asian ones (for example Confucianism). While it suggests possibilities then, postmodernism does not really seem to provide the tools from which to build indigenous forms of Asian social science, certainly not unless it is radically reconstrued on a quite alternative epistemological basis (for example Buddhism, of which more below).

A third possibility arises from a "civilisational" approach, not in Samuel Huntington's sense, but in the sense of Asian civilisations as having distinct characteristics which create the possibility for a cultural dialogue between them which does not simply reproduce the hierarchical and repressive relationships between the colonising West and the colonised (Nandy 1998). Implicit in this model is a discussion of what Asia itself actually is. Nandy himself admits that it is a geographical rather than a cultural construction and this is indeed so. What he does not point out that even this geography is fought over by academic specialisations ("South Asian Studies," "Southeast Asian Studies" etc.) and is today constantly reconstructed by the economic forces of international capital ("globalisation") and its cultural agencies such as advertising, the tourist industry and publishing. The differences between Asian "civilisations" (a dangerously essentialist concept) are apparent enough. What the civilisational approach tends to occlude are the inequalities and tensions within such "civilisations"—caste conflict in India, the position of women under Confucianism, ethnic stratification, religious divisions, and widening income gaps. Dialogue between such civilisations all too often turns out to be conversation between privileged intellectuals often speaking or writing in a colonial language. Despite its moral appeal (who can argue with the desirability of dialogue?) the civilisational approach as it now stands sits rather oddly with other more theoretically informed approaches in cultural studies that are post-culturalist, non-essentialist and take a critical view of both the conventional understandings of culture itself and of the politics of culture within individual "civilisations." Part of the difficulty lies in the fact that the civilisational approach has its roots in psychology, a discipline that itself lacks a critical tradition and so which, when it tries to bring together psychology and colonialism, as in the work of Nandy himself and of his precursors Fanon, Memmi and Mannoni, puts into juxtaposition an underdeveloped subject with an overdeveloped object. The resulting uncovering of subjectivities, while ethnographically interesting, lacks the economic, political and sociological contexts necessary to turn it into a true critical theory with its roots in indigenous sources. In fact in its classical form (e.g. Fanon 1967, 166-199) it is actually a form of nationalism. In the historical situation of the 1940s and 1950s this made some sense; from the perspective of an increasingly post-nationalist and globalised world system, nationalism, whether political or cultural and especially when twinned with a language of nativism, can only appear as a retrogressive step.

A fourth approach has its roots not in psychology, but in literature. This is not surprising given that much of contemporary cultural studies has its own roots in literary studies (Easthope 1992) and that the analysis of literature (and by extension film) has provided the basic data for a great deal of cultural analysis. Indeed postcolonial studies has its origin directly in work on Commonwealth literatures and some of its most distinguished propagators have continued to make literary studies the keystone of their methodology (e.g. Said 1993). Here however I will focus on the work of the cultural studies and comparative literature scholar Rey Chow.

Chow sees the major fault line in academic life as running between those who espouse what she calls "theory" (by which she actually means simply poststructuralism and deconstruction) and which characterises cultural studies, and those who consider themselves "critical theorists" (i.e. who resist the poststructuralist turn). In common with many other cultural studies specialists, she also rejects both older anthropological definitions of culture (as lifeways) and class based conceptions of culture ("high" as opposed to "popular" culture). The root of the problem she sees (Chow 1998: xv) as being the separation of cultural studies from critical theory, in her reading because critical theorists see themselves as the repository of "high" theory while cultural studies is seen as a kind of vulgarisation and concentration on the ephemeral. In fact Chow argues, it is in cultural studies that the contemporary questions of gender, class, otherness and multiculturalism are most clearly asked and in the context of which Eurocentric theoretical assumptions are most directly challenged. The project for an Asian cultural studies is to draw on this field of theoretical possibilities while avoiding the dangers of slippage into disguised forms of Eurocentrism, of the use of inappropriate theory and of the temptations, all too visible in cultural studies, of "progressive" posturing—the rapid embracing and discarding of currently fashionable "positions"—all of which add up to a new form of Orientalism rather than its rejection (Chow 1998: xviii). While her work contains many problems—including the radical overdrawing of the "class" distinction between critical theory and cultural studies (she has evidently not been reading in the field of Asian development studies)—her approach suggests several important points. On the general front these include the actually critical functions of cultural studies when practised correctly, the dangers of Asian studies simply assimilating and reproducing the grand theory generated elsewhere and in totally non-Asian cultural contexts, and the conceptual problems involved in "Area Studies." But these are largely programmatic statements: they necessarily point beyond themselves to more concrete prescriptions.

Some of these Chow has embodied in her own work on Asian literatures and more particularly on Asian film (Chow 1995). Others are contained in more theoretical and methodological suggestions. The first of these concerns the status of the texts of Asian authors themselves:

> "The guideline that I follow in all these readings is a simple one. I feel strongly that, until and unless we grant non-Western authors and texts—be these texts fiction, theory, film, popular music, or criticism—the same kind of verbal, psychical, theoretical density and complexity that we have copiously endowed upon Western authors and texts, we will never be able to extricate our readings from the kind of idealism in which the East-West divide—which, I'd propose, is also the assailable divide between 'cultural studies' and 'critical theory'—is currently mired. Granting such density and complexity would mean refusing to idealize the non-West—be it in the form of a culture, a class, or a gender group: a text, an author or a character—and instead reading the non-West in such a manner as to draw out its unconscious, irrational and violent nuances, so that, as an 'other' it can no longer simply be left in a blank, frozen and mythologized condition known perfunctorily as an 'alternative' to the West" (Chow 1998: xxi).

This granting of equal "density" to non-Western voices arises from the perception that while Said's Orientalism quite correctly diagnosed the domination of the non-West by the West through images of culture and through patterns of representation, it does not really suggest any alternative.

Chow's solution to this is an interesting one: it is that cultural studies holds the key in that the essential quality of cultural studies is the identification of otherness. As such it both situates the essential problems of postcolonial Asia and of the marginalised within it, and it simultaneously subverts European theoretical hegemony by forcing the latest and apparently most radical and deconstructive phase of that theory—poststructuralism—to confront its own political naivety. Poststructuralism's claims to subversiveness and radicalism prove to be hollow once it is forced to confront both the realities of the non-Western world and the violence of European colonialism (Chow 1998: 5). This observation both flows back to the West—where the academic study of non-Western cultures is still mired in ideological and foreign policy concerns and where it is dominated by theory generated in the European/North American context (for which indeed it may well be valid), and to the East—where it suggests that the simple adoption of modish Western theory by "progressive" intellectuals will not work, but will merely create a form of self-Orientalising.

The obvious solution to this is a nativist one—a return to some form of "indigenous" values. But the problem here (quite apart from the essentialising and often retrogressive qualities of nativist movements) is that, as Gayatri Chakravorty Spivak tellingly points out, there is no pure indigenous theory since colonialism (Spivak 1990: 69). And as Chow goes on to note (1998:9) even if there were, such a return "masks … the violence of the cultural politics that is within an indigenous culture." A nativist programme (which may well conceal classist, fundamentalist or other features behind a return to, or more probably construction of, tradition) (Hobsbawn and Ranger 1992, Vlastos 1993) is, especially in a globalised world, at best an uncertain path to take. This is not because it is not desirable to enhance the quality and autonomy of local cultures, but because indigenous traditions and values are not only not necessarily (as Chow points out) egalitarian and non-racist/sexist, but equally fundamentally, because they do not necessarily contain the resources for building theory at all in its usual academic sense.

The Western project of modernity is predicated upon a certain world view, composed out of ideas of individualism, the primacy of rationality, the central significance (at least since the Enlightenment) of equality as opposed to hierarchy, residues of Greek thought filtered through Christianity, a political fixation on ideas of power and the dominance of the economic, a concern with binary modes of thinking and a preoccupation with language, a radical separation of nature from the social, a strong strand of biologism, a tendency to psychologise all forms of experience, including the religious, and a belief (at least until the advent of postmodernism) in the applicability of scientific or quasi-scientific (e.g. economic or sociological) techniques to "solving" the "problems" of the world. The genealogy of such ideas and its contemporary manifestations can easily be traced not only through classical Western philosophy since Descartes, but also through the role call of the contemporary luminaries of Western thought—think for example of Derrida, Lévi-Strauss, Lacan, Foucault, Althusser, Adorno, Habermas, Wittgenstein. The "alternative" high Western tradition—from Nietzsche through Heidegger to such contemporary thinkers as Morris Berman (e.g. Berman 1990)—with its much more somatic approach to human reality, while not unimportant, is nevertheless both the minor strand and the one that has fed (often via New Age thinking) or drawn inspiration from, Asian philosophies and religions (often in practice, unlike in the West, the same thing).

This vast project has not only produced luxuriant theoretical fruits, but theory itself, of a particular kind, is an essential part of that project. Western modernity and the production of theory are inseparable, and that theory is consequently of a particular kind—logocentric, obsessed with epistemology and assuming a particular image of human society. Asian social reality, particularly with its deep roots in religion (even economic success or failure is debated in religious terms) however has not generated the same issues. This means that a genuinely Asian form of social theory will have to be radically different from its Western counterparts and possibly deeply subversive of it (Clammer 2005). This also raises acute questions of academic politics since the incommensurability of these modes of theory and of the cultural soil out of which they have grown radically questions the reality of intellectual globalisation (although economic globalisation may well be taking place) and totally decentres the hierarchies of academic excellence. The centre of good theory may as well be in Benares as in Paris, and indeed it probably is, only the Hindu knowledge generated and transmitted there is not recognised as real theory by those who control the international networks of publishing and academic status and who only consider material in the so-called metropolitan languages to be significant. The "Kyoto School" of Japanese philosophy for example was arguably one of the intellectual powerhouses of the modern world. Its achievements are never mentioned in "standard" histories of philosophy, and when it is studied by Westerners it is almost invariably not as philosophy, but as "Asian thought." At the same time the "Frankfurt School" will be known to every serious Asian scholar of social theory. It is very revealing that the one area almost entirely ignored by cultural studies, something that indicates its still Western theoretical bias even in its Asian manifestations, is that of religion, clearly one of the deepest realities of Asian cultural life.

What is clearly indicated here, although different people use slightly different languages, is the primary importance of what both anthropologists and "development" specialists have taken to calling "local knowledges." The conjunction of these two disciplines is not fortuitous, since both the empirical failure of so many development efforts and the recognition that this frequently results from false cultural assumptions, Eurocentric biases, inadequate social analysis and simple failure to listen to the local people to find out not only what they want, but what they already know, has caused something of a joint crisis. And the way out of this crisis is perceived to be the privileging rather than the suppression of local knowledges, understood not only as technical abilities, but also as a set of values, a relationship to nature and cosmic forces and a set of functioning and functional social relationships. The questioning of conventional anthropological knowledge (as a field of theories, assumptions and pre-given methodologies), especially by indigenous anthropologists working on some aspect of their own society and also acutely aware of larger global forces producing substantial social transformations, is consequently taken as a first step towards the recovery and representation of local knowledges and the subsequent reformulation of anthropological knowledge, the context in which such knowledge is published to a wider audience, discussed and almost inevitably subsequently theorised. The result is a necessary "demystification" of anthropology from within by the native anthropologist. Anthropology, while it does justify itself at least as the one remaining academic vehicle for the systematic study of indigenous knowledge, does also represent the paradigm case of the Western inspired study of "the other"—the primitive, exotic or simple or simply different. The possibility of accurate representation, a listening attitude and a willingness to let theory grow out of the field not just out of the (Oxbridge) study makes possible one version of indigenous social science—a "people's anthropology," whether this arises in one form in Malaysia (Karim 1996) or in another in China (Fei 1981), concerned however not only with accurate representation, but also with a critical stance to the globalising forces of cultural transformation and destruction, including "development" itself.

A concern with local knowledge certainly avoids the obvious pitfalls of naive nativism, but it is not clear in itself how it might set about the reconstruction of social and cultural theory except insofar as it is a valid form of social knowledge. So it is to this issue that we must now turn. Cultural studies must contain at least two equally important but balanced elements: a concern with experience that allies it with what are sometimes called "sociologies of everyday life" (and which form its raw material and ethnographic basis) on the one hand, and a grasp of the structural situation of that experience on the other (the macro-determinants of behavioural possibilities such as economic circumstances and global forces) on the other.

It is out of the interaction of these two that cultural theory emerges, an interaction mediated in practice by social groupings favourably situated to negotiate and systematise meaning (usually intellectuals, artists, writers, initiators of social movements, theologians and others who self-consciously comment on as well as produce culture). At the same time these culture-specialists often "discover" what was already there—such as popular culture—but which they had no part in creating. The result is that even when cultural studies emerges or takes root in Asian settings, it, like most other social science, is already a second order phenomenon. It is in other words commentary on what already organically exists—knowledge and practices that it feels called upon to represent or to discover through "research"—rather than an example of first order culture in itself. Of course in one sense all artefacts of culture, including the writings of intellectuals, are also "culture;" the common hubris of cultural studies is that it wishes to, or believes that it has, collapsed the distinction between itself as commentary and that upon which it comments. One profound reason for this is that intellectuals often do not participate in or deeply share the practices and beliefs the analysis of which keeps their rice bowls full, except for the most genuinely organic intellectuals such as the profoundly knowledgeable but untutored and unrecognised anthropologist in the Brazilian novelist Jorge Amado's *Tent of Miracles* (Amado 1989).

It is presumably for this reason that although some Asian cultural studies specialists do discuss social movements (e.g. Im and Muto in Chen 1998), they do not discuss religious ones, and Western social movements' theorists interestingly do the same. Sidney Tarrow's near classic volume on social movement theory for example (Tarrow 1996) contains no references at all to religiously based social movements or to new religions as social movements. Such discussion is left mainly to sociologists of religion (e.g. Saliba 1995) or to a sub-speciality which deals exclusively with social movements in the "South" (e.g. Wignaraja 1993) mostly by sociologists from that very region since their existence has apparently escaped the notice of sociologists in the "North."

The religious issue in fact constitutes something of an acid test for the possibility of a genuinely Asian cultural studies as although, it is not a fashionable item on the international social theory agenda, the absence of any discussion of the fundamental religiosity of Asian peoples does violence to the actual cultural experience of those peoples. In a sense slightly different from that implied by Chow and discussed earlier, the cultural politics of Asian cultural studies has effectively excluded one of the primary facets of Asian cultural experience. Those that have attempted to do so are almost exclusively outside the academy and work in the field of

Islamic economics (e.g. Naqvi 1981), in Buddhist inspired social criticism (e.g. Sivaraksa 1992), from the perspective of Christian theology of liberation (e.g. Pieris 1992) or from within Hindu-based social movements such as the Indian Swadhyaya movement (e.g. Srivastava 1998). There are clearly two elements in such a vital addition to Asian cultural studies. The first of these is the ethnography of the place of religion in cultural experience and the generation of systems of meaning. The second is the linking of religion to the other more traditional aspects of cultural studies—popular culture, the economics of everyday life, power and class (or caste), gender and race—without which these themselves frequently do not make much sense.

Amongst these issues are precisely again the ones that cultural studies' close cousin, postcolonial studies, also largely ignores such as the interactions of religion as part of the colonial process itself and the profound effect that both colonialism and its intellectual cousin Orientalism have had on the formation of the concept of Asian religions themselves and their supposed content and belief systems. How far Orientalism itself is responsible for in a sense "inventing" Hinduism or Buddhism, categories which are now used relatively uncritically by Asianists East and West, is a fascinating example. Yet despite Said's own lead in placing the analysis of representations of religion at the forefront of his critique and construction of Orientalism, few have followed his lead, although a notable exception is Balagangadhara's more recent account of Christianity in the self-definition of the West and of the export through colonialism of the religious categories of (Western rather than Orthodox) Christianity to construct definitions of the East and especially of its "religions," assumed to be bounded and coherent entities (Balagangadhara 1994).

Here two issues arise, and they are rather different. One is that of the representation of religions and their social construction by those who are outside of them; the other is that of the incorporation of religion into the analysis of actual cultural practices by real people operating in everyday contexts. There are real dangers in conflating the two. The problem with Chow's approach to cultural studies is that her data consists exclusively of texts (literary or cinematic) not of actual behaviour or even of the reception and renegotiation of those texts by audiences. With literature the problem is reduced somewhat by the fact that the sources after all actually are texts. But when the same methodology is applied to religion the dangers are very much greater—of confusing the texts with practice and their authors with authority. For this reason much popular or "folk" religion has escaped altogether the attention of scholars of the religious cultures of Asia, except again for anthropologists whose prioritising of behaviour over texts avoids this problem. The other danger is that of not pursuing the very agenda which cultural studies has set for itself, in particular the critical aspects of that agenda. Thus Pieris for example (1992) links the issues of the religiosity of Asia with its poverty, not as cause and effect but as a cultural pattern in which one gives meaning to the other. He goes on, as a Sri Lankan Catholic theologian, to plea for the development of a cultural studies approach to Asian religions and Asia's "indestructable religiosity" (pp. 69, 80) which retains a critical stance towards religious imperialism while encouraging dialogue between Asian religions as a route to a future in which the serious social and economic problems of so much of the continent can be creatively addressed without succumbing to the exhaustion of modernity in the post-Christian West which has only succeeded in finding postmodernity at the end of its "Enlightenment" project.

But there are several ways in which this might be done. One is through what Homi Bhabba calls movements of "counter-modernity"—resistance to globalisation and its locally destructive or transformative powers. This is important, but not radically different from what goes on in many social movements, although these too have the potential to produce new social knowledge and new subjects of that knowledge and consequently of concern ("women in development" or other excluded or marginalised groups). The more radical possibility is to go back to our earlier discussion of the nature of social theory. If such theory is rooted in and refers to the site of its production, then if this is true in the West then it is also true in the East. If Western theory has grown out of an individualist, rationalist, egalitarian, secular (despite or because of the presence of Christianity) compost, then Asian theory should grow out of a soil permeated by religion, a concern for a more relational understanding of the self, a central place for the emotions and a greater comfort with ideas of hierarchy. If Christianity does lie at the root of Western individualism as Dumont argues (Dumont 1985) then it should follow that very different images of the self (which will be fundamentally reflected in social practice and in disciplines designed to examine this practice such as sociology, anthropology and psychology) will likewise emerge from other religions. Indeed Dumont himself struggles to make explicable the caste system as an intelligible system of holism (rather than as a system of extreme injustice and inequality) to a primarily Western readership in precisely these terms (Dumont 1980). It is this line of thought that we must now pursue in a little more detail.

A religion creates a "root model"—a habitus out of which emerges a whole set of second order constructions: hence Islamic science, Buddhist psychology, Hindu logic and metaphysics and the modes of technology and relationships to time and space characteristic of classical Chinese civilisation, and so forth. Likewise embedded in religious conceptions of the world are ideas about the nature of culture and social relationships. Every religion implies a sociology. But whereas in the West this sociology has been a primary derivative of metaphysical thinking, whether explicitly religious or secular (i.e. as defined against religion), and consequently a body of social thought has emerged which in itself largely contains or expresses the Western intellectual project: Hobbes, Rousseau, Marx and so forth. Much of this thought has taken a specifically political form and in any academic bookstore in the West the interested reader can find histories of political ideas, of social thought and of sociological theory. In Asian traditions of thought however, while social ideas are present they are not for the most part on the surface (Islam and Confucianism being the major exceptions). And even when ideas about the ordering of society are fairly apparent, they take a form highly unfamiliar to Western sociologists. This is not surprising since the notions of agency, structure and of the human self are radically at variance with Western conceptions of these "same" things. An Islamic sociology must inevitably be Theistic in character and, unlike almost any form of Western sociology (including the sociology of religion), must incorporate divine agency as a key explanatory factor. A Buddhist sociology poses even greater challenges as the Buddhist conception of the no-self and of causality as "dependent arising" goes far further than the most radical poststructuralism in decentring the human individual and deconstructing metanarratives. It is in fact the most advanced form of "postmodernism"—a fundamental undermining of the epistemological categories on which Western reason is based and a radical anti-foundationalist method which leads to an "Enlightenment project" of a quite different kind organised around a non-rationalistic direct perception of the nature of reality (Batchelor 1998).

Buddhist metaphysics, based on this deconstruction of the ego-self and constituting a methodology for transcending this illusory identity, not only undermines traditional truth-claims (based on the assumption of an objective, continuing world perceived by and acted upon by an equally objective and continuing individuality, but it also calls into question what can be thought of as "religion." The dialogue of Western and Eastern forms of social thinking or cultural analysis as a result in many ways parallels the discussions between scholars of comparative religion. As Balagangadhara points out in his seminal study of the place of religion in the West's construction of itself and of its subsequent construction (or distortion) of Asia, even critical and reflexive varieties of cultural analysis in the West have developed a language of "difference" and the "other" which, while it does allow the other to occupy her/his own space, does not at the same time recognise that what constitutes the experience of difference can itself be different in different cultures. In "normal" academic discourse Asia, or some part of it, is compared with the West; it rarely occurs to analysts to compare parts of Asia (or of Europe) with each other. Yet it may make much more sense to compare, say, India with Japan, or Japan with Thailand rather than India with the West.

Insofar as these cultures are rooted in religion and to the extent that, as McGrane argues (McGrane 1989) since the Renaissance concepts of the Other have been moulded by the prevailing theologies of religion (i.e. the ways in which Western Christian theologians have related to and attempted to understand non-Christian religions), then concepts of the self and other do indeed have metaphysical sources. McGrane further suggests that the tendency within this movement (theological in origin, but profoundly social in its implications) has been to treat the Other in one of two broad ways—as the object of subjugation and control (the colonial option, expressed also in many varieties of development studies and some forms of anthropology), or as sameness, in which the other is tamed and assimilated (through universalism, multiculturalism and some varieties of cultural studies). The counter-option: the recovery of indigenous concepts of the self—transcends both the destructive forces of colonialism and globalisation, and avoids the assimilation of genuine local identities into a homogenised sameness in which differences are effaced. The foundation of any indigenous social science must consequently be this recovery of indigenous conceptions of the self and with them the genuine differences that separate cultures. Self-knowledge and self respect can only come from this source, from which "higher-level" social theorising must derive as it is always secondary to the experience which underlies it.

Fundamental to all ideas of indigenisation is a concept of identity. Even in Western sociology there has been a shift, largely by way of a discussion of the identity politics involved in the so-called "new social movements" that identity is contextual, local, complex, implicated in cultural notions of space and of occasion, closely linked to notions of lifestyle choices and is performative rather than essentialist in its expression and conception (Hetherington 1998). The drift towards the study of "subjectivities" in poststructuralist cultural studies surely reflects the perception of the foundational status of notions of the self in any discussion of identity and identity politics. This is fine provided only that such subjectivities are also situated in the wider social order (economic, religious and political forces) in which they are caught up. The whole notion of identity politics not only transforms cultural studies from within, it also forces it to be comparative, since it turns out that there is not one (Western essentialist concept of the human person and of the relationship of those persons to space, time and nature), but many.

The critique of Orientalism (deepened in turn by postcolonial studies) quite correctly identified the unequal power relationship between colonisers and colonised as embodied in an asymmetry of representations, although it did not always adequately pursue the question of the economic and other systems that created and sustained such inequality. But it also raised the crucial question of what is beyond itself, a question that it did not answer. There is of course a plurality of answers, only one of which is suggested here: that it is in the recovery and privileging of local knowledges that relate to notions of identity (often if not always rooted in complex ways in religion) that the beginning of an indigenous social science resides. To date it is cultural studies and some critical forms of anthropology (and to a lesser extent some styles of history influenced by them) that have come closest to recognising this, not least because their professional agendas are sufficiently broad to allow the unconventional questions to be asked (of selfhood, the body in relation to culture, the place of the emotions, of consumption as self-construction and as cultural resistance, of local knowledges encoded in myth or in popular cultural expressions) and to theorise these in relation to more universal trends of modernity and postmodernity (for example Zito and Barlow 1994). As such cultural studies potentially offers Asian studies some powerful tools and perspectives which greatly help to overcome the essentialising, high-culture and textual biases so often reflected in conventional scholarship on the East.

But at the same time my argument has also been that the current (but not insurmountable) limitation of cultural studies is that it too tends to identify "theory" with Western theory (Rey Chow is a very good case in point) and to avoid the reflexive move necessary to recognise that theory is itself cultural. This not only decentres theory itself (it can no longer be seen as purely Western without self-contradiction), but it radically alters the recognition of what can be seen as constituting theory in the first place. Buddhist thought for example (an example that we have dwelt on because of its radical implications) fundamentally reposes in a totally different frame the basic questions of all social theory—the self, causality, purpose, meaning, agency and method. This suggests that an Asian cultural studies must not only turn its sights on religion as a real cultural phenomenon, but must go far beyond the reactive agenda so far reflected in many of its publications so far. Copying the postures and language of Western cultural studies can of course be ironical—a playful subversion of the dominant discourse through parody—but one suspects that it rarely is in current Asian cultural studies. Cultural studies in itself does not indigenise local social sciences or totally transform "metropolitan" Asian studies, but it begins to move in this direction by taking seriously the self-representations and local knowledges of those who support its enterprise by producing and consuming culture in real local situations. To totally transform and truly indigenise local social sciences it has also to take the final steps of redefining the meaning of "theory", of creating a new sociology of knowledge prepared for the challenges of rethinking from first principles rooted in the integrity of the cultures that it explores, of listening not only to the texts, but also to both the voices from the field and those from other disciplines (for example critical perspectives in development studies) where similar issues are being raised and are often rooted in harsh reality.

The current disciplinary boundaries are themselves a late Western academic invention and do not in any case necessarily reflect either the way in which knowledge or the world has to be divided up, assuming it has to be divided at all. The very rich indigenous social science traditions that already do exist—in Japan, in India or in China, for example—while themselves largely unknown in the West, provide many models for the reconstruction of Asian social theory and practice. Such a reconstruction need not only serve a local sense of cultural nationalism, but is a substantial gift to the wider intellectual community, since it can only transform cultural studies internationally and with it Asian Studies too. Marxism (a Western project) has transformed the face of Asia, not necessarily for the reasons that Marxists themselves assume, but because it is in Asia that Marx's own dictum that it is from praxis—the unity of practice and theory—that the true field of social knowledge emerges—has most faithfully been observed. Here there is a lesson for Asian cultural studies since it is precisely from the soil of practical strategies that local knowledges, and with them indigenous fields of social knowledge, appear and are rooted.

3

Asia in Europe's Imaginary

Disciplinary Knowledges and the (Mis)Representation of Cultures

One of the foundational assumptions of "modernity" is universalism. This assumption is expressed or concealed in a number of forms—of a universal history based essentially on Western notions of progress, of the inevitable and history-terminating triumph of capitalism, or of the methodological and theoretical primacy of a scientific world-view and with it certain understandings of causality and a single model of rationality. Reality itself of course has begun to interrogate these assumptions—in Asia at least in the form of self-conscious attempts to define alternative modernities outside of or in opposition to Western notions of a universal history (in Japan and China certainly and to a degree in Thailand and Burma for example). Postcolonial theory, attempts to discover or create a distinctive indigenous tradition of social inquiry, or critiques, whether practical as in the form of the various fundamentalisms, or theoretical and philosophical, as in the many regional varieties of liberation theologies, of secularisation, modernity and "development," all suggest the level of discontent with one-sided universalising claims.

The apparent epistemological hegemony of the West then is contested both by those subject to its homogenising tendencies and particular hierarchies of value in the not-West, and by cognitive minorities within the West—for example by both ethnic minority citizens whose cultural roots are outside of Europe, and by members of the dominant cultural/ethnic group who have relativised their own position by acquaintance with other traditions (New Agers for instance or the growing number of converts to Buddhism). But contesting is not easy, partly because of the variety of forms by which hegemony is extended, including colonialism, missionaries, global capitalism and its attendant consumerism, technology and its associated patterns of rationality, and perhaps most recently "development" and "globalisation." It is also not easy because of the cognitive legitimacy that the Western knowledge-mode obviously has, so much so that it is the alternatives that have to defend themselves as reasonable and interesting vis a vis the habitus of the dominant global model and the huge cultural capital that is acquired with mastery of it. Many Asian nationalisms, while anti-colonial, nevertheless adopt the techniques, languages, institutions and even, as non-Western social critics from Fanon (1961) to Nandy (1983) have pointed out, the psychology of the colonisers.

Not unnaturally then, given the profound historical impact that European colonialism has had on Asia, and its continuing influence in forms as diverse as the organisation of local universities (Clammer 2001a), architecture and the organisation of space (Kusno 2000), languages, political forms, diet and patterns of religion (one thinks of the Philippines and the absolutely transforming effects of Catholicism on the whole society and its sociological make-up (e.g. Racelis 1998), many progressive commentators have suggested that the subject for study in Asia-Europe relations is and should continue to be colonialism/postcolonialism (Chen 1998), particularly considering the hardly declining cultural and economic influence of the West, again both through market forces (disguised as "globalisation": Greider 1998) and through the active intervention of such agencies as the IMF and the World Bank (called "development": Sachs 1995). This view is not necessarily incorrect. Where it errs is in its too limited view of what constitutes not only colonialism but of postcolonial hegemonic practices concealed within globalisation and which may in fact have even deeper consequences for the accurate self-understanding of contemporary Asian societies than the more obvious forms of "McDonaldisation" (Ritzer 1996, Watson 1998) of culture. What I will argue in this chapter is that one of these practices, and indeed an absolutely key one, is the structure and epistemology of the very disciplines used to undertake the investigation and interpretation of Asian societies, both by outsiders and today by insiders themselves—the so-called social sciences.

Ever since Edward Said's now classic work Orientalism (1978) it has been recognised that the (Western) social sciences and their precursors in the form of Eighteenth and Nineteenth Century topographies and geographies constructed rather than described the (Asian and Middle Eastern) cultures that they were investigating and spatialised them according to Western generated geographical categories that had no necessary relationship to linguistic, religious, ethnic or other realities on the ground (Lewis and Wigen 1997). Said furthermore, and no doubt reflecting his own profession of literary scholarship, sees the attendant European and later American readings of "Oriental" societies largely in terms of a distortion of representations. Again this is correct in so far as it goes, by drawing attention to the ways in which the emergent social science disciplines created a body of Orientalist "knowledge" frequently based on exoticised, eroticised, or barbaric images of the Asian Other and on an implicit denigration of Asian religions (especially Islam) compared to the assumed "truth" of Christianity. What it occludes however are two vital factors: the emergence of the disciplines themselves and their creation of hegemonic methodologies for the study of societies through the creation of both categories of social phenomena and knowledge about them (for the sources of this in early French sociology see Clammer 200lb) and of an epistemology concealing both certain ontological assumptions and certain views of what constitutes rationality on the one hand, and, equally significantly, the adoption of these disciplinary assumptions by Asians themselves in the self-investigation of their own societies.

This latter process contains within itself not only the dangers of self-Orientalising, but the even more fundamental one of self-interpretation employing the (already distorted) categories of the colonising Other. The problems that this engenders can be seen in the attempts to adapt Marxism to Asian conditions (e.g. Banerji 1985), to assimilate psychoanalysis to Asian understandings of therapy and of the self (Doi 1973), or to attempt to indigenise Christianity in Asian settings (for example Mullins 1998). Where this is perhaps most apparent on a macroscopic scale have been in attempts to interpret Asian religions using Western categories. This is so central that it is worth reflecting on in more detail.

Western social sciences of Asia have adopted extremely ambiguous attitudes to religion. The subject is largely ignored in Western cultural studies and this creates major problems when such an approach is applied to the analysis of Asian cultures where religion continues to play a major role (Clammer 2000d). In Orientalist discourse religion was indeed noted, but primarily as an element in the exoticism of the Other—to be denigrated as a factor in the backwardness of the Orient or to be praised as the source of its mystique. Relatively rarely, except in anthropology, struggling with its own crises of postcolonial legitimacy and methods of representation and interpretation (Marcus and Fischer 1986, Wolf 1994), were studies made of actual religious practice rather than the textual, historical and doctrinal studies of comparative religion, the history of religion and the various specialised sub-fields such as Buddhist Studies. The problem however goes deeper that this, since even where Asian religions were or are treated sympathetically and as integral parts of a larger cultural fabric, the critical problem arises of what can be said to constitute religion. The Indian scholar S.N. Balagangadhara for instance has recently argued (1994) that South Asian "religions" are largely the construct of Western scholars operating with Christian notions of truth and identity (the non-commensurability of ideas from different sources for instance) together with the colonist's desire to classify, count and control. Thus "Hinduism," found as a discrete entry in the encyclopaedias and dictionaries of religion in the West, was in fact an invention of that same West. The actuality was a vast and amorphous collection of local practices, deities, animist or quasi-animist beliefs, scriptures, monastic and pilgrimage traditions spread over a huge geographical area (now known as "India") of great linguistic and cultural heterogeneity.

A similar argument can be made for Japan, but with an interesting twist. Many a semi-informed foreigner might assume that Zen is the dominant form of Japanese religion, an assumption deriving from the mass of scholarly, semi-scholarly and popular books available in Western languages on the subject and from the common argument of a more traditional school of Japanologists that it is Zen that underlies almost all of the classic forms of Japanese cultural activity from the tea ceremony through archery and flower arranging to calligraphy. In fact Zen has always been a minority religion in Japan, historically confined to the Samurai class and today practised by almost no one. Yet it has attracted probably the bulk of English language writing on Japanese religion, especially that concerned with practice rather than anthropological analysis, although there are probably more Zen Buddhists in California than there are in Japan. The exoticism of Zen, a certain romanticism attaching to the austerity of its practice and its association with traditional Japanese culture has ensured that an extremely sociologically minor expression of Buddhism has been taken for the whole. It is as if a Japanese scholar of the West, in undertaking an analysis of European or even just British religion, had concluded that the Quakers were the dominant expression of Christianity. Galen Amstutz has concluded from his survey of the sparse Western scholarship on what is actually by far the largest and most significant expression of Buddhism in Japan—Jodo Shinshu or Pure Land Buddhism—that the paucity of such work is because to Westerners with its paradise, its salvation through faith, its church-like structure and its Messiah like figure (the Amidah Buddha). Pure Land is simply too much like Christianity to be interesting (Amstutz 1997). So a paradox emerges at this point: that which most challenges Western epistemologies, discursive practices and notions of the self becomes in a sense incorporated into that epistemology rather than subverts it by becoming an object of study; while that seemingly most like the cosmology of the West is excluded from the realm of interest. Much Western scholarship on Zen turns out as a result to be Orientalist: the construction or representation of the praxis of the Other in accordance with one's local

(Western) categories which are in no way displaced or called into question by what is actually a very much one-sided encounter.

The examples can be multiplied. But to take just one more, it is also a commonplace of much Western scholarship on Japan, that the country has three religions (although individual Japanese may adhere in different contexts to all three): notably Buddhism, Shinto and various forms of local folk religions. In fact it can be shown that the three overlap, draw on each other and are in some cases indistinguishable (Fujita 1998) and also that certainly to the case of Shinto, the religion is twice-constructed (again, like "Hinduism," out of numerous local cults, harvest and nature rituals and popular folk deities) first by the Japanese government after the widespread arrival of foreigners and Christian missionaries after the Meiji restoration of 1868 in an attempt to modernise, centralise and control popular religiosity, and later by Western scholars concerned to conceptualise Japanese religion along systematic lines in keeping with the expectation that religions must indeed have a coherent theology and body of distinct practices.

Religion (a factor almost entirely missing from Western cultural studies and studies of international relations) here is taken as paradigmatic of a larger and two dimensional process. On the one hand there are the Western attempts to construct "Asia," not necessarily in their own image, but certainly in line with certain epistemological principles which allow Europe to interrogate Asia (on the possession of valid religion, on human rights, on environmental concern, on gender relationships, on medical practices, on its art), while not permitting a reciprocal interrogation, certainly not at the level of allowing its fundamental rationality and philosophical premises to be seriously and systematically questioned. On the other hand, through the agencies of colonialism, efficient instrumental and technical rationality, and economic domination, in Asia a confused negotiation, quite asymmetrical with that of the West's encounter with Asia, is initiated, largely centring on issues of identity and on the possibilities of maintaining or regaining the cultural integrity of local cultures in the face of globalisation and "development". (The local literature even in the metropolitan language of English, is vast and is an industry in itself: for two examples see Sulak 1979 and Itty 1984; in the vernaculars, for example in Japanese, it is even bigger; see Clammer 2001c, Yoshino 1997). This negotiation of identity is a large and complex issue involving many factors from the rise of religious fundamentalisms to agonising over the nature of local literatures and the languages in which they should be written and on to the debates throughout the region of "Asian values" and whether they even exist. Here I will take up just one aspect of this: the way in which such identity debates are muddied or even rendered insoluble by the incorporation into indigenous social science thinking of the very disciplinary epistemologies created in the West and which were in the first place responsible for the (mis)representation of the East. The "enemy" as it were is internalised and then used as the very agent through which the self is to be interpreted. It is disciplinary knowledge as much as any other aspect of contemporary colonialism, neo-colonialism or globalisation that continues to render problematic not only European readings of Asia, but also Asian's reading of themselves, when that reading takes place through the very prisms created by the erstwhile dominators. A local social science that is local only in the sense that its content is endogenous and that its practitioners are native is not likely to be a true alternative if its methodologies (widely taken, especially amongst positivists as being universal in application) and fundamental presuppositions are no different from those of metropolitan European ones, I will now attempt to unpack this idea and to show how it might work if a search for an Asia centred or dialogic methodology for the social sciences, and in particular my own discipline of sociology, is seriously entered upon. I will also try to show that this matters and is not simply another move in an academic game.

Mapping the Self with the Cartographies of the Other

Let me first restate my thesis. This is in essence that not only are there the by now well known dangers of the misrepresentation of Asia by Europe (Orientalism)—something so evident that it is for the most part consciously guarded against, but that, much more insidiously, Asia, having co-opted and internalised the disciplinary assumptions of the Western social sciences has frequently and as a direct result, misrepresented itself. The Self is presented back to the Other in the categories of that Other. Not only is the Self misrepresented to the Other, but is also misrepresented to itself. The hegemony of the Western social sciences promotes in other words an intellectual colonialism, which like all colonialisms is most damaging when it operates at the psychic rather than the purely material level (Mannoni 1990).

Oddly however the social sciences themselves in the West are largely unwilling to deal with this psychic level. They are not at all reluctant to discuss more macroscopic themes, and the interesting phenomenon of the former colonists developing a cottage industry out of postcolonial studies, especially in university departments of literature (e.g. Williams and Chrisman 1993), is not without its ironies. It is indeed probably no accident that it has been in the fields of history and geography and the interfaces between them, in addition to comparative literature, that the "outer" dimensions of the intellectual impact of colonialism has been addressed, without however for the most part drawing out the full epistemological significance of this. The US-based Thai historian Thongchai Winichakul for example in his in many ways masterful examination of how modern Siam was created as a national, cultural and political entity through discourses of colonial geographical knowledge in which certain notions of space (obsessed with notions of margins, unambiguous boundaries, mapping and control) superimposed on indigenous notions of sacred space and hierarchical relations between essentially unbounded political units, hints is essentially a question of a clash of rationalities (Thongchai 1997: xvi). This insight however is not pursued and mapping itself, actually the epiphenomenon of a deeper epistemological struggle finally won by Europe (France and Britain in particular), is seen as the major mechanism which succeeded in suppressing local cultural concepts of spatial ordering. Having been defined however by somebody else's social science conceptions, while it may lead to the adoption of those conceptions as reality, this also typically creates other effects. One notes with interest for example the number of Thai and other Southeast Asian sociologists who, when they go abroad for graduate study, choose departments that are highly quantitative in orientation, or who in pursuing political science go to get trained in rational choice theory. What happens to the economists can easily be imagined! The critical question then becomes not simply the noting of this clash of rationalities, but exploring its implications. For mimicry is not the only possibility. Several others exist. These include a kind of dual-economy model—the Western trained social scientist in the office, but the committed Muslim at home or in the Mosque, without ever systematically connecting the two worlds or thinking through their mutual implications. Another is the possibility of carrying on a socially relevant and often critical discourse without realising that it is actually social science (for instance many of the debates about Confucianism in East and Southeast Asia, of engaged Buddhism in Thailand or liberation theology in the Philippines). Yet a third is the development of a conscious nativist discourse, a prime example being the *Nihonjinron* or "theories of Japaneseness" widespread in Japan (Sugimoto 1999). A fourth is the attempt to construct or to articulate an indigenous social science—one recognising its continuities with more universal examples of such inquiry while remaining rooted in local cultural traditions and ontologies (Alatas 2000). These possibilities are not mutually exclusive, but in fact in many cases are engaged in a complex conversation with each other, the nature of which I will try to reveal in more detail in what follows.

It is true that it was usually colonialism that started this process, often beginning, as Thongchai intuits, with the distortion of indigenous notions of space and their subsequent reincorporation back into local notions of architecture, city planning and political cultures (Kusno 2000) or even into the restructuring of local traditions of land-tenure, clan organisation and sacred space (for an early but I hope still pertinent example see Clammer 1975a). Subsequent patterns of globalisation have certainly often reinforced or extended these tendencies through cultural mechanisms—whether the spread of Hollywood to the detriment of the local film industries or the world domination of the metropolitan music industries, through the gate-keeping functions of international publishing or through the image-industries in general with their profound effects on behaviour, relationships and conceptions of the self (e.g. Featherstone 1997; Kiely and Marfleet 1998). Smuggled in with this economic and cultural globalisation is academic globalisation, not only in the form of the power and attraction of the metropolitan institutions, but more subtly through disciplinary globalisation—the idea that there is really only one correct way to do or "perform" the social sciences, and that is the Western way. How this works in practice I will now attempt to demonstrate.

The actual nature of the contemporary social sciences is revealed by the questions that they do not ask as much as the ones that they do. In what follows I will restrict myself largely to sociology and anthropology, although I suspect that similar points could be made about many other disciplines. A brief glance at the contents pages of any standard introductory textbooks reveals what their common agenda normally is: in sociology methods, status and roles, socialisation, deviance and social control, stratification, gender and age, the family, education, work, health, religion, political life, and social change, the latter probably including population, urbanisation and perhaps something on "collective behaviour" (e.g. Kammeyer, Ritzer and Yetman 1990). Anthropology texts, with the very rare critical and innovative exception (e.g. Cheater 1989) follow a not dissimilar pattern with the expected conventional disciplinary emphases (more on kinship for example and a slightly different range of founding fathers, Durkheim for example appearing in both, but in a slightly different guise). If one goes into an academic bookshop in Japan, Korea, Malaysia, Taiwan and probably anywhere else throughout the region, one might of course find imported (probably English language) texts. But what one will also find are two items of rather more interest—foreign textbooks simply translated into the local language with no local content, or local versions of foreign textbooks following exactly the same structure as the foreign texts, and recommending identical methodologies and frequently citing the foreign founding fathers while including more local content. The student in a Japanese or Korean university is likely as a result to be getting the same methodological fare based on the same theoretical presuppositions as her counterpart in a British or North American university. It is even possible to buy, certainly in Japanese, Chinese and Bahasa Malaysia, sociological dictionaries that simply explain and define the standard Eurocentric sociological concepts in the vernacular without in any way debating the appropriateness of those concepts or the ways in which they are being employed in discourse. What is missing however is likely to be any account of indigenous conceptions of culture, social relations and social institutions, either because they are not thought to be especially interesting or significant to mainstream sociological (i.e. Western) discourse, or because they are invisible, being difficult to capture in terms of that discourse.

Two or three examples might illustrate this more concretely. Social inequality in Japan is often conceptualised by both foreign (e.g. Steven 1983) and local scholars (e.g. Ishida 1992) in terms of class. This is facilitated by the pervasive Marxism of large areas of Japanese academic life, although the actual analyses of class employed are usually closer to conventional sociological (socioeconomic status) ones than they are to serious Marxism. But there are problems with this, notably that Japanese themselves rarely if ever use a language of class, employing instead a language of hierarchy, and that objectively Japan is a remarkably equal society with low income differentials, distinctive rather age-grade like and education linked mechanisms of social mobility, fewer patterns of social exclusion and widespread popular and subjective conceptions of class convergence. In conventional Western sociology class is seen as a quality of industrialised societies, while patrimonialism and similar forms of hierarchical organisation are seen as characteristic of "traditional" societies, i.e. ones that have not fully entered onto the path of modernity (cf. Anthony Giddens: "Modernity is a post-traditional order": Giddens 1991:14). But actual acquaintance with Japan reveals that it is a society that combines both these qualities of class and hierarchy, not as alternatives, but combined into distinctive sociological patterns that make Japan "Japanese." The conventional sociological vocabulary however has no term for this, so either the notion of class is employed despite its doing obvious violence to the facts, or analysts fall back on the common language of suggesting ad nauseam that Japan somehow uniquely combines "tradition and modernity." Local understandings of social stratification, which does indeed empirically exist, either (especially amongst professional social scientists) takes the same methodological and conceptual form as in Western sociology, or appears in the guise of nativist discourse rarely taken seriously by Western social scientists or Japanologists although it clearly represents an indigenous mode of self-representation (Clammer 2001c). This problem is not unique to Japan, but applies in different ways to rapidly developing societies such as Singapore, where conventional class analysis is widely used despite the complexity of cultural notions attaching in such a multi-racial country to idea of status, and to the high levels of social mobility which mean that empirically several different "classes" may well exist within the same household, but along generational lines, In South Asia and amongst expatriate Hindu communities overseas an analogous problem arises in respect of caste. Louis Dumont has argued on a number of occasions that Western commentators on caste almost always misunderstand it, seeing it from the perspective of a system of socio-cultural domination rather than as (from the point of view of many Indian sociologists including such major figures as the late M.N. Srinivas) a system of inclusion that has kept the vast and heterogeneous social landscape of India together for centuries, allows the assimilation of minorities into a totalising social structure, protects sub-castes from economic competition and provides a primary identity forming mechanism far more psychologically realistic than Western style individualism, which for its own ideological reasons greatly downplays the extent to which people are actually socialised and are much less free than they imagine (Dumont 1980, 1986).

Another example, and one closer to the psychic level identified by Ashis Nandy and other indigenous postcolonial theorists, is that of conceptions and images of selfhood. Foundational to ideas of personhood and identity are notions of the self. It is revealing that with the advent of the "risk society" (to use Ulrich Beck's term) in Europe and elsewhere in the West, there has been a significant revival of interest in the nature of the self in European and to a lesser extent North American social thought (for example Cohen 1994, Barglow 1994, Seider 1994, and Clecak 1983). This is clearly linked with the whole "cultural turn" in the Western social sciences and is tied in with a whole group of tendencies manifesting in cultural studies generally, including a preoccupation with a new understanding of politics—as cultural politics, the politics of culture, identity politics or, in Giddens's phrase, "lifestyle politics" (as opposed that is to the old style "emancipatory politics") and a sudden concern with the body, which has been rediscovered as a central site of cultural practices—of fashion, decoration, meditation, sexuality, medical procedures, dance, and so on. It is in this zone of selfhood that a convergence between some forms of Western "postmodern" thinking and certain Asian (and certainly Japanese and Chinese) conceptions has been taking place, particularly in the largely unexplored interface where deconstructionism meets Buddhism (see however Odin 1995) and appear to be speaking a rather similar language.

Some commentators trace this not to a sudden enlightenment on the part of a West that has suddenly discovered the epistemological and ontological challenges of the East, but to a breakdown in the transcendent structures of Western religion and philosophy, a breakdown that has forced the realisation that there are and have long been viable alternative models (e.g. Hall and Ames 1998) based on quite different principles.

Anthony Giddens has argued that there is an intimate relationship between modernity and the self (Giddens 1991), an idea that is correct, except that Giddens appears to think that Western conceptions of the self are universal. This has the effect of either occluding alternative understandings of personal identity or of putting non-Western societies outside of the possible scope of modernity. Interestingly Giddens has been extensively translated into Japanese and his earlier book on modernity (*The Consequences of Modernity* 1990) is widely read in Japan, and much of his work is also available in Chinese. Giddens's view of the "Western" self as bounded, permanent, rational and essentialist may well be true of Europe and the North Atlantic societies. Whether it works for the Asia-Pacific ones however is moot. This is important not only for the accurate ethnographic delineation of cultural conceptions, but also for the consequences both of cultural mistranslation and of the undemocratic hegemony of certain people's concepts on social science communication and on positive communication between cultures. The centrality of this issue, in which questions of selfhood are paradigmatic, warrants a little further attention.

Selfhood, Identity and the Limits of Western Social Science

Western notions of personhood are characterised by individualism, permanence and an atomistic approach in which selves are free-floating monads (Morris 1991). They are essentially lonely and indeed the basis of European existentialist philosophy is exactly the alienation that the autonomous self experiences and which can only be overcome by the creation of meaning in the face of an essentially meaningless universe (Jean-Paul Sartre's *Being and Nothingness* standing as a paradigmatic example). The view emerging, in slightly different but historically closely linked configurations, in China and in Japan and in contiguous cultures influenced by them (Vietnam in particular) is very different. If Dumont is correct in arguing that the root of Western individualism is to be sought in Christianity, then it may well be that the roots of East Asian views of the self lie in Confucianism, Buddhism and Taoism.

So what, crudely sketched, are the characteristics of these alternative views of the self? Firstly a clear distinction must be made between individuality and individualism. If the latter refers to a notion of the autonomous and monadic self, the first refers to the construction of character through self-cultivation. In this model, while some basic qualities of selfhood are indeed givens, they are not permanent, but are capable of transformation through ethical endeavours, which, by their very nature cannot be solipsistic but require the integration of the self into a community. The Confucian exemplary cultivated person (*junzi*) while unique is not autonomous, and is irreducibly social (Hall and Ames 1998: 25-27). This is true also in Japan where the self is seen not as a monad, but as a "field," as the focused point of a web of relationships. What appears to many outsiders as a culture characterised by a weak sense of self and highly situational ethics, is in fact better understood as "situational" (Bachnik and Quinn 1994), "relational," or "interpersonalistic" (Hamaguchi 1982), in which the self only exists in a dialectical relationship to the other and in which either practical or ontological autonomy are illusory. The self then is seen as social, dialectical rather than binary, dependent rather than autonomous, embedded in a network of civility, reciprocity and responsibility and as much emotional as rational. The "decentred subject" of French deconstructionism has actually always existed in Asia.

The nature of ideas of selfhood is a fascinating ethnographic subject in itself and has provoked some extremely interesting comparative work (for example Kondo 1990), some of which I have reviewed elsewhere (Clammer 1995). My point here however is to point up the theoretical and methodological implications of such comparisons. What are they? Briefly the first and probably most important is that they radically change the concept of agency. Notions of agency are foundational to all social science (including historical and philosophical) endeavours: who acts? by what means? on whom? through what notion of causality? Anthony Giddens has argued (Giddens 1983) that the problem of the relationship between agency and structure is the key problem of the social sciences. He may well be right, although unfortunately he assumes that the agents (human individuals) are the monadic entities of classical Western individualism. If one however understands agents and their mode of relating to the world in radically different terms, the whole nature of the "problem" changes. There may in fact not even be a problem. For example, much Western social science and its underlying philosophy is still essentially Cartesian in character. It assumes in other words not only the monadic individual, but also that those individuals are essentially rational (Cogito ergo sum) and are creatures deeply divided between body and mind, which then, as maybe the central philosophical problem, have to be related somehow to one another. Japanese thinking on the nature of the person however is holistic and non-Cartesian seeing body/mind as simply two aspects of a single entity which do not need relating, but rather expressing. It is consequently in practice rather than in cogitation that the self discovers its true nature, whether through work (as in Kondo's ethnography), through the merging of art, sport and religion (all separate categories in Western thinking) in such activities as Zen archery, or in the practice of indigenous psychotherapies such as Naikan which are based on techniques of meditation and the recovery of memory, not in order to accuse the other, but for the ethical purpose of rediscovering and reaffirming nuturative relationships (mother, teachers and significant others) who have helped the individual to grow (a small but expanding literature exists in English, for example Yuasa 1987, 1993, and a substantial but as yet untranslated one in Japanese, for example Ichikawa 1991).

Such a view of agency has many other implications only a few of which I can indicate here. This essentially dialectical and non-ego view of the self creates a view of social causality which is very like, and may well be based on, the Buddhist conception of "dependent arising" in which all phenomena are in a sense "causeless" since they are all interlinked and mutually interacting. This idea is not unlike that of some varieties of Western chaos theory (the minute disturbances caused by a butterfly flapping its wings in Bermuda may be the ultimate cause of the typhoon in the Bay of Bengal...) or of some of the ideas emerging from quantum physics (Capra 1983), except that there is no first cause at all: the universe is an intricate web of relationships—the "net of Indra"—not a system of linear causality. A second consequence is that the Western obsession with categories is also dissolved. In the Zen example cited above, art, sport, spirituality, and what in the West would probably be called psychology, are all blended. The "body" and the "mind" are integrated. Emotion and reason are no longer juxtaposed. A third and extremely important one is that in Western thought on the whole (an exception being some varieties of "New Age" thinking which have however borrowed heavily from Asian thought) human society is seen as entirely separate from and over against nature. In indigenous Japanese social thought however this is not the case. Humans as embodied beings are intrinsically part of nature, not merely observers of it. Not only are Western inventions such as socio-biology unnecessary to account for the relationship of humans to the rest of nature, but there is a cultural link too, via aesthetics. The traditional Japanese concern with an aesthetics assimilating the human to the natural is well known, although rarely related to the indigenous understanding of the self. And aesthetics plays a major role in Japanese culture as it not only ties humans into the material environment, but also represents a major basis for ethics, and, through the assimilation of ethics and aesthetics to each other, links Japan to debates on postmodernity as they have occurred in the Japanese context (Miyoshi and Harootunian 1989). The language of postmodernity, appropriated from Europe, has however been in many respects turned against its originators as it has allowed Japanese social theorists to both argue that its cultural characteristics have always made it postmodern, long before the West even thought of the idea (and so in a sense ahead of the West), and that Japan stands outside of "universal," i.e. Western, history and as such has either been exempt from modernity, or alternatively has achieved modernity by a quite different route from that taken by the West.

These rather abstract observations might be made more concrete at this point by trying a small thought experiment using one of the key elements in the cultural make-up of East and Southeast Asia. What would a Buddhist sociology look like? How in other words would notions of agency, selfhood, causality, institutions, history, justice, rights or social ethics look from the point of view of a non-transcendental, non-materialist dialectical position which has no conception of a permanently existing discrete self and which is non-Cartesian in its understanding of the constitution of the human person and in which enlightenment takes the form of an unmediated, non-cognitive grasping of the fundamental nature of reality? Few attempts have been made to work out what this might mean, but let me suggest just a few thoughts.

Buddhism might be thought of as the most advanced form of postmodernism. It is clearly anti-foundational, decentres the position of the human individual through its radical notion of "no-self," and undermines conventional truth-claims based on the assumption of an objective and continuing world perceived by and acted upon by equally objective and continuing individuals. It also contains a methodology for overcoming the illusory world-view of the ego infested mind, and with its totally non-Theistic cosmology, radically undermines Western conceptions of what constitutes "religion." Such views cannot but have substantial impact on ideas of ethics, social justice, human rights, "development," social policies, notions of human responsibility and personality, of ecology (through the Mahayana notion of the potential Buddhahood of all sentient beings, which may include plants) and of the good society (a consumer one being a little hard to justify when a doctrine of non-craving is basic to the whole Buddhist system). Concepts of time, space and, to take an example that has attracted substantial attention in Western social sciences in the last decade, memory, all require fundamental rethinking from this alternative perspective. What, after all, are the sociological implications of the doctrine of reincarnation? Masao Abe, in his study of the work of the seminal Japanese Buddhist thinker and practitioner Dogen, has the following to say:

> "Thus, Buddhism, in interpreting human existence as something that undergoes birth-and-death, or 'something that undergoes arising-desistance'...does not necessarily view humans as distinct from other animals. Rather, it sees humans as part of impermanent existence undergoing the vicissitudes of arising-desistance... Human existence is grasped in the dimension transcending the limits of 'human' defined as a being that has a beginning and an end. That is why Buddhism discusses the vicissitudes of birth-and-death in terms of *samsara*, or transmigration...Therefore Buddhism transcends humanism and anthropocentrism... and it also discloses the way to a fundamental emancipation of human existence." (Abe 1992: 146)

One could go on. The point is to show that a view of knowledge not based on the categories of Greek philosophy and its logocentrism is possible, and not just as a theoretical project, but one that exists over huge areas of Asia. This project is not only a theoretical one, since it also contains its own emancipatory agenda very different from that of the European Enlightenment project (Batchelor 1998). Its non-Cartesian nature and its views of the self also go a long way towards explaining both the failure of psychoanalysis and for the most part the failure of Christianity to penetrate those parts of Asia dominated by Buddhism and never directly colonised by the West (Japan and Thailand for example).

A parallel analysis could be carried out for other living religio-social systems of Asia too—Taoism, Confucianism, Islam or Shinto. But hopefully using the Buddhist example the point has been made that it is entirely possible to envisage alternative social science and modes of social thought based upon local epistemologies and which view the world in very different terms from Western disciplinary knowledge and methodologies. Yet in practice these systems have become not a challenge to Western intellectual hegemony, but its objects of study, or worse, regarded as simply "nativist" forms of thought of no universal significance. In fact of course in a genuinely polycentric world the centre is everywhere and there are no peripheries. The reality of this however is still far from informing or transforming the fundamentally Eurocentric biases of mainstream social thought.

A similar analysis has indeed been developed for related traditions, as Hall and Ames have attempted to do for Confucianism and Taoism in their Chinese settings. Again my intention here is not to recapitulate their arguments, but to point out their methodological and theoretical implications for the reading of cultures under the sign of globalisation. Speaking primarily of religious culture, they suggest that "having had

Judeo-Christian assumptions imposed on them, even the Chinese have in large numbers become persuaded that they are not a religious culture" (Hall and Ames 1998: 233), a process symptomatic of the larger problem of the smuggling in to readings of Chinese religion and philosophy "a worldview and a way of thinking that is alien to the tradition itself" (*ibid.* 237). What they term (following the Cambridge philosopher I.A. Richards' discussion in his book *Mencius on the Mind*) "our implicit syntactic apparatus" (*ibid.* 239) have entailments. But whereas Richards attempts to develop a methodology for comparative studies is based on decentring or "fuzzying up" key concepts in order to allow their full range of meanings to emerge without imposing predetermined definitions on them (a laudatory aim), the suggestion being advanced here is that this is not necessarily enough, since it does not allow for the operations of the sociology of knowledge. Encouraging latitude in the usage of concepts is fine, except that it does not see the extent to which the usage of such concepts is not determined by individual preferences or linguistic competence, but by institutional factors: the permitted usages within a given discourse in other words. A Japanese university student is likely to be taught the received definition of key disciplinary terms, but not, unfortunately, encouraged to explore the full range of possible meanings. The determination of meaning, as Wittgenstein rightly pointed out, is one of usage. But that usage is embedded in discourse and discourses are embedded in institutions embodying and reproducing the disciplines that they claim to represent. The actual sociology of intellectual production (for example the critical analysis of the university) in Asian settings (Pierre Bourdieu and a few others have done it for the European and US universities) is as necessary as the deconstruction of texts and discourses themselves. It is surely no accident that Edward Said concluded his *Orientalism* with an examination of knowledge production and reproduction (research and teaching) in the major US universities that study the Middle East.

Cultural Communication in a Polycentric World

Is this an argument for incommensurability? Not at all. What is hopefully being opened up here is a sketch for the foundations of a methodology that might move beyond the temptations of either Orientalism or Occidentalism on the one hand, and the necessary but self-limiting moves of postcolonial theory on the other. The elements in this methodology can be briefly set out as follows. i). The recognition of the extent to which local readings of Asian societies using the disciplinary frameworks of Western academic subjects with their built in epistemological biases is at the basis of self-misrepresentations, as much as it is the source of Orientalist misrepresentations. ii). The paying of serious attention to indigenous social theory and refusing the temptation to dismiss it as "nativist." It may be, but in a polycentric, multivocal and non-ethnocentric world one should at least begin by assuming that it represents the local voice, in much the same way that anthropologists presumably treat any form of local knowledge. Western social science in fact turns out to be just as local and nativist as any Asian or African body of knowledge, it has simply had power behind it, hence its now near hegemony. Local social sciences that do not simply ape the postures and language of their Western counterparts and which are willing to seriously question the disciplinary boundaries of those metropolitan versions and of the rationalities that underlie these, are core components of the "local" or "indigenous" knowledges that Western social science (for example development studies in a big way) has just begun to rediscover and applaud. iii). It is necessary to question the language of "flows," "travelling cultures" and "hybridity" that are currently fashionable ways of talking about what an older vocabulary used to call culture contact or cultural communication. In talking about culture there is a strong tendency to essentialise. In fact all cultures are processural and the West consumes the East even as the East consumes the West and as the East consumes other parts of itself (Japanese pop music in Hong Kong and Singapore, Chinese food in Japan and the constant use of Chinese imagery in Japanese advertising, comics, animated movies and video games, Thai motifs in Malaysian architecture, and Islamic ones in Singaporean, and so on). The issue is not just the existence of flows, interesting as they are (Europeans becoming Buddhists, Asians becoming Christians), but of the ways in which these flows are negotiated and the processes by which they are incorporated into local intellectual, emotional, somatic and political cultures. While the whole thing cannot necessarily be reduced only to power, it is the case that without this epistemological investigation into the basis of cultural communication (one in which culture itself is increasingly open and pluralistic), globalisation simply becomes the continuation of colonialism by other means; the imposition of alien forms, again emotional, religious, subjective as well as economic, by means of consumer capitalism, and dare one say it, academic discourse.

This statement however needs some qualification, along at least two lines. The first is that the older Orientalist critique assumed (like its child, postcolonialism) that the problem of the (mis)representation of cultures was primarily a Western one—politically motivated misreadings stemming from unequal distribution of power. The preceding analysis however suggests that the problem is now more subtle in that involves not simply politics in the narrow sense, but also on the one hand the politics of academe and the hegemonic and gatekeeping influences that disciplines exercise over the production, categorisation and recognition of knowledge(s), and on the other the pervasive effects of globalisation which amongst its many effects, and amongst its more profound ones, transforms subjectivities. Its effects are nowhere more powerful than when it can persuade a Tokyo office worker to model her hairstyle on that of Princess Diana, her pout on that of Madonna and her emotions and social attitudes on those of the Spice Girls. Bryan Turner is correct when he argues that the biggest threat to traditional forms of religion (and he has Islam particularly in mind) are not the attacks of secularising intellectuals, but as he puts it, Tina Turner or that same Madonna (Turner 1994: 10). The problem is still a Western one insofar as that is where academic disciplines have their origins, but the problem of representation is now internationalised through the assimilation of those same disciplinary models into both the self-perception of Asian societies and the ways in which the social scientists of those societies "read" their neighbours. Japanese readings of China, Korea and Southeast Asia are extremely revealing, not only for the ways in which historical tensions colour perceptions, but for the ways in which Western categories of social analysis structure these readings. This does not go completely unchallenged—one thinks of the local critiques of Western conceptions of Thailand as a "loosely structured social system," of Srinivas's critique of Dumont's interpretation of the caste system, or of at least partial attempts to rethink Southeast Asian kinship outside of the categories of Western anthropology (e.g. Karim 1995). But the basis of the problem has shifted from direct inequalities of power (Asian scholars are very capable of talking back to the West and to its scholars who think they know best), to the autonomy of the disciplines. While certainly the role of subjects like anthropology or sociology is challenged in at least some of the relatively newly independent societies of Asia such as Malaysia (Shamsul 1999), they are enormously popular with students who in turn carry the categories that they have learned in the classroom out into the analysis and management of their own societies. The root of true intellectual independence consequently lies in challenging the autonomy of the disciplines, for this is where one of the most subtle and pernicious influences of globalisation is to be found.

If one examines the responses to this globalisation within the practice of the social sciences in Asia, it is possible to see a range of reactions: the filling in of the disciplinary structures with local content, attempts to create or define indigenous alternatives, postcolonial thinking, and anti-modernist movements, whether taking the form of fundamentalisms or attempts at autarky, or on the other hand as principled rejections not of modernisation, but of the package that is often taken as constituting Western style modernity—as seen for example in the Chinese revolution or the 1940s attempts by Japanese intellectuals for finding the means of "overcoming modernity" (Najita and Harootunian 1998). Recent critiques of "development" as representing simply the latest phase of neo-colonialism provide yet another example. On the Western side attempts to address misrepresentation in turn range across the sudden rediscovery of "indigenous" knowledge, discussions of "culture and development," the emergence of comparative philosophy as a serious field and participatory methodologies of various kinds. Interestingly some of the most interesting attempts to really address these issues have taken place outside of the conventional academic disciplines altogether—in the New Age movement, serious Western attempts to grapple with Asian spiritualities, in chaos theory and in emerging Western models of the self that are attempting to link personhood to ideas from quantum physics (Zohar 1990) to ideas long embodied in the major Asian religions (Capra 1988).

To conclude then we might note that cultural relations requires not only a dynamic and processural understanding of culture, but also one that is both critical and aware that cultures are not just sets of habits, but are the embodiment of underlying ontological and epistemological presuppositions. No search for a new order, world or otherwise, is sustainable if based on false philosophical premises. What appear to be simple cultural misunderstandings or disputes may actually turn out to be people actually talking right past each other, quite unaware that what appears to be a mundane disagreement in fact contains deep ontological divergences. For example when Louis Dumont, the French scholar of South Asia suggests that Western culture is "permeated by nominalism, which grants real existence only to individuals and not to relations, to elements and not to sets of elements" (Dumont 1986: 10) he is pointing to exactly this kind of factor. The basis of alternative modernities is not only differing political or economic systems, but cosmologies, the integrity of which are paradoxically being eroded by globalisation at the very moment when the possibility of their being more than one route to modernity is finally being seriously discussed. A key way of discovering a cosmology is to find out what a people's utopias are like, something more likely to be revealed in their literature, film, art and religion than by conventional social science style research. These utopias, or their fundamental dreams or collective aspirations, represent the most interesting and least explored dimension of inter-cultural dialogue and is where both commonalities and existential differences most clearly express themselves and where the most basic social categories actually indigenous to that culture reveal themselves—the relationships between religion and culture, of emotions, body and self, of rights and freedoms, of individualism and collectivism, of nature and society and where notions of rationality, ethics, gender relations, wisdom and possible futures are expressed.

The question then becomes whether the debates that entrance Western sociology—class, constructivism v. biologism, functionalism or structuralism and so forth, really exhaust the total field of possibilities. The answer is clearly not, yet the world is still largely read from these limited theoretical perspectives and their assumptions—for example that philosophy and the empirical sciences are different, the former simply clarifying the presuppositions on which the latter is based. Subjects that fall outside of the positivist presuppositions of that science—intuition, mysticism, meditational states, ESP and so forth are consequently not considered to be forms of knowledge at all. If this view is challenged, as it has been from within Japanese philosophy for example, conventional sociologies of, say, the body or of medicine, are radically undermined or extended, once the body is seen as and field of energy and as fully integrated with the mind for instance (Ozawa 2001).

None of this should be taken as an argument against critiques of Orientalism, attempts to develop indigenous social sciences, postcolonial studies or continuing attempts to theorise the relationships between anthropology and colonialism in Asia (e.g. most recently Van Breman and Shimizu 1999), or to discuss the geographical "construction" of Asia (e.g. JAS 2000) Rather it is a question of levels and a question of identifying what is missing. To recapitulate: this means my argument that one of the major but least identified sources of the misrepresentation of culture—Asia by Europe and Asia by itself—lies in the local assimilation of originally Western, but now hegemonic modes of social science theorising and methodology embodied in the various social science disciplines. To overcome this problem it is not enough to simply replace foreign content with local, or to search for "relevance" (development issues such as poverty, or the critical posturing of much cultural studies work in Asia). The harder task is the deep inner work that both attempts to discover the sources of misrepresentation in the hegemonic intellectual systems of the social sciences, and to explore sympathetically the alternative sources that exist within local cultures themselves and to not only respect the differences in world-view that may exist amongst them, but to see these as the sources of new theoretical insight rather than of problems. Even after colonialism Europe still flourishes in some of the deepest levels of Asia's being—in its imaginaries. These may appear in the representations of popular culture (film, comics, fashion, advertising) as part of the normal traffic between cultures. They may also appear in the self-representations constructed out of the vocabularies of the social science disciplines, a level at which some of the most fundamental self-imaginings are formed and where hegemonic systems can very easily drive out the cultural creativity embodied in the local realities beyond those systems. Any real politics of identity is, after all, contingent upon intellectual autonomy and the validity of the cultural forms that constitute the frameworks for everyday life and meaning creation.

4

After Orientalism

Postcolonialism, Culture and Globalisation

Asia and Europe: Reframing the Debate

Linkages between Asia and Europe exist, and have long existed, at a number of levels—economic, political and social. Underlying and reflecting these is the cultural—the perceptions and representations of Asia by Europeans and of Europe by Asians. There are older and now perhaps less sophisticated models for characterising this mutuality (often a distorted one based upon differential access to power), notably "Orientalism" (Said 1978) and "Occidentalism" (Carrier 1995). Both these approaches assume (as does the even older field of "International Relations") two broadly defined blocs or entities between which interchange takes place.

The limitation of such conceptualisations is that they predate or deflect the immense shifts in the understanding of the concept of culture itself which have accompanied late modernity and the globalising forces that it has set in train. Leaving aside for the moment the disputes about the precise meaning of the term "globalisation" and its significance for the critical analysis of the contemporary world system, most commentators would agree that it contains and implies profound implications for culture, whether this is understood in terms of the migration of peoples, symbols or objects, of attitudes to selfhood and subjectivities or of the implications for everyone of such powerful Eurocentric concepts as "development" (Friedman 1996, Robertson 1992, Giddens 1991). This concern is not only that of establishing the place of culture within globalisation, but more profoundly that of questioning the meaning of culture itself in these new circumstances.

While the argument for the centrality of culture to the framing of questions in political economy is not a new one (Clammer 1985), it has re-entered debate through the three portals of firstly, postmodernism, secondly, anthropological disputes over the means (and the legitimacy) of the representation of the "Other" (Clifford and Marcus 1986) and thirdly through attempts to create a new vocabulary to ensnare the phenomena that have emerged out of postcolonial studies, the study of international migration and "travelling cultures" and the increasing visibility of transnational communities such as the Overseas Chinese—a vocabulary that now contains such celebrated and disputed terms as "hybridity" and "creolisation." The cumulative effect of these conceptual and methodological shifts has been to both re-centre culture in debates about the nature of the world system and to at the same time problematise the concept of culture itself, by seeing it as no longer the relatively fixed possession of spatially and temporally bounded groups, but as a processural and highly dynamic strategy of identity negotiation, by its nature open-ended and without points of closure.

The primary consequence of this is that to talk at all about cultural relations between Asia and Europe it is necessary to reframe the debate. The outlines of how this might be done constitutes the body of the chapter that follows, an endeavour which involves essentially the attempt to formulate a new vocabulary as a consequence of the fact that the study of European-Asian cultural relations needs resiting in the context of the realities of globalised cultural complexity. This must necessarily bring into question the language of "flows," "values" and "identities" and especially of the whole language of "development" through which the formerly postcolonial West has continued to impose itself on the rest of the world in the postwar decades, as suggested in the previous chapter.

To undertake this critique and to suggest an alternative conceptual reconstruction there are four elements that need to be taken into primary account. The first of these is the notion of postcoloniality. There are those in Asia as we have seen (e.g. Chen 1998) who argue that understanding decolonialisation is the key question for cultural studies in the region. The basis for this claim is not only the huge empirical impact of colonialisms on Asia economically, politically, linguistically and institutionally, but also its continuing impact long after its formal demise in the creation of mindsets, definitions of reality, creation of institutional forms and in the guise of "development" programmes. Postcolonial theory, while it has certainly taken its own peculiar polemical turns, raises some fundamental questions not usually addressed in the context of the globalisation debate.

The second is the notion of contemporaneity: the coexistence of cultures and social systems in what is actually a single world system (Augé 1999). Western anthropology, in former incarnations at least, was inclined to treat "other cultures" as spatially remote examples of the temporal past of its own social evolution. Now it increasingly recognises that supposedly "other" cultures are in fact deeply implicated with its own, through their real even if remote relationships created by the world system and through the mental means through which it constructs those "others" and through which its itself is reciprocally constructed. There are not simply "relationships" between "East" and "West": those relationships are constructed and mediated, today largely by the social "sciences" which purport to study but in fact largely simply construct models of the societies in question and their supposed linkages. The assumptions that the East somehow represents the Other of the West, and that, from the perspective of the East, the West necessarily represents its future are deeply questionable. The "reality" of these societies and their challenge epistemologically and politically to the West's philosophical and historical hegemony (largely expressed through colonialism) is a necessary precondition for any talk of "relationships."

Thirdly, and related to the foregoing, is the whole question of globalisation as the West's modernising project—a project founded in fact on the assumption of a Westernising and homogenising civilisational process. Such a conception has of course not only sparked debate about the extent to which globalisation spawns intensified localisation, but also the question of alternative modernities at the macro-level, modernities which may take the form of reactions to globalisation in such forms as the Islamic revolution in Iran (Beyer 1997) or the defining of routes to postmodernity which bypass modernity altogether, as in the case of Japan (Clammer 1995).

Finally, the actual content of culture and of cultural "flows" must be carefully examined. While Easterners do indeed consume the West (fashions, food, education, literature and film for example), the West now also increasingly consumes the East—both those same items and more, religion being a conspicuous example. This not only involves the wholesale export of spiritual alternatives (especially Indian forms of neo-Hinduism and Japanese new religions), but also the assimilation and transformation of Asian religious traditions into distinctly Western forms, as with varieties of Sufism now popular in the West (e.g. Vaughan-Lee 1993) or with the emergence of a whole variety of Buddhism now called "Western Buddhism" (Kulananda 1997). Just as indigenous intellectuals in the East have in the past negotiated, assimilated, rejected or modified the cultural offerings of the West, so now as that process continues in Asia, a parallel process is occurring in the West in respect of Asian cultures at an accelerating pace. At another level film, literature and popular culture represent points at which complex cultural negotiation takes place on an everyday level in the attempt by Asian peoples to define postcolonial identities (Chow 1998), something which also occurs in the context of everyday consumption activities (Clammer 1997b). Even as the Pacific war is being weekly refought (and won) in Japanese *manga* or comic books, so housewives in Kuala Lumpur or Colombo daily negotiate their relationship to the world through the contents of their shopping baskets. The relationship between Asia and Europe then is not simply one of increased cultural flows, it is also and predominantly an issue of the ways those flows are understood and assimilated into broader cosmologies. If globalisation has changed the nature of culture, then a fresh appreciation of the subtleties of these changes on inter-cultural and international relationships has to be taken into account. Without these new possibilities for regional cooperation will be fraught with representational problems not so dissimilar from those analysed in the older critical literature on classical Orientalism, but this time simply transposed into a postmodern key.

Fragmentation or Cultural Flows?

A conventional approach to the cultural situation of the world at large is to characterise it through a language of fragmentation (Featherstone 1997: 1). But a more accurate picture would be not of disintegration, but of new and unacknowledged patterns of flows, fresh recombinations of elements and, as chaos theory so tellingly suggests, of small differences in initial conditions leading to large differences in outcomes of situations. The high volume of travelling and physical interaction between Asia and the West leads not only to the mobility of bodies, but also to the travelling of images. A language of syncretism however is inadequate for describing the outcome of these interactions: some things blend, some are adapted, but also totally new cultural configurations emerge out of unexpected and almost random conjunctions of ideas, styles, events or modes of behaviour. A view of global culture as decentred assumes that there was originally a centre somewhere (presumably in the West?).

In fact the Westernisation of the world is paralleled by (and indeed contested by) the Japanisation of the world. And attention to regional zones rather to the total global system demonstrates more restricted but on the ground equally significant interactions. Hong Kong is simultaneously an heir to British colonialism, to Japanese popular culture and modes of consumption (the departmental store for example), to linguistic and cultural (to say nothing of economic and political) input from mainland China, from Taiwan and from the Chinese of the diaspora. At the same time Hong Kong exports itself through tourism, through its large film industry (Lii 1998), its global airline (Cathay Pacific) and. its own substantial economic impact on the region. It is a society that both imports labour to serve its own middle and upper classes (Filipina domestics), and exports its skilled labour to Singapore and elsewhere in Southeast Asia, Australia, Canada and the Gulf and its unskilled labour as illegal migrants to Japan. Different but structurally similar models could be constructed for Singapore, Malaysia and other societies within Asia-Pacific. Star TV, transmitted from Hong Kong, is seen all over Asia, the Japanese NHK transmits to Europe and CNN and BBC news can be viewed all over the region. Anyone with a satellite equipped TV can watch on a Sunday morning in the Japanese countryside the news in English, Japanese, Chinese, Korean, Russian, German, French and Spanish.

The question then becomes one of what all this means specifically for an analysis of "cultural relations" between Europe and Asia. The basic assumption of classical Orientalist discourse was that it is the West that constructs the East, the East itself being essentially the residue, that which is left over beyond the edges of Western definitions of civilisation. Postwar political and more especially economic changes that have led to Asia-Pacific emerging as a powerful bloc and international actor in its own right have profoundly changed and even reversed this: the progressive project and even modernity itself becomes an Eastern prerogative and Europe and its erstwhile colonies or colonised spaces (Africa, Latin America) decline (Sakai 1989). The daily cultural problematic of a worker in England, Ireland or continental Europe may be, whether consciously recognised as such or not, negotiation of Japanese culture and management techniques, assimilation of Indian or Chinese foods and mastery of Taiwanese technology, while planning meanwhile a holiday in Thailand. Globalising images arise as much now in the East as they do in the West. The West's modernising project in other words has effectively reached its end, an end signalled by its own internal exhaustion (of which postmodernism is the major symptom); the glaring ineffectiveness of "development," its main postcolonial mechanism of influence on the non-Western world; and the reversal of cultural flows and economic power which, combined with sheer demographics and control of raw materials places the definition of the global future effectively in the hands of the East.

This brings into play several new factors. Paramount amongst these is the perception that history is not only chronological, but also "spatial and relational" (Sakai 1989:106), in which case the temporal metanarrative leading universally from premodernity through modernity to postmodernity in which "postmodernity is in effect accorded the status of being the latest stage in a master logic of historical development, notwithstanding all the obligatory homilies paid to the critique of development" (Featherstone and Lash 1997:1). Societies which place themselves outside of this logic (Japan, Thailand, China, Burma before the generals, would come to mind) create different historical spaces for themselves in which alternative projects of civilisational construction take place which are in no way Eurocentric, but on the contrary on which the West impinges merely as a distraction and as the inappropriate route to the future.

Secondly, as Jonathan Friedman so cogently argues (Friedman 1997) analyses of creolisation and hybridisation have tended to concentrate on cultural artefacts themselves and the ways in which they are "transformed" through "culture contact" (cf. Tobin 1992), whereas if indeed culture is to be seen as process rather than as substance, then the real focus of attention must be on cultural practices that produce and reproduce identity spaces of an ever shifting nature. East/West cultural flows need recasting consequently in this form—not as the exchange of objects or even of ideas, but as a complex network of identity strategies in which artefacts and commodities are employed not as "essences" but as counters in a game with no fixed rules.

Thirdly, cultural analysis frequently ignores the underlying economic realities. In this context there are three of these: that it is international capital (both Eastern and Western) that currently dictates the fundamental context in which social and political action takes place (it is the locus of power in other words); that this power is not merely "material," but takes symbolic forms. either in the creation of meaning systems and systems of values, or in the creation of symbols which are themselves commodities (Lash and Urry 1994); and that this capitalism is itself protean, diverse and possessed of distinct national characteristics (British let us say, as opposed to Japanese capitalism). All debates about culture and all debates about East/West relations must be placed in this frame. The coding and decoding in which cultures and individuals are constantly engaged in a globalised world is not, as in a culturalist model, autonomous, but takes place in the context of the prevailing international political economy, which is a capitalist one.

Finally, there is little left, in a globalising world, of "pure" cultures, one in which, despite a whole popularising literature to the contrary (*The Japanese Mind*; *Thai Culture*; *The Ways of Thinking of Eastern Peoples*), the "essence" of particular geographically defined cultures can be discerned and packaged. This is true of the West as much as of the East, and if the cultures of the Orient were transformed by colonialism, so the cultures of the West are being transformed by hybridisation occasioned by the movement of artefacts, foods, symbols, peoples, literatures, arts and technologies from Asia, Africa, the Caribbean and Latin America. The actual polycentrism of the world system is matched by the actual hybridisation of the cultures in each of these shifting "centres." Even under colonialism, seen by many largely as the self-export of the West to the rest, counterflows of resources, ideas, language, people, artefacts and arts occurred widely. Classical Orientalism not only failed to grasp the extent of these flows even (or especially) at the moments of high imperialism, but also did not realise the existence or extent of counter discourses. Subaltern studies is actually only the contemporary surfacing of a tradition which has long been present in Asian societies, but which has only been able to fully articulate itself with the demise of colonialism and the conceptual decentring of the world system.

For this reason post-colonial studies have come to occupy an important place in the intellectual landscape. The language of postcolonialism is also of significance for two other reasons. The first is that it represents the way in which the debate about East West relations has been framed in much of Asia, especially in India and East Asia (Chen 1998). This is significant both as an indigenous discourse (however much it has been co-opted by Western scholars and publishers as a politically-correct intellectual option—e.g. Williams and Chrisman 1993 amongst many others) and for the extent that it avoids any of the language of "development" so prevalent in the West. The second is that it allows into the discussion themes which have been largely excluded from conventional political science or sociological approaches to "international relations"—such as memory and the emotions of dispossession and domination. Europe in Asia is still a haunting legacy, and if Europe itself and its vaunted version of modernity still has to fully digest the implications of the Holocaust (Bauman 1989), so Asia still has to fully digest the experience of colonialism, including Japanese colonialism and to integrate it into a balanced understanding of the present and possible futures.

Significantly postcolonial studies began in literary studies and since then has continued to be a discourse largely about culture and about the exclusion from the West's master narratives of modernity (e.g. Habermas and Giddens) of any discussion of colonialism itself or of the profound cultural transformations that it wrought on subject peoples, through its creation of massive diasporas and through its many and often subtle effects on the colonisers themselves (Thomas 1994). It calls into question both the universality of the modernist project itself and of the notions of culture which it generated and which are themselves part of the technology of domination, notions which essentialised identities ("Japanese," "Indian," "Hindu") while actually displacing and confusing them through an inevitable process of hybridisation. As Featherstone puts it, "(H)ere we think of the need to investigate the ways in which particular European notions of culture were generated within modernity which presented its culture as unified and integrated, which neglected the spatial relationships to the rest of the world that developed with colonialism, in effect the dark side of modernity that made this sense of unity possible" (Featherstone 19911:12). As Featherstone goes on to point out, Sociology, the "science" of this modernity, itself came of age in an era of the formation of nation-states and created a disciplinary culture which, passing through functionalism to structuralism via Talcott Parsons, revealed, like its sister science Anthropology, a mania for discovering the principles of "integration." In an at least partially post-national world in which global complexity has swept aside any simple notions of functional integration and in which the dark underside of late modernity itself (continuing global "underdevelopment," Eurocentrism in social and economic theory, racism and other abiding social issues) both this disciplinary focus and the assumptions that underpinned it are obsolete. The necessity of matching this with new notions of culture which are spatial as well as temporal, processural rather that categorical, recognise hybridity rather than essence as the normal condition of being, which arise from multiple understandings of modernity which conceptualise human subjectivities and understandings of selfhood differently and which are in many cases conflictual in that they continually contest received notions of social reality (new social movements in the "South," Asian theologies of liberation, Buddhist socialisms, indigenous conceptualisations of identity such as the Japanese *Nihonjinron*, for example) and are based on fundamentally different philosophical premises from those of the Enlightenment project. Globalisation itself is consequently a paradoxical phenomenon in that while it integrates at some levels (primarily economic), it creates differences at others and indeed creates the pluralist context in which the previously subaltern can speak and can expect to be heard as equal voices, as occupants of different spaces even if of the same time as the colonisers.

What then in summary are the implications for Europe-Asia relations of postcolonial analysis? The first is the obvious one that flows of people, ideas, ideologies, religions, arts and material goods are not only from the former colonisers to the formally colonised, but that this flow is now not so much simply reversed as deepened in its complexities and ambiguities. There are more Muslims in Bradford than Christians in Kuala Lumpur; but there are also probably more Christians in Africa than there are in the whole of Europe. Turkish is the de facto second language of large areas of Germany, even as Mexican Spanish is of southern California. Identity in any simple sense has been finally shattered by the cultural impact of globalisation. This, and secondly, together with expanding knowledge of Asia in the West and of the West in Asia, finally does away with any notions of cultural superiority or inferiority on either side. With probably more Westerners becoming Buddhists than Asians are becoming Christians, the very philosophical underpinnings of the Enlightenment model begin to dissolve. And since postcolonial theory has as a basic premise the assumption that academic knowledge—its nature, production and dissemination—has been historically involved in the colonial project, even as it is now implicated in the project of "development," so Western academic study of the East faces serious questions as to its purposes, methods and political or business linkages. For scholars in Asian academies the problem is oddly similar; not that of simply reproducing a mirror image of Orientalism in a reactive Occidentalism, but rather the more subtle danger of having so internalised the preconceptions of the West that the indigenous scholar becomes a postcolonial orientalist, reproducing and perpetuating European concepts of the East, not least because of the still Western-centred distribution of academic power, prestige and influence. Who even today will do his Ph.D. at the University of Hanoi if he has the opportunity to do it at Harvard? (Behdad 1994).

The Eurocentric power to define, characteristic of both classical Orientalism and most of its successors (most notably "development studies"), is also visible in much of the contemporary globalisation discourse, which, while again purporting to generate a universalist theory, is often a triumphalist and (like its cousin postmodernism) partial account of the world. The apparent globalisation as seen from Wall Street looks a little different when seen from a Calcutta slum. A key lesson of postcolonial theory is that the vocabulary of differences must be and remain a critical and self-critical one as the language of Westernisation, and to an increasing extent of Japanisation, is a pervasive one that has dominated Europe-Asia cultural relations for too long and can easily reappear in new forms (such as in the domination of cultural studies by European modes of thought).

Postcolonial theory then sets out the basic model for examining relations between West and East and must do initially because it draws attention both to the structural levels (economic, political and military power, and to the cultural, not only in the sense of empirical flows, but also of images, representations, memories, prejudices and subliminal linkages. Until the colonial is fully exorcised and relations can be established on a wholly equal basis, the critical dialogue embodied in postcolonial theory must continue. This is not to say however that it is the final model, for if the present is encompassed in a postcolonial framework, the future need not necessarily be so. So while Kuan-Hsing Chen unequivocally identifies the subject of cultural studies in Asia to be colonialism (Chen 1998) he also admits that a postcolonial reaction, given the economic success of much of

East and Southeast Asia (at least until the collapse of 1997), can easily be a facile triumphalism which simply replicates in reverse the earlier triumphalism and Eurocentrism of the past. But having admitted this, Chen's own analysis of the alternatives is dated and anachronistic, leaning heavily on the discourses emerging from the colonial psychology/identification theories of Mannoni and Fanon on the one hand, and on the nativist and civilisational models of Memmi and Nandy on the other, leaving it a very open question as to whether these really constitute the basis for a fresh identity politics.

For there is clearly no one unitary "Asia" any more than there is a unitary "Europe" or "the West." The main contemporary difference in political direction between the two broad areas is that, with the formation of the EU, Europe (or at least much of it) is striving through concrete institutional means (including a common currency) to bury old hatreds and to create a new collective identity. This is a very different model, for all its problems, tensions and degrees of commitment, from the "pan-Asianism" of politicians like Lee Kuan Yew and Mahathir Mohammad who are attempting to create unity on the basis of "Asian values" which clearly do not exist in any collective sense. So while Asian leaders seek effectively to create Esperanto like values, it is assumed, paradoxically both in Asia and in Europe, that pan-European values do exist, since these are thought to be precisely the philosophical foundations of the "Enlightenment project," despite the obvious dangers of ascribing to a whole continent the same values and the atemporality of somehow assuming that these values have remained constant since the 18th century despite the radical social changes that have taken place since then. In any case a major flaw in both Eurocentric and pan-Asian models is that they ignore the presence of the United States, whose global presence is felt economically, militarily and culturally (especially in the area of popular culture) just about everywhere and which provides both a source of cultural and economic input and a force to be opposed in both Europe and Asia.

Europe in Asia's Imaginary

Chen (1998:31) rightly as a result suggests that "The West has to be dealt with not so much as a geographical entity but as an emotionally charged imaginary" from an Asian point of view. The dynamics of identity politics within the EU consequently both resonate and contrast with formally similar processes in Asia. The "re-Europeanisation" of Europe that some commentators see as being generated in the search for a collective European identity is part of this, but is clearly not the whole story as some Asian critics have effectively suggested. The "new Europe" is not simply returning to its past: it is to a great extent engaged in exorcising that past (its old nationalisms for example) while at the same time facing totally unprecedented new problems that have arisen in the search for a common political and economic (but not necessarily cultural or linguistic) identity—and these levels while related should certainly not be confused with each other. The new Europe is not only engaged in constant dialogue with its own past, but also with its relations to the "Rest"—and especially to emergent Asia-Pacific, as well as to its "Others within," many of whom are of Asian origin.

In this respect the approach of some prominent cultural studies scholars of Asian origin (although revealingly not necessarily actually living in Asia) is subtly misleading. An excellent case in point is the acute but distorted analysis of Ien Ang (Ang 1998) of contemporary Eurocentrism, as she sees it located in, and indeed reviving in, the context of a Europe faced with the paradox of its own economic and international resurgence on the one hand at the same time as its loss of transcendent superiority and the recognition of its own "ordinariness" with the demise of colonialism. Her argument is sufficiently important to deserve a little specific critical comment.

Ang is correct that Europe is engaged in a search for a new collective identity. This is indeed based on a kind of "civilisational" approach (which oddly Chen Kuan-Hsing earlier in the same book sees as characteristic of Asian attempts to transcend the colonial era) as evidenced by EU reluctance to countenance the admission of Turkey on the grounds that it is not really "European." But this identity seeking does not as she implies necessarily imply a new and revised edition of Eurocentrism. On the contrary a substantial amount of humility is necessary to come to terms with Europe's own recent history and to confront on the one hand the political differences within the EU and the very real economic inequalities that still exist within the Union; and on the other Europe's empirical place in an interdependent (read "globalised") world system, in which Asia-Pacific is very much a major actor. This identity formation is itself hesitant and fitful and has none of the neo-triumphalism that Ang seems to ascribe to it, and does not involve any assertion of European culture identity vis a vis the rest of the world, large minorities from which it harbours within itself and many members of which are no longer "African" or "Asian" but are themselves hybrids of several generations depth, transformed by their own European sojourn into new Europeans themselves. So while there are no doubt still individuals throughout Europe who decry the loss of their former colonies, these are an anachronistic minority, and to link a mythical resurgence of cultural superiority to a defensive posture resulting from this loss is strangely to impose on Europeans an inverted form of Mannoni's colonial psychology. In fact in a tripolar world (in terms of economic power) a united Europe is operating from a position of strength not of postcolonial demoralisation, but Ang provides no evidence (other than that in the writings of a few European intellectuals) that this is accompanied by assertions of cultural superiority in relation to the rest of the world. By its very existence the EU proves the presence of a hybrid place, a site of pluralism and an experiment in multiculturalism. Ang's subjective feelings of never quite belonging after a quarter century of residence in Holland do not add up to a thesis about Europe as a whole. Indeed her subsequent relocation to Australia is revealing: as a Chinese she would have no doubt discovered that a common Asianness did not necessarily protect her from discrimination in her own native Indonesia.

The idea that Europe is the sole motor of modernity, progress, historical change and economic leadership in the world is a straw man, not only given the contemporary role of the US and Asia-Pacific, but also because of all the contrary historical evidence largely ignored by cultural studies scholars, but widely available—for example studies of East Asian trading systems and their world role (Frank 1998) or of complex systems of accounting and managerialism in South Asia and elsewhere (Goody 1996). Indeed Frank's compendious demonstration that global trade based in Asia long predates or runs parallel to European commercial hegemony and that even during high colonial times the imperial economy was run largely on resources and networks centred in Asia, leads him to oppose what he calls "real World History" to "Eurocentric Social Theory." The result as he sees it (Frank 1998: 8) is globalism not Eurocentrism as the better factual description of the world economy, even during the heyday of colonialism itself, That a certain subliminal Eurocentrism still shapes contemporary attitudes and thinking even after the demise of formal colonialism is not in doubt (Shohat and Stam 1994), but the very existence of postcolonial theory (amongst many other discourses such as pan-Asianism) reveals that this is highly contested terrain, from within the European academies as well as from within the Asian ones. In fact a more nuanced view sees Europeans as struggling to move beyond Eurocentrism of the superiority variety in both its practical manifestations (e.g. racialism) and in academic discourse (vestigial Orientalism) just as Asians are hopefully moving beyond what elsewhere Ang calls "counter-othering" (Ang 1992: 318) and vacuous claims about "Asian values" to alternative and more open relations with the West and with more realistic and less triumphalistic or subordinated searches for viable new identities. Europe's view of itself and its place in the world does not then directly parallel the search for "Asian identity": the legacies and historical experiences have been too different, the language of internal discussion is too diverse (e.g. Kearney 1992 or Morio 1987 for Europe, Itty 1984 or Sivaraksa 1991 for Asia), especially when one listens to the discourse of the intellectuals as Ang does, rather than to the discourse of the politicians, or most important of all, to the discourse of actual average Europeans or Asians.

For even as the "Asian subject" was undermined by the depredations of colonialism, so too the "European subject" is being undermined from within by the spread of Asian religions and a host of Asian inspired cultural movements in food, fashion, the arts and myriad other ways. The new non-transcendentally superior culture that Ang signals is in other words not brought into being by academic discourse, but by cultural practices. To speak at all of "European subjectivity" or of "the European structure of feeling" (Ang 1997: 92-96) is in fact essentialist and is also grossly simplistic. European culture is already transformed by centuries of contact with the rest of the world and is deeply hybrid whether it sees itself that way or not. The circuits of power in the modern world are now multiple, economically and culturally. Indeed what is most conspicuously missing from the cultural studies approach is a grasp of political economy and of the intimate connections between cultural change and economic shifts, so it is to these that we must at least briefly turn.

The Political Economy of Culture

If it is a persistent shortcoming of economistic approaches to social transformation that they ignore culture, it is an equally persistent shortcoming of cultural studies that it ignores economics. As I have suggested elsewhere (Clammer 1985) the bringing together of these approaches, not through mere addition of one to the other, but through genuine conceptual integration, is a major theoretical question for the contemporary social sciences. Preoccupation in cultural studies with issues of race, gender and multiculturalism has brought about huge theoretical (and political) gains, but these themselves to advance further need to be placed in the context of the new capitalisms that are now, I would argue, the major determinants of discussions of cultural or other kinds of relationships between West and East. Indeed I would also contend that most of the contemporary language of "globalisation," "postmodernism," "late modernity," "risk," "ambivalence" or even the "third way" is actually a code for "late capitalism." Even as Frederic Jameson has argued that postmodernism is the cultural logic of late capitalism, I would extend this to suggest that all these key words of current cultural debate are in fact part of that same logic. The world-wide spread of commodity forms, the shaping of subjectivities and emotions through consumer capitalism, the penetration of capital into every kind of human culture and almost every form of relationship within those cultures, is symptomatic of this. What is new about this new capitalism is not only its increasing reliance on new technologies, especially those associated with information technology, but the fact that it itself takes cultural forms. Advertising is now regarded as art, "lifestyle politics" have largely replaced emancipatory politics, entertainment is now almost wholly delivered through technology by corporations and "popular culture" is in fact mass produced and mass marketed. This new capitalism also penetrates the political, determines the parameters within which "development" is supposed to occur, sweeps away traditional forms of life or co-opts them ("ethnic fashion"). To speak at all of "cultural relations" in the absence of this overwhelming reality is meaningless.

To talk then of "alternative modernities" is simply idealistic unless it is realised that these "alternatives" are themselves varieties of capitalism: Japan pre-eminently, but also Taiwan, South Korea and the other little "tigers," and that those striving to join this club (Thailand, Malaysia, Vietnam, China) are in fact and paradoxically moving along exactly the route prescribed for them by the much vilified modernisation theorists of two or three decades ago. This route may not be seen as Westernisation (since all these societies are eager to keep at least some of the trappings of their traditional cultures without which the tourists do not come), but is certainly capitalist. The "failures" (Burma, Laos, Cambodia, the Philippines, Bangladesh and so forth) are not those who are creating or discovering genuinely alternative routes for themselves, but those which fail according to the criteria of World Bank and IMF defined "development." What has changed is the fact that this capitalist norm is no longer necessarily Western in origin, but is locally or regionally produced. "Postcolonial" has unfortunately not translated into "postcapitalist," and nor, except in micro-level social and economic experiments, is there any sign of it doing so. The failure to perceive this is the fundamental theoretical blindness of postcolonial studies. This is not to argue against either the profound effects of Western models (in particular Marxism and capitalism) or against the significance of local attempts to transform, adapt or reject these through social movements and religious and intellectual experiments, but rather to argue that "alternative modernities" turn out to be primarily the local transformation of these macro forces into regional socialisms or into regional capitalism and the subsequent historical ouster of the former by the latter.

Certain general conclusions can be drawn from this. The rather romantic idea of "counter-modernity" held to characterise the postcolonial situation by some of its theorists (e.g. Bhabha 1994) is not in fact, except in some primarily religious forms, anything that really exists in this hegemonic context. Rather forms of and large pockets of "underdevelopment" prevail within existing patterns of modernity. Sites of resistance to the dominant order do indeed exist, but the problems they face in transforming or displacing that order are largely themselves defined in terms of the nature of the order that they are struggling against (a consumer capitalist one). Change of course often begins with new ways of defining reality and this is what is happening within modes of critical theory that have been applied with telling results to "development" discourse (e.g. Munck and O'Hearn 1999) which has developed a vocabulary of critical globalisation, an analysis of regionalism within the current world system, and ways of seeing that system from outside of the paradigms of modernity and developmentalism altogether.

The assumption that modernity began and expanded as a purely Western project (that famous Enlightenment one) is the final myth that needs to be exploded here. That idea is itself a profoundly Eurocentric one which overlooks the permanent historical polycentrality of the world. Models of Europe-Asia relations which talk a language of flows in which a dominant West exported itself in the form of its religions, ideologies, arts (i.e. classical Orientalism), but in which now sees that flow as being reversed (classical postcolonialism) are naive. What is dominant undoubtedly is the commonly shared idea that Western modernity was the only version, an idea as much believed in the East as in the West, as the discourse of scholars like Ang so tellingly reveals.

The way beyond Orientalism is not by the blind alleys of triumphalism (based, like the "Asian values" debate, on false premises), nor by the subtle self-denigration of Asian cultures by Asian scholars, but by a change of paradigm. That shift involves several elements: the recognition of historical polycentrism; the extent to which Western modernity, far from being a totalising and successful world process has always been partial and uneven (including in Europe), and contained from the beginning the seeds of its own destruction. Intellectually what has displaced it however as we know has not been a model genuinely beyond the discourse of modernity, but rather a language of postmodernity. This is simply a slippage, not a true revolution. What postcolonial theory has correctly grasped is that while Western modernity (and Western societies) saw themselves as primarily economic and political entities (hence the language of rights, democracy and power), Asian modernities were based on radically different principles—of society before the political, of the primacy of the cultural and of the subordination of economics to values not economics as the generator of values. The shying away on the part of both postcolonial theorists and cultural studies specialists in and of Asia from the subject of religion is very revealing here, not only for its suppression of what is a vital element of life in many Asian societies, but because taking religion seriously would expose the really alternative cosmologies upon which differing civilisations have built themselves. A Buddhist epistemology is a much greater challenge to the philosophical assumptions of the West than any amount of political posturing by Asian Marxists, who in reality share a Western ideology.

This is not of course to argue for a shift from a political-economy model to a "pure" culture one—a move that would simply reinstate culturalism. It is to argue that these cultural processes have different relationships to the political and economic than do their putative counterparts in the West, the very definition of "religion" itself for instance differing widely from one society to another. But at the same time as these deep, and essentially epistemological confusions and opportunities in dialogue between Europe and Asia need to be identified, clarified and absorbed into academic debate on the nature of the relationship and its future directions, it needs also to be recognised that the "contemporaneity" of which Auge speaks is both made possible by global capitalism, and is yet an ambiguous process. "The world's inhabitants have at last become truly contemporaneous, and yet the world's diversity is recomposed every moment: this is the paradox of our day" (Augé 1999: 89). The constant negotiation of that paradox is both the daily lot of modern people, and the basis of a wider identity politics. As Allen Chun suggests in discussing identity politics in East Asia: "If one can view discourses of identity as interpretative mechanisms through which specific people, institutions or cultures localise (or indigenise) diverge global flows in order to negotiate a meaningful life space or position themselves within a situation of power, then it would be possible to see how in different localities specific institutions and practices serve as strategic sites for meaning and power" (Chun 1996:69). This observation applies as much today to Europe as it does to Asia.

Discussions of "relationships" are in fact discussions of identity. My purpose here has been to suggest that the specific field of Europe-Asia relationships as a paradigm of broader global process cannot be adequately treated without what amounts to a politico-philosophical clearing of the ground. Failure to do this creates simply more empirically flawed studies and theoretically flawed assumptions. To blend the critical and deconstructive with the creation of new and constructive paradigms is not an easy task, but it is a necessary one if the fundamental heterogeneity but unitedness of the contemporary world is to be simultaneously grasped, while recognising that the future itself, while constrained, is nevertheless fundamentally open to redefinition, through theoretical debate certainly, but also through new forms of academic and social practice.

Part Two

Japan and the Globalisation of Religion in Southeast Asia

5

Changing Worlds

Transnationalism and the Flow of Religious Symbols and Beliefs

The study of conversion has played a central role in the sociology of religion for very understandable reasons. Conversion implies not only the subjective embracing of an alternative set of beliefs, but is also likely to involve the transformation of personal practices—in diet, dress, social and cultural networks, time schedules to name some of the more conspicuous instances—as well as potentially major political ones. Imagine for a moment the changes in lifestyle attendant on the decision of a Malaysian Chinese to embrace Islam, of a middle class Westerner's determination to adopt Buddhism, Sufism or one of the Japanese "New Religions" now spreading far beyond their geographical homeland or of a local person's decision to convert to Christianity in much of the contemporary Middle East, or even in India for that matter. Such movements of religious affiliation, conventionally called "conversion," while they may or may not be marked by any geographical relocation or transformation of class position, are most certainly accompanied by substantial shifts in subjective identity, cognitive and affective orientations and even ethnicity. These shifts will slowly or more rapidly be encoded into everyday practices and political affiliations and will become very visible in the subsequent socialisation of the next generation.

While sociologists of religion have been forced to recognise the multiple social consequences of religious conversion, they have often responded to this widespread phenomenon in terms of a rather conventional set of sociological categories—the social backgrounds of convertees and the presence of "crises" in the lives of converts that might precipitate such major shifts in identity—being amongst the most favoured ones. Theological perspectives have similarly been informed by a particularistic agenda—often one very similar to that of the sociologists, but with the additional twist of the active desire to promote such identity shifts—but naturally in particular directions only. In this chapter an attempt will be made to extend these limited agendas in four directions. The first of these is to incorporate a more anthropological perspective—one that concerns itself with transformations of cultural meaning and material, spatial and temporal practice. The second is to examine an Asian case as opposed to the Western and African perspectives that have empirically dominated the field and to explore what difference this might make to more general theories of conversion. The third is to examine a situation where the direction of conversion is not from a local or indigenised world religion to Christianity—the subject of the bulk of conversion studies to date—but rather of movement between non-Western religions. The fourth is to incorporate as an integral part of anthropological analysis the political dimension of conversion, since in multiethnic societies in particular (such as those found throughout Southeast Asia), I will argue that religious transformation always carries with it political implications. The fact that the significance of changing patterns of religious affiliation is of profound interest to the modern state, an interest paralleled only by the concern with structurally similar secular identity transformations (for example to or from some form of socialism), clearly signals this political sensitivity of shifts in belief systems, particularly if they begin to involve large numbers of people rather than only isolated individuals.

If the question of the politics of religious transformations is and has long been of particular interest to the state in Southeast Asia (Van der Mehden 1968, Haynes 1993), the concern with identities has become of particular interest to anthropologists. This concern, while it certainly involves ethnicity, does not confine itself to it, but extends to transformations of subjectivity of a much greater range and consequently incorporates themes as diverse as gender, multiculturalism, individualism versus corporate identities, changing notions of relationship and intimacy and the very notion of the self as a foundational category (e.g. Cohen 1994, Giddens 1991). Very important although it is, what very little of this literature acknowledges is that one of the most significant sources for the decentring and destabilisation of essentialist notions of identity and selfhood is religion. This can take several forms—the decline of formal religious affiliation and with it the collapse of any identity rooted in such categories and values (that is to say, secularisation) being one, but the resacralising of the world (signalled not only by the rise of fundamentalisms, but also by orientations to the spiritual contained within the "New Age" movement) being a quite opposite one. Both however are contained within a bigger context—that of globalisation.

While globalisation is often understood as a primarily economic process of integration it is worth noting that it first emerged out of the work of scholars in the sociology of religion such as Roland Robertson (1989) and has remained an important notion in recent and contemporary studies of religion, whether framed in terms of modernisation (Berger 1979) or in relation to the original idea of globalisation as a cultural process (Beyer 1997). In all cases what remains central is the fact that religions travel: they migrate well beyond their points of origin and in doing so offer a range of religious choices to people who would once have had few if any cultural options in terms of their religious identity. In areas such as Southeast Asia, where cultural flows and global influences have been the norm rather than the exception not only in the recent past but over long stretches of the region's history, religions have profoundly influenced each other (Indonesian Muslims incorporating large amounts of mystical material from non-Muslim Javanese and Hindu sources and Malaysian ones from pre-Islamic animist belief systems, Theravada Buddhists in Singapore adopting Christian organisational patterns and forms of worship such as hymnals and so on in myriad forms of syncretism and borrowing). Religious pluralism equally offer possibilities to the individual or even to whole communities (such as the Malaysian Orang Asli Temiar people, whole villages of whom have converted from indigenous animism not to the more obvious options of Islam or Christianity, but to Baha'i) for the self creation of identity along religious lines.

Southeast Asia has throughout its history been subject to waves of successive religious influences which have had a profound effect on its cultures and ontologies. Hinduism, Buddhism, Islam and Christianity have all in succession swept across the region leaving layers of belief, symbolism, social order, languages, architectures and values, all of which still exist in endless permutations and are constantly refreshed by new ideas, theologies and practices spreading from the Middle East, India, China and, in the case of Christianity, from North America rather than Europe. Numerically smaller religions—Judaism and Baha'i for example have in turn interacted with and fertilised these larger world religions. Others such as Subud and strands of Javanese mysticism (*Kebatinan*), the spirit cults (*Nats*) of Burma and the forms of "animism" that characterise the hill peoples of Thailand and the native peoples of Sarawak and Sabah are wholly indigenous in inspiration.

The geography of religion in Southeast Asia has consequently always been complex, a complexity deepened and animated by the historical wholesale conversion of peoples (the Malay peoples to Islam, the Thai to Theravada Buddhism for example) and the innumerable crossings of religious boundaries by individuals for reasons of conviction, intermarriage, conquest or advantage, and the not infrequent crossing back again. The most recent of these waves of influence has been Japanese. Japan has been a major actor in Southeast Asia since at least the 1930s when Japanese businesses, farmers, dentists and prostitutes began to appear in sizeable numbers. In the 1940s most of the region was occupied by the Japanese and the subsequent postwar economic growth of Japan has ensured that the country has become and remained a massive economic presence. With the export of Japanese capital have come Japanese expatriates to manage that capital, their families to accompany them, schools to educate their children and Japanese food, fashion and culture to keep them happy. With them also came religion, inconspicuously practiced until the advent of the so-called "New Religions" (*shin shukyo*) initially as missions to the growing Japanese expatriate communities and then spreading, with other elements of Japanese culture, into the host societies. The Japanese economic presence has brought with it a parallel cultural rather than directly political presence in the region, and a significant element of that cultural presence has proved to be religion (Ben-Ari and Clammer 2000).

The New Religions and their latter day off-shoots or successors the "new new religions" (*shin shin shukyo*) have become major actors on the Japanese religious, cultural and social scenes, particularly since the ending of the war. Some, such as Soka Gakkai with its affiliated political party (*Komeito*) have become direct political actors. Others, such as Aum Shinrikyo, have become notorious for their violent tactics or deceptive advertising of the efficacy of their spiritual or physical cures. Originally confined to Japan and practiced by nobody except the Japanese, a number of them such as the aforementioned Soka Gakkai (a Buddhist-based movement, Tenrikyo (a Shinto-based one) or Mahikari (a syncretic movement) have spread overseas, along with some of the smaller sects such as Omotokyo, Seicho-no-Ie and most recently Sekai Kyusei Kyo which has attracted members in Thailand (Derrett 1987), PL Kyodan and the Kofuku no Kagaku, the latter often known in English as the "Institute for Research in Human Happiness." Confined initially to Japanese expatriate communities, either ones of recent origin such as the business community in Singapore, or long established ones such as the large Japanese populations of Brazil and Peru and then again beyond these into the local "native" communities where they are increasingly taking root and in some cases establishing themselves as amongst the fastest growing in the veritable supermarket of religions now available to seekers around the globe, (on new religions in general see McFarland 1967, Thomsen 1963, on their spread abroad see the case studies in Clarke and Somers 1994). In many parts of South East Asia they have proved to be a great success attracting numerous converts from the local populations and competing very effectively against their major rivals and in particular Christianity and modernised forms of Buddhism. While some of the more general aspects of their presence has been explored (Clammer 2000c, Hamrin 2000) the particular question of what motivates conversion to this latest in a long history of religious innovations in the region has not yet been systematically explored, and this I will endeavour to do here.

The "traditional" religious scene in much of Southeast Asia has been transformed postwar by a number of major forces. Some of these are external religious forces, either ones entirely new to the region (the Japanese New Religions for example) or radically revitalised and socially accessible forms of older ones—Pentecostal forms of Christianity, the Dakwah movement amongst Muslims, and neo-Hindu movements such as that of Sai Baba to name some conspicuous examples. In some cases quite traditional and conservative forms of religion have been changed substantially by theological trends originating elsewhere—the impact of Latin American liberation theology on Philippine Catholicism for instance, or the recent debates within Islam about economic responsibility and the possibility of an Islamic economics. In some cases a debate within one religion—such as liberation theology—has spread into others, in Southeast Asia and internationally into Buddhism where attempts to find the basis for a socially and politically relevant and ecologically responsible Buddhism have been stimulated largely by earlier and parallel debates within the Catholic Christian community. In yet others global movements such as feminism have impacted all religions in various ways with local movements such as the Sisters of Islam springing up in Malaysia to challenge the patriarchal biases of the historical religion. Quite traditional religions have as a result modernised their practices, liturgies, buildings, social outreach and language, often with profound effects such as the revival of Mahayana Buddhism in Malaysia and in Singapore, a spiritual path that a couple of decades ago some commentators were writing off as in irreversible decline. This has both made the traditional options more attractive to many people and in a pluralistic social context has legitimised newer options often no longer tied to their cultural and ethnic sources: hence Chinese in Malaysia flock to Sai Baba meetings, Indians make up a substantial proportion of Pentecostal congregations in Singapore and Subud (which began in central Java) now has probably more Caucasian than Indonesian members, both Sufism and Buddhism have founded Western orders culturally adapted to Europe and North America and Theravada temples in Singapore are staffed by English speaking Thai and Sri Lankan monks to cater to their ethnically Chinese but English speaking middle-class clients.

But these forces and the patterns of syncretism which they provoke are certainly not the only ones, and changes within religion cannot be explained by internal factors alone. Again prewar and with accelerating speed the whole region has been transformed by the secular forces of nationalism, capitalism, globalisation and in some areas socialism. The identity politics formed around older patterns of ethnicity, gender and caste and traditional patterns of social stratification have been largely destroyed and remade under the pressures of revolutions, nation-building and consumerism. To understand conversion at all adequately it is necessary to situate it in the context of these secular forces as much or even more so than it is to situate it in terms of religious ones, as it is in the interplay of the sacred and the secular that the reformulation of identities appears.

Japanese New Religions and Japanese Cultural Presence

Japan is not noted as a society that has either effectively assimilated its own ethnic minorities into its social fabric or which has desired to export itself culturally in quite the ways that other former colonial powers in the region have done. Despite this, Japan has become an immense cultural power in the region—its fashions are worn, foods increasingly eaten, TV dramas avidly watched, comics read in ever larger numbers, its cars fill the roads and its electronic gadgets fill the homes of Southeast Asians. It is essentially as a consumer power that it is visible. Most Southeast Asians know little in detail about Japanese culture or history and even less about its politics. While the language is widely learnt, this is primarily for pragmatic reasons—to deal with the tourist trade and to do business—rather than from any real love of Japan. While hordes of Southeast Asians have adopted Japanese material objects they have not for the most part adopted Japanese values or world views. And a major reason for this in the past has been the absence of any kind of conversion-oriented religion that might act as a mechanism for assimilating non-Japanese to a Japanese ethos. Japan is often compared with Thailand as two societies that began their process of modernisation at the same time and to the relative exclusion of foreign influences (Yoshihara 1989) and they do indeed possess certain remarkable parallels. But in one very important respect they differ fundamentally: Thailand has for the most part very successfully assimilated its ethnic minorities—and most notably its large Chinese population—by means of religion. While certainly legal and civic mechanisms have also long been in place, Theravada Buddhism has provided both a key element in Thai identity and a profound force for incorporating groups and individuals who would otherwise have remained outside of the national fold as potentially destabilising forces from the state's point of view. It has even become a modest export product, and Thai temples now dot the Malaysian and Singaporean landscapes bringing with them many elements of Thai religious and aesthetic culture. Japan however has never until recently had a religious tradition that easily assimilates the outsider. Shinto has remained a largely nationalistic and particularistic religion despite recent attempts to make it look contemporary and ecology-friendly (International Shinto Association 1995) and in the past was a tool for the expansion of the imperial vision rather than a benign means of incorporating the Other into Japanese culture. Japanese Buddhism has fared little better as it has developed a variety of Mahayana schools very different from the forms of Buddhism found in Southeast Asia some of which (Zen for example) are closely associated with very nationalistic and even militaristic aspects of Japanese culture.

This religious insularity has changed however with the advent of the new religions all of which began as deeply rooted in Japanese society and religious cosmology, but a number of which have successfully internationalised themselves, attracting not only some members of Japan's own minorities at home (in particular Koreans and Chinese), but large numbers of foreign adherents as they have spread abroad. In Latin America and North America where there are large populations of people of Japanese descent, this perhaps makes more sense, but becomes sociologically even more interesting in Europe and Southeast Asia where there are quite substantial Japanese expatriate populations of business people, diplomats or members of international organisations temporarily resident, but no assimilated Japanese communities of long standing. But since they have substantial local memberships, the interesting question arises of what, given the range of indigenous and newly imported religious options available to Southeast Asians, might motivate conversion and then sustain commitment to religions emanating from the erstwhile enemy and not fondly remembered occupying power? It is to this specific question that we will now turn.

The first classical issue in sociological studies of conversion is of course "who converts?" And the short answer here is—Chinese. The New Religions have made almost no inroads at all amongst the Muslim populations of Southeast Asia and have had relatively little success amongst either ethnic Indians—who tend, if abandoning Hinduism at all, to migrate to Christianity or to a neo-Hindu movement (which keeps them effectively within Hinduism) and only rarely to Islam, except for occasional cases of conversion for facilitating religious intermarriage, or Buddhism (although large numbers of low caste Hindus and Untouchables have made precisely that move in India)—or amongst ethnic Thais who tend to remain loyal to the Theravada tradition. Eurasians in Malaysia, Indonesia and Singapore tend to be and remain Roman Catholic. This creates an interesting ethnic pattern—it is the Chinese who are the great converters, followed by the Indians. Indians however tend to convert only to Christianity in any large numbers, a faith both well known to them from the colonial past and with its own ancient Indian representatives, such as the Mar Thoma and Syrian Orthodox Churches which date their origin to the first century of the common era. The Chinese however are prepared to convert in at least small numbers to most of the options now available—to Christianity in large numbers, to Islam in much smaller but still significant numbers, to neo-Hindu movements in small numbers, and most recently, to Japanese New Religions in very significant numbers. Two of these—Soka Gakkai and Tenrikyo, one a Nichiren Buddhist movement and the other a neo-Shinto one—as they have grown and operate in Singapore have been discussed in detail elsewhere (Clammer 2000c and Hamrin 2000). Rather than repeat here that detailed ethnography, I will attempt to move to a more theoretical level, to ask the question of why it is in particular Chinese who are converting and sustaining these new religions in such numbers that they are ceasing in the region to be Japanese at all in majority membership, but are becoming truly local organisations.

To do this requires attention to several factors. Some of the more sociological ones were cited in the above mentioned papers and can be briefly summarised and extended here to a more general picture of the attractiveness of the Japanese new religions before we move on to consider other factors. Attractiveness in itself does not necessarily lead to conversion—a step that requires the re-figuring of identity and the sustaining of a commitment beyond an initial moment of enthusiasm—but we still need to briefly consider what that attractiveness is as it is certainly a necessary if not sufficient condition for conversion.

The Japanese new religions are from the point of view of Southeast Asians post-colonial (although in fact many existed prewar and during the war and occupation years) and so on the one hand are not tainted with the long standing colonialism of the British, French, Dutch, Spanish or Portuguese, and on the other are representative of postwar Japanese economic power and its cultural accompaniments in the region, conveniently forgetting Japanese wartime colonialism. They allow, in other words, an identification with the regional economic superpower while distancing that allegiance from any hints of colonial subservience. As such they allow Southeast Asians to simultaneously participate in an attractive form of internationalism while stressing the "Asian" identity currently politically in favour. One can see in particular how this might appeal to ethnic Chinese: the supreme networkers of the region have through membership in a JNR both a place in a new and international network different from but intersecting with their own economic one, and a tool for asserting their own identification with the region: it allows them to be simultaneously global and local.

Any choice of religion in Southeast Asia has political implications. Christianity is perhaps too linked to the former colonial powers. For a Chinese to become a Muslim is to "masok Melayu"—to enter Malaydom and for a Muslim to contemplate conversion to any other religion, even where it is legally possible, is to face expulsion from the community of origin. Every religious choice is consequently not just a theological one, but is fraught with political and sociological consequences, especially as ethnicity throughout the region is closely tied up with religious affiliation. A Filipino colleague who deliberately challenged these boundaries by declaring himself to be a "Catholic Malay" was not surprisingly met with considerable shock and disbelief that any such category (in fact technically possible) could possibly exist.

Until quite recently Christianity was indeed the religion of choice for most converts from another religion in Southeast Asia generally because (other than purely theological considerations) it is in principle non-ethnic (i.e. universal), associated with modernity and linked to the possibility of forms of individualism denied to the members of more communally based religions. While these characteristics are still present, they have been eroded both by increasing disenchantment with the Western model of modernity and with an awareness (embodied in much of the "Asian values" debate throughout the region) of the limits to individualism as a basis for either social order or personal happiness and fulfilment. The JNRs however offer both a religious identity that is modern but neither Western nor Christian and which allows new forms of individualisation and self-expression within a supportive community. They are also attractive because of their almost universal peace message, they have roots in existing Asian cosmologies (especially the Buddhist-based ones), they are generally not puritanical with respect to material consumption, they are politically acceptable to local national governments, they are lay movements and are in many cases (Soka Gakkai being a good case in point) blue collar in class membership and stress the use of Chinese language, unlike Christianity which tends to be middle/upper middle class in membership and often to be English speaking or uses a local vernacular (Indonesian, Tagalog, Thai or even very local ethnic languages such as Sundanese in West Java). Most emphasise social action, often of a social work kind, without being overtly political, and most have distilled their teaching into clear and codified forms and organisational structures through which measurable progress can be made and which involve fairly simple daily religious practice. In Japan a key element in the expansion of the JNRs has been their emphasis on healing, something also highly attractive in Southeast Asia and amongst Chinese who participate extensively in healing activities at spirit-medium temples and in Charismatic Christian contexts, both Catholic and Protestant. That an extensive set of disposing factors exist then is without doubt. The question is why specifically do individuals convert to the JNRs, given that to do so usually requires them to participate in a much more regimented and required regime of activities and performance than that expected in the traditional forms of religious observance, and may also precipitate conflict with family members and friends who may oppose the move or be fearful of its consequences on behaviour and/or of observation of the ancestral cult, marriage or burial expectations and other features of the traditional religious landscape which have significant social implications.

Cultures of Conversion

Indeed I would argue that there is a complex sociological basis to conversion based essentially (amongst Chinese) in class and resulting, after conversion, in a retrospective narrative of justification. Let me set this out in a series of moves. Evidence from the field suggests that predisposition to conversion can be envisaged as a series of concentric circles. The outermost one consists of the broadest sociological, economic and political contextualising factors, which include the intense urbanisation, industrialisation and commodification associated with the "development" process and the personal and social disruptions and recoalescings, the ecological and environmental degradation and the sense of living increasingly in an over-complex "risk society" that characterise late modernity. The second consists of the class cultures from which converts come and the effects of this on "conversion style"—the predisposing causes, the event itself and the subsequent rationalisations and life-style adjustments that are made. Highly significant here is the educational background of converts with there being a continuum from the least educated who tend to find the healing and ancestral emphasis of the JNRs most attractive to the most educated who tend to experience "intellectual conversion" in which attraction to doctrines is predominant. The former are also more likely to visit Japan as pilgrims or as package-tourists, the latter as business people, scholars or on professional visits. The degree of knowledge of Japanese culture and history also varies with the latter having the greater formal knowledge, but with the former being more likely to have actually learnt at least some Japanese language. The JNRs themselves provide avenues of social mobility to the potentially upwardly mobile and are thus most attractive to those not already at the top of the social totem-pole. Mobility within the religious hierarchy and organisation, the possibility of subsidised trips to Japan on pilgrimage or for study and the seeking for educational credentials by way of the internal theological training possibilities are also strong attractions.

The third circle is cultural and can primarily be thought of in terms of the structural parallels between the JNRs and the various forms of Chinese religion available in the region. Some of these are directly religious in nature and suggest why Buddhist-based JNRs tend to fare better in Southeast Asia than Shinto based ones, as the transition to another variety of Buddhism is easier than the transition to a totally different cosmological system. Others are concerned with similarities in emphasis, especially health, exorcism of spirits and material success. A third, and I would argue a centrally important one, is the JNR's concern with the ancestors and the management of the spirits of the dead, a core element in all forms of Chinese religion. The syncretic and inclusive nature of the belief systems of almost all JNRs (Soka Gakkai being perhaps the main exception) is also an attraction to most adherents of Chinese religions, almost all of which are themselves highly syncretic.

The fourth circle is that of involvement. While most traditional Chinese religious practices are highly individualistic and there is little congregational life outside of monastic settings, the JNRs move in the opposite direction. They are communal, provide hierarchies of groups and activities—religious, social and educational—in which members are expected to participate and converts often comment on their warmth, level of support and caring and the extent to which an entire social life and a new lifestyle can be formulated around the activities provided by the JNR, which create in effect an entire alternative social network in the case of the larger and better established ones. But again there is a class difference here. Working and lower-middle class Chinese tended to be more fully incorporated into the social networks of JNRs than professionals and business people who tended to maintain extensive social contact outside of the particular religious group to which they belonged. The fifth and final circle is, as with all studies of religious conversion, that which lies beyond sociological analysis, notably personal conviction. Whatever predisposing and contextual factors may be present, there is still the actual decision made by the individual convert, often knowingly a momentous one given the social implications and the changes in lifestyle and subjectivity that will inevitably flow from it.

To highlight this very general model of conversion to the JNRs however three additional factors must be introduced. The first of these is simply to note that while Southeast Asians may indeed join JNRs for the same reasons that Japanese do, there may also be substantial or even fundamental differences. For example, a number of commentators writing about the expansion of JNRs in the West have noted that many of these religions see Japan as the centre of world peace and future spiritual development and the Japanese as the real chosen people, elements that are very much played down in seeking (foreign) converts and which may not even be revealed at all to non-Japanese members until they reach quite advanced stages of study and assimilation, by which time they are presumably too thoroughly socialised into the movement to particularly care about these nationalistic revelations. The position of JNRs within Japanese society itself, the social position of converts (for example Japanese housewives situated themselves within a particular set of social roles and gender expectations) and the particular and peculiar social problems that Japan faces are obviously not simply reproduced in Southeast Asia which as a region is culturally very different from Japan, and which has substantial variation within itself, sociologically and politically.

The second is to compare conversion to JNRs with what I would see as being their closest rival, notably Christianity. While some of the same factors appear to apply in the two cases, and while there are some similar patterns of class-specific affiliation in Christianity in Southeast Asia, there are also some significant differences. I will shortly return to some of these as they highlight both parallels and important divergences. The third is to more fully locate the process of conversion to JNRs in the specific cultural and sociological settings within which it occurs in Southeast Asia and the particular nexus of historical and political forces that are in play and have been in the past in forming cultural complexes and religious geographies in the region.

The Subject of Conversion

The standard battery of explanations for the rise of the JNRs in Japan itself usually involve a set of basically functionalist considerations—defeat in the war, the subsequent social and demographic dislocations followed by a period of rapid social and economic change, the inability of the established religions to anticipate, address or cope with the existential stresses resulting from these profound shifts and the alienation of the sick, the poor, the lonely and the socially marginalised which the JNRs very successfully spoke to. All of these are correct up to a point, although as Winston Davis points out in his seminal study of Sukyo Mahikari, one of the major NRs in Japan and one which has subsequently spread abroad, the key question is how members construct what he calls their "world-of-meaning" in a social and cultural context in which to adhere to a JNR is an act of "cognitive deviance" (Davis 1992: 9). In generalising from his particular case study two important factors can be derived. The first is that the immediately prewar and postwar conditions of Japan differ substantially from those of Southeast Asia during the same period. The prewar years were ones of relative stability, with few except local activists anticipating the forthcoming and rapid collapse of western colonialism throughout the region. The postwar ones, while, as with Japan, marked by profound and rapid social change, were of a very different character—marked by decolonisation, nationalist and revolutionary struggles, the creation of a number of quite distinct political, social and economic formations, largely socialist in Indo-China, capitalist in Thailand, Malaysia, Singapore, the Philippines and Indonesia (in each case in a unique configuration derived from the local political culture, ethnic patterns, role of the military, social structure and "development" level) and with special cases in Brunei (Royalist Islamic) and in Burma (a form of populist Buddhist nationalism succeeded by military rule) on the periphery. In each particular case existential responses to these immense changes (compounded in some instances by rapid urbanisation and internal migration) were naturally filtered through the dominant local cosmologies—Muslim, Buddhist, animist or Christian. In only a few cases did local new religions arise in response to these tensions—Subud in Indonesia, Baitiangong in Malaysia or more conspicuously the Cao Dai and Hoa Hao syncretist movements in Vietnam—for example. This is partly because Southeast Asian religious traditions have always tended to syncretism and so adaptations of existing local traditions are easily made, and partly because the major traditions, which are all world religions or branches thereof, have moved with larger international tendencies in their parent faiths and have as a result been always more or less "up to date" (Pentecostalism amongst Christians, Dakwah amongst Muslims, the various forms of "protestant Buddhism" amongst Buddhists and Chinese Religionists all being instances of this). But into this situation have come the JNRs which have drawn away substantial numbers of adherents to the older religions. How can this be explained?

Some of the factors have been enumerated above (the attraction of Japan as the major economic power in the region etc). Others parallel the Japanese situation—the presence of sickness and social alienation and marginalisation amongst those whose labour has contributed to the construction of modernity and its artefacts, but who have not necessarily been included in its fruits. In some cases adherence to a JNR does not, at least in the mind of the new member, imply separation from the prior religion, but is seen as an extension of it, a fulfilment of it or as a useful alternative in a religiously plural cultural situation. A popular explanation of JNRs within Japan is that they are essentially antimodernist movements—reactions on the part of the powerless and marginalised to a social system which has excluded them. Given the power and visibility of some of the larger JNRs (Soka Gakkai, Rissho Kosei-kai for example) this not entirely an easy argument to sustain, although it may have been true in the immediate postwar years when JNRs were rapidly growing and it may still be true of some movements such as Mahikari, the subject of Davis' detailed ethnography. But does it work in Southeast Asia?

Keeping in mind the background explanations noted above, I would suggest that the answer is "no"—that JNRs in Southeast Asia are not responses to modernity, but rather attempts to appropriate it. We have noted the class stratification of religious affiliation and this again needs to be stressed: the JNRs tend to attract people of lower and working class Chinese ethnicity in the greatest numbers. This is partly because they have successfully targeted such people and have organised their activities, language and structures to suit them while providing an avenue for upward social and educational mobility. It is partly because of the association of the JNRs with modernity itself—with Japan, with the encouragement of material success and with simple and updated ritual requirements. And it is partly because of the relative failure of the established religions (especially Christianity) to meet the needs of this large social sector. But even as I write this there is evidence that the established faiths are striking back: Pentecostal Christianity has spread throughout the region and has penetrated much further into the excluded classes than its more wordy Evangelical forms, Theravada Buddhism has been self-consciously modernising itself (and borrowing many forms from Christianity as it does so) in an attempt to appeal to the Chinese, Sinhalese and Indian middle classes, and perhaps most conspicuously of all Mahayana Buddhism which has undergone tremendous revival with massive temple extension and building programmes, a large increase in the number of worshippers and a rapid extension of its ancillary activities (old people's homes, free clinics, educational activities) and which has its social base in precisely the same groups from which the JNRs have been drawing. The modernity of the JNRs is consequently being forced to compete with the updated expression of the traditional religions and the fact that, for Chinese Mahayana Buddhism, for Sinhalese and some Indians and for all Thais Theravada Buddhism and for most Eurasians Roman Catholicism are the culturally familiar religious options, which the JNRs are not (Muslims being almost entirely immune to their attractions).

Given then that there is no "need" to convert to a JNR—there are numerous competing alternatives and all of the spiritual services provided by JNRs (healing and exorcism being amongst the most conspicuous) are available through other channels, we must obviously look elsewhere for a fuller explanation. Here I will briefly sketch an alternative model. For Davis in his study of Mahikari, possibly the most "magical" of all the JNRs, the persistence of this magic is a problem to be explained—in the context that is of an otherwise industrialised and thoroughly modernised society. To a Southeast Asianist it is rather less of a problem as magic continues to pervade cultural life, even in the largest cities. Exorcism, healing, spirit-mediumship, amulets, special practitioners such as *pawang* and *bomohs*, spirit cults, widespread belief in demons, omens, belief in ancestral spirits and the paraphernalia of spiritual protection are commonplace and are in a sense even present in their absence—Christian converts who destroy "non-Christian" pictures and artefacts believed to harbour such spiritual entities for instance. The problem is not the persistence of magic, but the fact that whereas in the past it was modernity that had to protect itself from magic, it is now magic that has to protect itself from modernity. Paradoxically, while secularisation, in the sense of loss of religious affiliation, has most certainly not taken place, Weber's "disenchantment of the world" is proceeding at the cognitive level. The rationalisation and scientism of modernity threatens the viability of the spiritual real as an autonomous zone. What the JNRs uniquely offer is a "magical" system married to modernity: the perfect blend of the spiritual and the material, of consumption here and now with salvation hereafter. It is this blend that enables them, in Davis's terms, to the situation in which "Far from contradicting the practical achievement-orientation of industrial Japan, the practices of Mahikari seem to increase the capacity of its lower class members for responsibility, self-denial and toil" (Davis 1992; 13).

The magical/modern meaning systems of the JNRs, attractive as they are, are also supplemented by a variety of other sociological and cosmological factors. Buddhism, especially in its Sinicised varieties, is very much a salvation religion, and the salvic mechanisms of the JNRs parallel these and are familiar in their general form. Many of the JNRs (Mahikari and Tenrikyo for example) also stress karmic causality—that problems and illnesses in this life may have been caused by behaviour in previous ones—and so healing and wholeness must come from the undoing of or compensating for this karmic inheritance and clearing away the "dust" that accumulates on the soul because of sin and past experiences. Again this is a basically a familiar idea to anybody of Buddhist or Hindu background and is an idea that fits easily into many regional religious cosmologies.

Dramatic healings and exorcisms interestingly are less commonly reported than more general feelings of membership of a community, social or political empowerment and renewed sense of purpose or an engagement, that may never have happened before, with bigger global issues such as peace. Upward religious mobility, indicated by increased skill in the performance of rituals, exhibitions of the "appropriate" behaviour in religious settings, and knowledge and training in the doctrines and practices of the JNR, is, in Southeast Asia as much as in Japan, a major attraction. Most new members join a JNR not because of reading pamphlets or other more "intellectual" means, but because they are introduced by a friend, a colleague or a family member who is already associated with the group. This is largely true of Christians in Southeast Asia too, suggesting that given the plethora of choices, a major precipitating factor in joining any particular group lies in the coming together of acceptable and culturally appropriate beliefs or experiences, and the introduction to a particular group by a member of the potential convert's own social network. The validation or legitimising of the new affiliation is certainly related to the cogency of the particular belief system espoused, but it is also very much related to its efficiency in socialising new members into a social network. Whereas this almost certainly, involves, as in Davis's example the socialisation into the dominant values of the wider society, this latent function is not all that is at work. Together with the acceptability of the new cosmology goes reinsertion into a concrete social order and the specific and very practical meeting of real needs—whether of health, relationships, business or spiritual protection. In the configuration of possibilities, it appears to be the JNRs which most effectively, whether through strategy or accident, meet this particular constellation of desiderata.

But at the same time it must be recognised that the broader context of conversion has changed; it has in a sense, like so many other aspects of culture, become "globalised," not in the slower sense in which older world religions spread to the region, but in faster, more electronic and communication oriented ways. If one steps back from the scene it is indeed remarkable to find Southeast Asians practicing the religion of their former enemies and using it in turn as a springboard to learning the Japanese language (Tenrikyo for example having active "cultural centres" attached to or associated with its missions and which are in effect language schools) and often physically visiting Japan on pilgrimage or for religious-education related reasons. Rapid communication between Japan and Southeast Asia, the regular movement of missionaries, pilgrims, youth groups, drama troupes, the rapid translation of Japanese texts, scriptures, tracts and theological works into English, Chinese and national languages, all place the convert at the centre of a web of communicative forces which place him or her in a supranational context in which new subjectivities are moulded not only by the immediate religious community, but by communities which are themselves formed in this new postmodern setting. "Postmodern religion" need not only refer to the content of belief, but also to the forms in which it is transmitted and received.

So if conversion to a JNR is in a sense a "conversion to modernity," it is not, unlike most instances of conversion to Christianity, to be located in the "interplay between Europe and the colonised world" (Van der Veer 1996:4), but between Japan as the current economic superpower of the region and the former colonies of both itself (very briefly) and of the West. The relationship between Europe and its colonies (occupation, administrative and cultural domination and in some cases settlement) is structurally very different from Japan's current relationships with its partners and economic client states in Southeast Asia and the brief period of physical occupation which extended over little more than three years under war-time conditions, while it has left its scars, was too short to have had major or lasting cultural effects.

The current nature of the relationship between Japan and Southeast Asia is not one in which there is any obligation or immediate advantage in "subject" peoples adopting the religion of the conquerors. Local people in fact of course have both choice and agency: they are making choices not responding to either physical or ideological coercion. The ascription of agency has two consequences. Firstly it actually empowers the individual chooser who is free to perform what Van Der Veer calls "innovative practice": "Conversion is an innovative practice that partakes in the transformation of the social without being a mechanical result of it" (1996: 7). It is in other words both an expression of and a subsequent source of creativity in imagery, performance, the remaking of the self, the reinterpretation of history and the reformulation of social relationships. Secondly, and as a result of this creative character, it is subject to the imposition of local meanings. Just as a Christian convert in Chiangmai, one in Singapore and another in Java may all formally share the same religious affiliation but differ profoundly in the cultural mappings and social implications of their new faith, so do converts to JNRs "read" differently the meaning and consequences of their action. This is particularly so at the level of the remaking of the self, a project inevitably involved in the transformations entailed by a sincere religious conversion. But even where conversion involves the making of a "modern self" as is often argued in respect of Christianity, modernities themselves differ and a good case can be made that Japanese modernity differs most (Clammer 1995). The

Singaporean who joins Soka Gakkai or the Indonesian who is attracted to Mahikari is not subscribing unwittingly to the Western project of modernity, but may be becoming "modern" in radically different ways that may even contradict, subvert or relativise that Western reading of history. Modernity for a start does not necessarily imply secularisation, nor need it imply that the only model of political development is the nation-state in either its (fundamentally Western) democratic or totalitarian forms since there may be other possibilities that, as some argue Japan does, create social order on very different premises. Hence the ambiguous relationship between religion and the state throughout Southeast Asia: while religion is both a source of identity and a socialising agent to middle-class values of stability and labour, it is also the most powerful potential challenge to the state's ideological hegemony and its most cogent critic.

To convert then is to adopt a certain discourse as one's own. But the means by which this discourse is adopted is structured, and indeed without this structure the path to the new discourse in which one desires to be embedded and the new language of belief would be undiscoverable. The academic study of conversion narratives however has been dominated by Christian models in which radical "turnings" in which the past is rejected as evil and the new life as the redemptive reality predominate. And indeed it is not uncommon to hear Christians in Southeast Asia describing their "conversion experience" in the language of St. Augustine or St. Francis of Assisi. Such a model indeed implies that conversion is an "experience" and occludes the possibility that it is an evolution, a recognition, an adaptation or largely the reordering into a new configuration of already existing elements. Conversions to JNRs appear to fall into two broad categories depending on the type of religion to which the conversion takes place. Those attracted to the more "emotional" and spiritualist varieties (such as Mahikari) are likely to report a healing or an exorcism as the source of the new allegiance, while those attracted to the more "intellectual" or socially based ones (such as Soka Gakkai) tend to refer either to the validity of belief and/or practice or to the attractions of membership in a family-like community. In neither case is the sin-based model of Christianity emphasised, and where issues of sin do arise they are more likely to be understood in karmic terms (as in Mahikari and Tenrikyo) rather than in individual ones. The type of conversion narratives which "as a way of explaining personal change are deeply embedded in Western culture" (Pollmann 1996: 47) do not exist as a universal form and while equally profound transformations of identity occur, their mode of explanation in JNRs, both in Japan and in Southeast Asia, varies substantially from or makes no reference to the "classical" Christian model of conversion.

While conversion then is not just a social process, but may and often does involve radical reconfiguration of personal identity, as Gauri Viswanathan has been at pains to point out (1998) it is also a political act, and may in certain contexts be a highly subversive one of the expected social order (as with conversions to Christianity in Pakistan and elsewhere in the Middle East or of conversions to Islam or Buddhism in India). In refiguring personal identity a whole range of national, international, local and even gender allegiances may be formed with many cultural implications, provoking one to learn Japanese rather than a European language or another regional one, to take up the study of Arabic, to alter habits of diet, dress and leisure time activities. So while governments cannot necessarily control the rise and fall of NRMs, they rarely ignore them, either persecuting them or, as with the case of Soka Gakkai in Singapore, co-opting them.

Conversion then is not simply the adoption of a new set of beliefs, but the opening up of a whole range of possibilities, alliances, new social networks and symbolic vocabulary. In most Southeast Asian societies, and certainly all states, one must have an identity, an identity partly at least conferred by reported religious allegiance. JNRs create a new possibility in this regard, especially for Chinese members who struggle constantly (except in Singapore with its overwhelming Chinese majority) with the question of their political loyalty and cultural location in Southeast Asian societies in which they are seen still in many cases as interlopers. JNRs are "modern" (or at least intimately associated with the most modern of Asian societies, but one that is attractively and most definitely not Western), membership confers numerous possibilities of social advancement and community, they meet felt needs, are politically acceptable to local governments as they appear as positive socialising agencies, give members access to an international network and which confer a religious identity (very important in most societies in the region and vital in societies like Indonesia where atheism is equated with communism) while allowing ethnic minorities to both retain their ethnic identity while retaining a certain independence socially and politically by not having to identify with one of the local religions and hence with the particular dominant ethnic group associated with it (say Malays and Islam in Malaysia, Catholicism and the Filipinos in the Philippines, Buddhism and the Burmans in Burma and so on).

A JNR is socially acceptable to the surrounding majorities, is attractively international but post-colonial and allows the retention of ethnicity and most cultural practices. Furthermore they are pragmatic and problem-solving and even materialistic, all values dear to the overseas Chinese heart. Rationalisation of society may not, contra Weber, necessarily lead to the disenchantment of the world, but it does certainly, at least in the case of the JNRs, lead to the magical being proffered in this worldly packages. But that has never been a problem for most varieties of Chinese religion which share these characteristics while lacking the modernist orientation which the JNRs so abundantly possess. The conversion process itself—the formal mechanisms, learning of performative acts and reunderstandings of personal identity and relationship to the cosmos—is also generally shorter and easier than it is in many branches of Christianity.

Conversion, Transformation or Multiple Identity?

Studies of social change in Southeast Asia have tended for the most part (with a few notable exceptions, e.g. Mulder 1996) to ignore changing subjectivities. Modernisation, "development," urbanisation and globalisation bring with them not only shifts in material conditions, but also in social relations, cultural configurations, epistemologies, ontologies and the organisation of the emotions. New consumer cultures, the impact of media and the transformation of communications have as profound effects in the religious sphere as they do in any other. In such conditions the creation and management of identities changes in fundamental ways. Even where the old categories (such as ethnicity or nationalism) still apply, they have become relativised, deconstructed and fluid. One response to this is to move away from such categorisation altogether and to embrace instead the "self-religions" of the New Age movement. But interestingly while some of the superficial paraphernalia of the New Age has appeared in Southeast Asia (meditational CDs, books on communicating with dolphins, much of the rest—incense sticks for example—was already present) the movement as a whole has had little success in the region. The search rather has been for new religious expressions which combine solutions to existential problems with a sense of community and of global or at least international identity, something that the JNRs so abundantly supply.

But there are also a number of broader theoretical implications for the sociology and anthropology of religion to the study of conversion to JNRs in Southeast Asia, implications which speak to more general theories of conversion. Here I will note just a few of these. Talal Asad in an interesting recent paper (1996) suggests that agency—the choosing to convert—has been overplayed in studies of conversion. Rather, he argues, most people convert, just as they enter modernity, because of forces outside of their control. Here I have questioned this assumption and would rather suggest that, at least in the case of JNRs in Southeast Asia, conversion is chosen and the particular choice of new religion is made deliberately, partly because of the much greater range of choices available to the average Southeast Asian than to the average European, especially when classical theories of conversion were being formulated. Conversion to JNRs consequently suggests not lack of autonomy and irrationality, but rather a process of self-making and social mobility that is actually highly rational. Part of the confusion here arises from the fact that in European discourse and especially in the Christian world "conversion" is a common and relatively unproblematic term even although the process itself may signal major transformations (Hefner 1993).

This is not so however on the whole in Asia and in the case of new adherents to the JNRs it was rarely used. The Japanese term for conversion for example is mostly used in the context of secular ideological conversion, for example historically switching from a Marxist to a nationalist position in immediately prewar and wartime Japan (Matsui 1998). In a cultural context in which multiple religious affiliations is the norm rather than the exception, moving between religious options for functional reasons is unproblematic, and to a lesser extent this attitude extends to Southeast Asia. The pressures there for an unambiguous religious affiliation come principally from Islam and Christianity, although even in these cases the situation is fluid. Southeast Asian Islam is in fact syncretic and contains many elements of pre or non Islamic origin and while Christianity polices its boundaries perhaps more strictly one still encounters cases such as those of Catholic priests who also adhere to a JNR arguing that there is no incompatibility between the two systems (to say nothing of a substantial number of Catholics, lay and clerical, who meditate and follow forms of Zen practice). Religious transitions and displacements certainly take place and with profound personal and social effects, but they are not necessarily perceived or expressed as "conversions." The European/Christian model in particular assumes that conversion is about a change in belief. Our evidence here however suggests that it has just as much to do with the adoption of new forms of embodied practice and the contextualising and performance of these in a new social nexus as it does with simply cognitive change. But whereas Christianity in particular has tended to stress the break with the past involved in conversion, the JNRs permit continuities, for example in ancestralism. Even those JNRs that in the past took a militant approach to conversion (Soka Gakkai in particular) have softened and modified this, especially in their overseas manifestations.

A final point brings us back to the specific sociological characteristics of Southeast Asia, and in particular its multi-ethnicity and the association of particular major religions with specific ethnic groups, and through them, to a variety of political positions. As Ackerman and Lee point out in their study of non-Muslim forms of new religious movements in Malaysia (1990), such groups erode ethnic boundaries between their members (mainly Chinese,

Indians and Eurasians)—while possibly intensifying class differences—while simultaneously contesting the religious hegemony of Islam and providing the politically disempowered with alternative sources of social action and meaning. This is true too of the JNRs, only just at the time of their research beginning to become visible in Malaysia. It is at the meeting point of ethnic identity, cultural continuities, empowerment/mobility and the creation of new communities of modernity that the JNRs emerge as real religious options for Southeast Asians. As such they are part of the creation of modernity rather than its subversion, and consequently welcomed by modernising governments for whom non-politicised and (middle-class) value creating movements are very welcome, provided that they do not fundamentally upset the religious (or secular) balance of power. For this reason they are destined to be the religions of the ethnic minorities, and as such have two interesting futures—on the one hand as the focus of religious experimentation and syncretism within Southeast Asia, and on the other as a source of innovation within the JNRs in Japan itself as new ideas, conceptions of the world and organisational forms flow back to the source, underlining once again the protean nature of conversion and religious transformation especially in the context of globalisation.

6

The Local, the Regional and the Global

Soka Gakkai and the Spread of Japanese Religious Cultures in Southeast Asia

Throughout history religion has been one of the most formative influences on the cultures of Southeast Asia. In successive waves, religious ideas originating outside of the region have transformed indigenous perceptions of self, cosmos, kinship and political and social order, have created new patterns of ethics and aesthetics, have imposed new cuisines and fashions and have, in ways both obvious and subtle, irrevocably altered the spiritual landscape and religious geography of a whole sub-continent. Hinduism's immense influence on Cambodia, Java and Bali, Theravada Buddhism's transformation of Thai and Burmese society, the impact of Islam from southern Thailand east as far as the Philippines have been amongst the most important factors in the formation of world views, economies and political systems. The subsequent appearance of Christianity, which especially in its Catholic variant has had profound impact on Southeast Asian societies as diverse as Vietnam and the Philippines, and the coming of Mahayana Buddhism with Chinese migrants have woven yet further threads into the religious tapestry in an area which has both been the recipient of influences from the east and the west and the transformer of those influences into distinct local patterns—Javanese mysticism, Philippine folk Catholicism, or the Vietnamese Cao Dai movement for example, as we have seen above.

Since these deeply formative cultural periods, many newer varieties of religious doctrine, practice and experience have implanted themselves throughout Southeast Asia—Protestant Christianity and its so-called "charismatic" or Pentecostal expression and the neo-Hindu Sai Baba movement are examples—quite apart from indigenous sectarian movements such as the plethora of healing, divination and spirit medium cults amongst Chinese religionists (Clammer 1983). The latest wave of influence, in a process that shows every sign of upsetting or transforming the conventional theory of secularisation, has come once again from the east, but this time from Japan, in the form of the spread overseas of the so-called Japanese "new religions" (*shin-shukyo*).

The category of "new religions," or even their more recent manifestation the "new new religions" (*shin-shin shukyo*) comprises a very large number of religious movements some of which date from prewar and many from more recent years and which, despite the alleged non-religiosity of Japan, have attracted large numbers of adherents, have in some cases built large religious complexes and even universities, and which collectively have redrawn the religious portrait of contemporary Japan (Reader 1991). Many of these religions have their roots in the indigenous Shinto tradition of Japan (for example, Tenrikyo), others in Buddhism (for example, Rissho Kosei-kai). Almost all are syncretic, some even having Christian or Jewish elements despite the very minority status of the first and the almost total absence of the second tradition in Japan (the Iesu no Mitama Kyokai or the Makuya movement being major examples), some are largely regional in nature, such as Kurozumikyo which is concentrated in the Okayama prefecture of western Japan (Hardacre 1988), and many of the larger ones are now nation wide. Some have now begun to spread overseas initially amongst Japanese expatriate communities and Japanese permanently settled abroad, in Hawaii, California and Brazil for instance, and from there to the native populations (Clarke and Somers 1994).

This chapter will examine in more detail one already introduced example of this last category—the Soka Gakkai, a Buddhist-based "new religion" which, having established a formidable presence in Japan with several million members, extensive property, a publishing house, a university and an affiliated political party with substantial representation in the Diet (the Japanese parliament), has begun to spread abroad to North America, Europe, South America (where there is a large community of Japanese origin) and most recently to Southeast Asia. The influence of Soka Gakkai is being felt throughout the region, especially as suggested above amongst its ethnic Chinese minorities, but here its position and implications of its spread will be traced in the one society in Southeast Asia which has a Chinese majority—Singapore—in which the movement is reckoned by some commentators to be the fastest growing religion in a society which already boasts a veritable supermarket of faiths.

The choice of Singapore as the case study is not fortuitous for other reasons too. It is a small but ethnically very diverse society with a population of three million with Chinese, Malay, Indian, Arab, Eurasian, European, Japanese and Southeast Asian communities, economically dynamic, and politically highly controlled. It is a society that has long prided itself on being a cross-road of east and west and it is religiously complex with almost all the major and many of the minor faiths of Asia represented. It is also heavily influenced by Japan: there is a large Japanese expatriate business community, the city-state abounds with Japanese departmental stores, restaurants, karaoke lounges, language schools and bookstores selling translations of Japanese literary, scientific and managerial works as well as their Japanese language originals. Japanese made television programmes are common and there is a weekly hour long broadcast on one of the state run television channels, one half being about some aspect of Japan in English, the other half being news in Japanese. A large number of Singaporeans walking the streets are, unwittingly or not, wearing Japanese fashions and most who drive are certainly behind the wheels of Japanese cars.

Singapore is then, if not a microcosm of the rest of Southeast Asia (its high level of urbanisation, Chinese ethnic and political dominance and political system and culture make it unrepresentative) is nevertheless an ideal laboratory for both the study of religious change and of Japanese cultural influence (and of the links between the two). Very clearly in this case—that of the introduction, spread, assimilation and impact of Soka Gakkai—these factors meet, illustrating not only some of the qualities of Singapore society, but also very revealingly, deeper levels of Japanese cultural influence and penetration than can be uncovered by such more surface level phenomena as fashion behaviour or by simply studying the by now more familiar economic impact of Japan, important as these levels are. They are all in any case connected and interpenetrate, and a theoretical sub-theme of this paper will be to explore the connections, in a non-Weberian way, between religion, culture and economic activity as well as to deepen the understanding of the connections between religion and political culture in Southeast Asia.

Origins and Spread of the Movement

The Singapore Nichiren Shoshu Buddhist association was formally registered in the country as a religious entity in 1972. Aspects of its influence had already been felt in a rather indirect way as a small percentage of the rapidly growing Japanese expatriate community in Singapore were members of the home organisation of laity in Japan and brought their religious practices with them when they were posted to Singapore. The percentage was small largely because in their recruitment of staff large Japanese corporations of the kind that had a presence in Southeast Asia tend to avoid selection of known members of the new religions for fear that their involvement in an alternative organisation will dilute commitment to the company, the primary focus of loyalty and social identity for many Japanese workers (Rohlen 1979). Early interest in Singapore as a missionary field was initially restricted to these somewhat resistant Japanese. By the beginning of the 1970s, however, this was changing as increasing number of native Singaporeans were showing signs of interest in Japanese Buddhism, especially its more accessible kinds, as Japanese economic and cultural influence in Southeast Asia grew with Japan's industrial expansion and growing postwar confidence. So in 1972 the Singapore Nichiren Shoshu Buddhist Association (NSS) was registered with the Registrar of Societies and by 1975 had already begun to participate in the National Day celebrations that mark Singapore's independence each August. By the 1980s the NSS was very visible at this politically important occasion, supplying in 1987 2000 volunteers to take place in the torch-light grand finale of the National Day display and a further 200 marshals to help in the training and organisation of participants in other displays (Straits Times 1987). This signalled that the group had come a long way from the tiny group that used to meet in private homes in the 1960s under the influence of a Japanese expatriate and even from 1972 when the group with less than 100 members registered themselves as an association of lay believers in Nichiren Daishomin's brand of Buddhism (Chan 1988: 10).

Nichiren (1222-1282), a former priest of the Tendai sect of Japanese Buddhism, was the founder of a reformed Buddhism based on the supremacy of devotion to the Lotus Sutra. His reforms, though widely challenged, drew much of their legitimacy from the widespread belief at the time that the last era of the decline of Buddhism was in progress and Nichiren was believed by his followers to be reincarnation of the original Buddha returned to save mankind from its troubles.

After Nichiren's death the movement fragmented into a number of sects, one of which by way of the teachings transmitted through Nikko, founder of Taiseki-ji Temple near Mount Fuji, is now largely recognised as the orthodox one. Soka Gakkai, founded in 1930 as the Soka Kyoiku Gakkai or "Value-Creating Educational Society" was created as the organisation of lay followers of Nichiren Shoshu—the "orthodox sect of Nichiren." The founder, Makiguchi Tsunesaburo, was a school teacher who attempted to merge Nichiren's Buddhism with his own theory of value creation. Under its second president, Toda Josei, the word "kyoiku" ("education") was dropped from the title of the organisation and the association was reorganised stressing on the one hand its links with the Taiseki-ji and on the other vigorous proselytisation especially through the creation of Young Men's and Young Women's divisions. Under its third and current president, Ikeda Daisaku, Soka Gakkai has cultivated a new and less aggressive public image, has stressed cultural and even intellectual activities, Ikeda for example having published a book containing a dialogue with Arnold Toynbee (Toynbee and Ikeda 1989). Mainstream and conservative political activities have also been stepped up and the Soka Gakkai affiliated political party (Komeito or "Clean Government Party") has become a small but significant force in parliament. In 1975 Soka Gakkai International was formed to promote peace, culture and international understanding based on Nichiren's principles. Soka Gakkai has since spread world wide and has become a major participant in the carnival of religions that now fills the post-secular world (Saunders 1972; Thomsen 1963).

In Singapore the NSS exists to promote Nichiren Buddhism and recognises Taiseki-ji as the head temple, the priests of which are uniquely qualified to transmit the Gohonzon, the miniature copy of the Daigohonzon, a large wooden tablet bequeathed to Taiseki-ji by Nichiren and believed to contain universal power. It also recognises Soka Gakkai International as the parent organisation and members when possible make pilgrimages to Japan to visit Taiseki-ji, but is otherwise independent in its day-to-day running and organisation. This situation has since been complicated by a feud between the priests of Taiseki-ji and Soka Gakkai creating problems about the transmission of gohonzon to members. Several "centres," so called rather than "temples," now exist in Singapore and the organisation is financed through the contributions of its own local members.

Exact figures of membership are impossible to obtain, but estimations range from 6-10,000 families (membership being computed by family rather than by individual adherence). Organisation is very hierarchical stretching from headquarters down through chapters, districts and groups on the vertical axis and including units based on age, gender and special interests on the horizontal axis (Chan 1988). The four main divisions are the Men's, Women's, Young Men's and Young Women's divisions and the members of each local group are horizontally organised into the appropriate division. Sub-groups for students, teachers, medical workers, a dance troupe, Chinese orchestra, choir and a band form the daily points of contact between members and the organisation. The individual is tightly integrated into this intersecting network of vertical and horizontal ties. Full members (those who have received the *gohonzon*) are admitted after regular attendance at *gongyo* (recitation of the Lotus Sutra) and other meetings of the NSS, interviews and a conversion rite. After admission members enshrine their *gohonzon* in a *butsudan* or wooden chest in their homes as the focus of their personal religious devotions. Numerous activities—daily *gongyo* in the home, *daimokukai* or group chanting sessions, discussion groups, division meetings, special interest group meetings, study groups and the taking of examinations to proceed up the hierarchy, pilgrimages to

Japan, social work activities such as visits to homes for the aged and participation in public events such as the National Day celebrations provide a full and busy religious life for every member (and one can see why Japanese companies discourage membership).

What we then see in the NSS is the successful transplanting of a Japanese religious movement—both its theology and its social organisation—to Southeast Asian soil, where it has taken root, grown rapidly and attained substantial public visibility through its National Day performances, its glossy publications such as its magazine "Eternal Aurora" published in a bilingual Chinese/English format and its social work activities. Organisationally it is fairly tightly controlled and requires substantial commitment of time, energy and money from its members. In a country noted for its pragmatism and materialism the question naturally arises of what accounts for this phenomenon? What has caused its growth, how does it connect to Japanese cultural presence in the region and what are its wider implications for the development of Singapore society and culture?

Interpreting the NSS

Twenty-five years ago Joseph Tamney made the prediction that Buddhism was undergoing irreversible decline in Singapore (Tamney n.d. 261-264) on the ground that Buddhism was peripheral to the lives of most Chinese Singaporeans and as such it had never undergone a reform movement amongst the laity. Tamney's prediction seems to have been falsified on several counts—a revival of Theravada Buddhism has taken place, there have been protestant-like movements amongst Buddhists generally, partly because of the challenge of Christianity, another relatively successful religion in Singapore (Clammer 1991), and Japanese forms of Buddhism have spread in Singapore. Buddhism in Singapore in fact has undergone extensive modernisation in the two decades since the 1980s, and the popularity of Nichiren Buddhism is a major part of this process, both as an expression of activist Buddhism and as a threat to some of the more established forms and potentially even to non-Buddhist religions such as Christianity.

The question naturally arises of how this popularity is to be explained. The answer falls essentially into two parts. The first relates to the cultural impact of Japan in Southeast Asia, especially in those places—like Singapore—where there is a substantial Chinese population. Japan is of some interest to most Singaporeans, but especially to Chinese for a number of reasons. For Malays and Indians there is little cultural affinity with Japan—no linguistic or historical links, no commonalities of religion and not all that much interest in the organisation of business life. But for

Singaporean Chinese there are many points of contact: Japan is part of the "Kanji area"—its language is written using the Chinese characters, there have been many points of historical contact both between Japan and China and between Japan and Singapore, there is intense interest in Japan's postwar economic success, technology and management techniques and there are affinities in religion, both communities sharing the Mahayana Buddhist tradition, albeit in rather different forms. Interest, cultural links and proximity (Tokyo is only six hours away by air from Singapore) predispose many Chinese Singaporeans to considerable sympathy for both the material and non-material products of Japanese civilisation.

And then there are the specific characteristics of Soka Gakkai itself and of its social organisation as a religious movement. The emphasis on study for examinations in doctrine and the rewarding of success in these with diplomas appeals very much to the Singaporean love of educational advancement and constant (verifiable) self improvement. Most NSS members in Singapore are enrolled in study meetings designed to prepare them for the hierarchy of examinations stretching from the entrance examination to the advanced levels. Although in no way formally defined as such, Soka Gakkai is clearly seen as an ethnic religion—almost all its members in Singapore are Chinese, and in some ways as a class one. This latter point needs some explanation. The membership of NSS includes representatives of most social classes including professionals, but appears to be weighted towards middle and lower middle class Chinese. Its main rival in Singapore is seen as Christianity which is widely perceived as an upper/upper middle class religion. And indeed empirically Christianity has been relatively unsuccessful in attracting working/lower middle class adherents. Part of the appeal of NSS is that it is seen either as classless (something like a Chinese equivalent of Islam) or as a religion which is open to those of less education and less social status than Christianity. Conversion is thus seen as being intra-ethnic, from one form of Buddhism to another rather than into an alien religious tradition, and into a religion which is less cerebral than Christianity and which offers an attractive package of practical activities, an "Asian" identity, clear lines of advancement, a less class biased social pattern and a comfortable ethics which identifies the good not with self denial, but with what one desires.

NSS in Singapore also has some interesting sociological features which increase its attractiveness. It has an almost equal male/female membership profile, uses Chinese language to a greater extent than Christianity (Clammer 1991), has female leadership in the Women's and Young Women's divisions, and has links to the political leadership as evidenced by its high profile participation in National Day events, the very high level reception given to Soka Gakkai president Ikeda when he visited Singapore in 1988 which gives it substantial legitimacy. Other forms of revised Buddhism, especially the Theravada tradition, appeal (like Christianity) primarily to the English educated middle class and are seen in any case as multi-ethnic religions (many Theravada followers are of Sri Lankan origin for instance, or are Peranakan Chinese who speak Malay). Soka Gakkai also has, like its rival Christianity but unlike Mahayana Buddhism or the various forms of Chinese religion, a clear cut set of doctrines and practices. Its endorsement of earthly desires, absence of a puritanical moral code and its evangelistic and group oriented character make it attractive to pragmatic, materialistic Singaporeans who nevertheless desire support and fellowship in a highly urbanised and in many ways alienated society.

NSS and Japanese Cultural Diffusion

At the Singapore end of the Japan-Singapore nexus then the success of NSS at a time when the growth of the parent organisation is widely believed to have peaked is an extremely interesting phenomenon related to a wide range of factors including ethnic patterns, the politics of religion in a highly plural society, the desire to find a religion linguistically, ethically and socially compatible with lower middle class Chinese norms and also one which is not too different from Chinese religious and cosmological expectations. An analysis in these terms would be of interest mainly as an exercise in the internal sociology of religion in Singapore. But there are questions beyond these and in this context especially the interpretation of Japanese cultural presence in the region. NSS represents the successful localisation of what is becoming a fairly universal movement—an achievement that Bryan Wilson sees as being a major factor in the expansion of sect-like new religious movements (Wilson 1982:179). The universal movement in this case is precisely interesting because it is of Japanese origin and itself reflects a synthesis of Buddhism and aspects of Japanese culture. Does the overseas expansion of Soka Gakkai represent the genuine internationalisation of Japanese religious culture—its taking on a world role comparable to Christianity, Islam or even other forms of Buddhism—or the expansion of Japanese hegemony by other means than the purely economic (political expansion having failed dismally in the past and being in today's political climate in Japan domestically unacceptable)? What does it say about the future expansion of Japanese cultural influence in Southeast Asia and beyond?

Much of the impact of the new religions can be seen along two axes: the influence that they have exerted over the religious scene in the countries where they have taken root—on other religions, on social organisation and on attitudes towards things such as healing—and their power of influencing attitudes towards Japan. A number of the new religions, and most especially the "new new" religions have, despite their very distinctively Japanese roots, rapidly taken on an internationalist and even universal character. Soka Gakkai is a major exemplar of this trend, but there are other examples such as Kofuku no Kagaku, Mahikari, and the Seicho no Ie which have expanded internationally and which have an international department at their headquarters in Japan and which publish material in a number of languages. Interestingly in most cases this expansion has been facilitated by the religions in question playing down their Japanese origins and stressing their commitment to universalist programmes of world peace, intercultural communication and friendship between peoples, the promotion of culture and charitable, relief or development activities. The way in which their Japaneseness appears in these contexts is not as culture, but rather on the basis of Japan being somehow uniquely qualified to teach the world having been a "victim" (presumably of the atomic bombings of Hiroshima and Nagasaki) and having become a peace loving country, the only one amongst the major industrialised countries to have a constitution that specifically renounces war. The expansion of the new religions overseas is in no small way related to the postwar rehabilitation of the image of Japan. This is especially true in Southeast Asia: Singapore for example was occupied by the Japanese during the last world war and suffered substantially.

There is also some evidence to suggest that the overseas expansion of the new religions follows the same rules as the expansion of capitalism: when the domestic market is saturated, go overseas. There is some suggestion that membership growth amongst some of the major new religions in Japan, including Soka Gakkai, has peaked—the field is crowded, new entrants keep appearing and the crisis in early 1995 surrounding the "new new" religion Aum Shinrikyo and its link to terrorist activities has made many Japanese suspicious of the claims of all of these faiths. The economic success of Japan has also meant the availability of funds and the openness of Southeast Asian (and other) governments to Japanese investment and the perception of Japan as no real political threat means that there are no real ideological barriers to the acceptance of cultural influences from Japan, many of which—fashions, departmental stores, television programmes for example—have come anyway via the normal channels of international trade.

Almost certainly too the success outside of Japan of the new religions needs to be related to the international appearance of new religious movements. The Japanese new religions are well placed to exploit this trend: they already have efficient organisational infrastructures in place, possess coherent theologies, have the strong yen behind them, can associate themselves with other aspects of Japanese culture which have proved attractive to the rest of the world and they are beneficiaries of the extensive international interest in eastern spiritualities. For reasons totally unconnected to Japanese influence, Singapore has seen a revival of interest in religion across a wide spectrum for at least the last twenty years since the 1980s and which still shows no signs of abating. Since the 1970s the local Christian population has expanded substantially and has achieved high social visibility, the Muslim community has been heavily influenced by missionary movements within Islam such as the Dakwah movement, the Hindus have been stimulated by the appearance of groups such as the neo-Hindu Sai Baba movement and there has been substantial modernisation and revival within Buddhism, including the growing attractiveness amongst English educated middle class Chinese of Theravada Buddhism and the almost frantic building of new Mahayana temples and the refurbishing of old ones.

This supermarket of revived expressions of religion has been, however, by no means simply a return to the past forms. Revival has taken place in the context of a rapidly modernising and almost totally urbanised city state. This has brought with it demands for more coherence in doctrine and for more simplicity in practice—a kind of protestantisation of religion in general—at the same time as there is an opening by way of what is sometimes broadly called "new age" influences to ideas of spiritual healing and reincarnation. The Japanese new religions almost invariably contain these elements, but can present them, unlike the amorphous new age movement, as parts of a tradition. In relation to the spread of Japanese new religions in the west, two commentators suggest that "The modern garb in which they present Japanese core values such as the importance of the pacification of the ancestors and the spirits of the dead, notions of spiritual causality of illness, the emphasis on this-worldly success and happiness, also attracts many" (Clarke and Somers 1994: 7). This combination of spirituality eastern-style and pragmatism is a potent brew, which also explains why Japanese "old religions" have not spread like the new ones. Zen Buddhism for instance, despite the huge amount of publicity that it has received outside of Japan, has very few adherents in the West and almost none in Singapore. Its simplicity, discipline and self-denying ethics have not recommended it at all to the modern Singaporean.

Temples tend to express traditional Japanese culture, whereas the NSS worship centres allow a more selective filtering of Japanese influences, something that has also happened elsewhere, such as in the United States (Melton and Jones 1994: 42-3). This ability to turn Nichiren Buddhism in to a successful lay movement has likewise given Soka Gakkai the edge over other Nichiren based new religions such as Reiyukai and its own offshoot Risshokoseikai, and has enabled both the parent organisation in Japan and its branches overseas to survive the controversy and subsequent split with the Nichiren Shoshu temples in Japan without too much damage, the main problem being the provision of funeral and ancestral rites and the confering of the gohozon on new members. The effect of the 1991 "excommunication" of all the members of Soka Gakkai both in Japan and abroad by the high priest of Nichiren Shoshu is likely to speed up the "protestantisation" of Soka Gakkai in Japan and to confirm such tendencies amongst its overseas branches, especially those with a high degree of autonomy such as the one in Singapore. In this respect the separation may actually reduce the degree of Japanese influence on Soka Gakkai in Singapore, something that Brian Bocking predicts for Britain, where there is also a well established movement (Bocking 1994: 120-122).

This question also raises a deeper level issue for analysis. On the surface the spread of any new religion seems to contradict the theory of secularisation, and to suggest, on the contrary that a resacralisation of the world is taking place. If membership, attendance at worship or construction or usage of religious buildings are taken as the criteria of secularisation then NSS would seem to be an antisecularisation movement. But if the content of NSS is examined closely, and indeed seen as parallel to many other Japanese new religions with their this-worldly and success oriented ethics, another point of view emerges. In commenting on the spread of Japanese religions in Brazil (a country of high religiosity and a large ethnic Japanese community), Peter Clarke proposes the following idea in relation to one of the major internationalist new religions, the Seichono-Ie:

> For its members, Seicho-no-Ie ideas seem to have considerable explanatory power where the changing world of Brazil is concerned. Moreover, they are seen to empower individuals to take control over their own destiny in a world where all forms of authority and power seem to have failed. This enabling notion of the self as divine and in control of one's own destiny and all that affects it would seem to be one of the movement's chief attractions. These ideas however tend to relativise and marginalise faith in and reliance on the supernatural order and in this respect Seicho-no-Ie can be said to facilitate a move away from a faith in divine intervention from above, in an external source of supernatural power upon which humans depend for salvation and from faith in the miraculous, to belief in the enabling, energising, dynamic power of the god within. It also suggests that Seicho-no-Ie in

facilitating the change from belief in divine intervention in human affairs towards a faith in the idea of 'self' as god or divine and totally responsible for all that happens acts as a 'secularising' agency and is similar in this respect to other 'Self-Religions'."

(*Clarke 1994:160-161*)

Implicit in this comment, despite the author's own ill-concealed religious assumptions, is an interesting theory of secularisation as it applies to the case of the Japanese new religions. It suggests that, far from being a re-secularisation or re-enchantment of the world, the new religions, while undoubtedly meeting many very real human needs for order, healing, meaning and empowerment, actually accelerate secularisation rather than retard it, in which case they should be seen as new cultural or social movements rather than as religions. The fact that NSS is Singapore does actually present itself in this guise then becomes doubly interesting.

It also says something interesting about Southeast Asian perceptions of Japan. Japan is seen in the region as, compared with say the Philippines or Thailand, a "non-religious" society. In fact, as any Japanologist will know, levels of interest in and often practice of religion are actually high (the new religions themselves being evidence of this.) What is actually in contention here is not the presence, but the form, of Japanese religion. In Japan religion is frequently seen as part of everyday life, rather than apart from it. Formal religious institutions have played little role in public life since the postwar disestablishment of State Shinto. If it is not a contradiction in terms, it would be almost true to say that, to generalise, the Japanese practice a "secular religion" and that this deep religio-secularity stems from sources quite fundamental to Japanese culture and which do not stem from the same causes as secularisation in the west.

If this is true it puts the question of Japanese cultural influence in Southeast Asia in a new light. It suggests that this influence not only takes more obvious forms (e.g. fashion), but also changes conceptions of the self and of human nature and as such not only subtly reconstructs many aspects of Chinese culture in Singapore, but also undermines the legitimacy of the existing religious traditions not by attacking them as systems of doctrine (the famous Soka Gakkai evangelistic technique of "shakubuku" or "bend and flatten" or "break and subdue" or coercive persuasion being given very little attention in the Singapore movement for instance), but by undermining their cosmology and offering as an alternative one that appears to be "Buddhist," but which also contains large doses of Japanese concepts of the self as person, as body and as actor-in-the-world (for discussion of which see Kasulis; Ames and Dissanayake 1993 and Ames, Dissanayake and Kasulis 1994).

This argument also parallels that of two Southeast Asian scholars who, in a book that otherwise surprisingly does not even mention Japanese new religions, develop a similar theory of secularisation in relation to non-Muslim religious movements in Singapore's immediate neighbour, Malaysia (Ackerman and Lee 1990). In this work the authors suggest that "As a social process, secularisation individualises participation in religious activities. The new religious movements reflect this process in the sense that they attract followers on a voluntaristic basis, offering concrete methods both of problem-solving and of meeting personal needs in everyday life" (1990:163). In this view participation in religious activities is not the issue: the central question is the movement towards individualisation of religious expression. And paradoxically it may be the case that religious movements that seem to be communal in orientation like NSS may, despite their high level of organisation, actually promote pragmatism and individualisation at a more fundamental level.

As in Malaysia, ethnicity and religion are central to the definitions of social identity employed by Singaporeans. But whereas "The conjunction of ethnicity and religion in Malaysia dichotomises the religious arena into a Muslim and non-Muslim field" (Ackerman and Lee 1990: 4), in Singapore it separates people into primarily a Chinese/non-Chinese division, and secondarily into Chinese who have converted to a "non-Chinese" religion (mainly Christianity) and those who retain their allegiance to a "traditional" religion. But in the context of rapidly modernising Singapore close association with a traditional religion has until recently at least implied some kind of backwardness. With the reforms within Buddhism and with the appearance in Singapore of Nichiren Buddhism, this equation no longer holds: it is now possible to be Chinese, Buddhist and modern at the same time through membership in a reformed branch of Buddhism, and especially through membership in the NSS with its positively progressive and desirable Japanese features reinforced by the government's "look East" policies. Ethnicity and religion can be brought together in an attractive package that now separates the progressive and modern Chinese from the traditional ones.

The NSS alternative also has other attractive features. It shares many of the organisational characteristics of Christianity without sacrificing a Buddhist content; it is similarly a high commitment religion membership in which, unlike many Chinese sectarian movements, is incompatible with multiple religious affiliations. Its ethical pragmatism, high level political connections, hierarchical structures and education (even exam) oriented approach make it both attractive in itself to many Singaporeans and an attractive alternative to Christianity, its main rival. The ethnic dynamics of

Singapore, government fear of the over-expansion of Christianity and the constant search in post-colonial Singapore for a set of "Asian values" which will provide a basic ideology for the whole society while being based if possible on Chinese Confucian/Buddhist principles (Clammer 1993a) provide a tailor-made environment for the expansion of Nichiren Buddhism in Singapore.

This is not to say that the movement has been without its critics. It has been attacked quite naturally by Christians who, given the very evangelical nature of local Christianity, see it as a major threat; by those still suspicious of Japan's real intentions and interests in Southeast Asia; and, perhaps most significantly by local Buddhists of non-Nichiren persuasions. This latter group also quite naturally see the NSS as a threat to their own specific doctrinal positions and as drawing away membership and revenues from the longer established denominations. This opposition to the NSS has provoked a literature of critique which sees the Nichirenists as attempting to displace the centrality of Shakyamuni Buddha's position as the source of true Buddhism, as materialistic and intellectualistic, as copying the Christians with their emphasis on evangelism, as being exclusivist, aggressive and sectarian, as being doctrinally selective, and as being based too closely on inappropriate characteristics of the Japanese. In one anti-Nichiren text these last are interestingly described as dependence, anomie, regimentation, materialism and ignorance of true Buddhism (Piyasilo 1988:119-122).

This very negative evaluation of NSS from a practitioner of (presumably) Theravada Buddhism of course represents a position which to someone outside of Buddhism altogether appears merely as sectarian squabbling of a kind very familiar to anyone who has studied the development of Christianity for example. But it is also of sociological significance, not only because it indicates that the NSS is operating on contested terrain, but also because of its very unflattering depiction of Japanese society. In Piyasilo's book, while it might of course be argued that he has misunderstood and caricatured Japan, the position that the Japanese have joined Soka Gakkai in such large numbers mainly because of social problems in their own society represents a real counter-trend to the Japan flatterers. Representations of Japan in Southeast Asia are themselves contested, partly because of old memories of war and occupation, partly because of the perception of contemporary Japan as pursuing imperialism by economic and now cultural means rather than by military ones, and partly because readings of the nature of Japanese society are not uniform. To many Singaporeans Japan, despite its technological achievements, is seen as far too group oriented to be attractive. On other grounds the same Japan that produces elegant fashions and state-of-the-art computer games is also largely responsible for the rape of the Southeast Asian rain forests because of its insatiable demand for timber. Many Singaporeans have by now visited Japan as tourists or for working purposes, and many bring back mixed reviews.

If at the everyday level the images of Japan shared by Singaporeans are mixed ones, so they are also by intellectuals and professional interpreters of Japan. Again while some of these are negative evaluations of past history or of present society, others are attempts to evaluate the specific role of religion in accounting for Japan's economic success. The question of Japan's achievements and what might be learned about the mechanisms underlying this and discovering what might be applied to Southeast Asian societies has become something of a local industry. Perceptions of the NSS naturally fit into this discourse, which is certainly not restricted to Singapore, but has also occurred in those societies in the region such as Thailand which are largely Buddhist in religion and which are also undergoing rapid modernisation. In this light Japanese Buddhism has been evaluated, contrary to Piyasilo's view, in a very positive light as being highly functional to effective development through its virtues of compassion, honesty, endurance, diligence, tolerance, simplicity, purity and high regard for aesthetic values (Pensri 1989: 14-27) which have exercised decisive influence over the development of Japanese politics, nationalism and social welfare policies. This reading too can be criticised for its essentialism, simplicity and lack of detailed understanding of Japanese history and the complex role of religion within it, but it does also indicate a desire in Southeast Asian scholarly discourse to understand the linkages of religion and economic development.

The introduction of Nichiren Buddhism into Singapore and its subsequent expansion and consolidation makes a fascinating case study of several social processes: of religious change, of religion and ethnicity, of the secularisation process. In this context it is also, or is primarily, an illustration of the expansion of Japanese cultural influence. Following the growth of a Japanese economic presence in Southeast Asia has come the spread of fashion, cuisine and media. Religion is rarely one of the early things to spread in societies where missionary zeal is lacking. While in the past Japan has certainly tried to export its economic and political influence, it has not been a society that has attempted to export its religions. And nor for the most part could it be, as Japan has either been the recipient of continental religious influences (Buddhism and Confucianism) or has been the possessor of an indigenous tradition (Shinto) which has been too national in character—or even quite literally nationalistic—to make an export product. Nichiren Buddhism however has reversed this tendency by evolving a form of Buddhism evangelistic and potentially universalistic in character. By the 1960s this became linked with the widespread desire in Japan to begin to put the past behind and to play a positive role in promoting world peace and harmony. Given Japan's political history and past record, this would be difficult to do by political means, and the rise of the new religions and their own desire to internationalise at exactly this point in time provided the mechanism through which a benign cultural influence, riding on the skirts of economic influence, could begin its spread.

The question remains of finally interpreting this phenomenon. At one level the spread of the new religions can be seen as a positive thing—as Japan genuinely putting a new face on its relationships with the rest of the world, as a symptom of internationalisation within Japanese society, as part of a world-wide resurgence of interest in religion and as part of a pattern of non-political influence in the world on the part of its second biggest economy. Quite apart from its role in the internal dynamics of Singapore society, the spread of Nichiren Buddhism in Southeast Asia can be read in this way. On the other hand the same evidence can also be seen in a different light. In all of the new and new-new religions, despite their universalist pretensions, Japan has a clear role as the promised land and as the centre of the world. This centrality may now indeed be seen in spiritual rather than in political terms, but centrality it remains. This vision as Japan as the centre is naturally played down in material that the new religions produce for international consumption—rather the message is of Japan as victim and peace-loving carrier of eastern spirituality—but it is very much present in material in Japanese designed for internal consumption at home. In almost all cases what is stressed is the spirituality, not the underlying Japanese social organisation that accompanies in practice full incorporation into the world view and organisation of the new religions. It is still an open question of the extent to which these aspects will spread—something very much dependent on the extent to which overseas branches of the new religions begin to assert their autonomy, become themselves more "protestant" and follow the logic of their parent bodies in breaking free of a Japan centred "papal" system of centralisation. This is indeed likely to happen unless and until Japanese society itself becomes more international and incorporates into itself influences flowing from Southeast Asia and elsewhere, including religious ones, rather than seeing itself as the new and exclusive fountainhead of culture in Asia. The case of Soka Gakkai in Singapore, whose central mandala and object of worship, the gohonzon, was once described by Toda Josei, the second president of the parent organisation, as "the happiness making machine," demonstrates very centrally the attractiveness of Japanese cultural influences in Southeast Asia, but also the ways in which these are adapted, incorporated into local ethnic stratification patterns and political cultures, and of the ways in which these influences can become the basis of a critique of Japanese society itself. Japanese cultural influence in Singapore is extensive, but it is not unitary or uncontested, and it is to a great extent on the field of religion that its eventual role in Southeast Asia is being worked out and which will determine the extent to which Japanese patterns of thought and social organisation can ever be expected to take root.

7

Globalisation, New Religions and the Contemporary Re-Imagining of Japanese Identity

Social scientists are wont to announce "crises" in the societies that attract their scholarly attention. While it might be stretching the evidence a little too far to suggest that contemporary Japan is in a state of crisis, it would certainly not be untoward to argue that Japanese society in the first decade of the new millennium faces unprecedented challenges, parallel in their magnitude to the vast shifts in social structure and images of self-identity that accompanied the opening of the country after the Meiji restoration and the defeat of 1945.

The collapse of the "bubble economy" of the 1980s and 90s, when Japan was announced as "Number One" by academic and popular pundits and when the world flocked to Tokyo and Osaka to discover the magical ingredients of the "Japanese miracle," the great Hanshin earthquake and the utter unpreparedness and logistical and administrative disarray of the government that it so starkly revealed, the Aum Shinrikyo cult's gas attack on the Tokyo subway system shocked the world. A series of brutal murders of children, including one perpetrated by a child only a little older than his victim, and the drawing of Japan into both UN peacekeeping operations in Cambodia and elsewhere and latterly into both the Gulf War and the US led occupation of Iraq, have thrown open a new round of the self-questionings that accompany major seismic shifts in Japanese society, in the past mostly occasioned by outside forces, but this time, while encapsulated within the bigger framework of globalisation, by events within Japan itself. These new and mostly unexpected events and the debates that they have triggered—including discussions about the long taboo possibility of revising the (US imposed) postwar "Peace" Constitution, the legitimacy or wisdom of sending armed Japanese troops abroad or participating in even UN sanctioned peacekeeping (PKO) activities, the effects of Japanese ODA, local attitudes to the presence of large numbers of illegal (and legal) foreign workers in the country for example (Mori 1993, Shimoda 1994), are layered on top of older but still smouldering debates about Japanese postwar identity.

An archaeology of such debates would go back to the Pacific War itself and the internal debates at that time about *kindai no chokoku* or "overcoming modernity," the postwar psychic, cultural, emotional and political negotiations of defeat, the management and constant reconstruction of the collective identity effects of the atomic bombings and more recent discussions of the ecological effects of the post-1950s economic boom years (of which Minemata is undoubtedly the best known, but by no means only example). The Comfort Women issue, and the whole furore triggered by the efforts of the "revisionist" school of historians and other prominent intellectual figures to reassess Japan's recent past and to either reject current readings that attach blame, or to attempt to come to terms with that past and integrate it into a new sense of Japanese identity that will allow the country to move forward and to become a "normal" nation once again are symptomatic of this malaise (Morris-Suzuki 1998).

Interestingly, a fairly recent collection of major essays on recent Japanese intellectual history devotes every chapter to what might be termed Japan's earlier primary encounter with globalisation in the form of its encounter with the West after the Meiji Restoration (Wakabayashi 1998). This approach, legitimate as it is in its own terms, has created however a template which has formed the model for much of the scholarship on Japan's relationship to internationalisation. The more recent work that has explored in great detail the impact of Japanese popular culture on the rest of East and Southeast Asia (Ching 1994) fits essentially into this same intellectual model. What is missing to a great extent are attempts to map the internal transformations of Japanese self identity brought about by these new forms of engagement with the world and by the intersection between the inevitable globalisation of Japan and the internal debates of the kind cited above. Here I will argue that it is exactly at this intersection of the "global and the local" that new imaginaries are emerging and that the fluid dynamics of this interface provide important clues as to the ways in which contemporary and emergent Japanese society might be thought.

There are a number of ways in which this could be done, and to some extent have been tried: the debate about historical revisionism and its associated and seemingly eternal debate about *nihonjinron* being a major example (Dale 1995), or preliminary attempts to chart the relationships between the penetration of globalised economic forces and transformations of Japanese emotional life (Clammer 2000e). Here however another approach will be taken. A growing literature is charting the expansion and impact of the Japanese *shin-shukyo* or "New Religions" abroad (e.g. Clarke and Somers 1994), and indeed they have become, along with Japanese technology, popular culture, food and fashion, a major export product to much of the rest of the world, having had an especially notable impact in Europe, North America, Latin America and parts of Southeast Asia where there are substantial Chinese populations (e.g. Clammer 2000c, Hamrin 2000). And while a great deal of scholarly and popular attention has been paid to the New Religions within Japan, not surprisingly given their visibility and collectively very substantial membership figures, little has been paid to the nexus formed by the interface of their expansion overseas and the internal transformations that this new internationalism is having upon Japanese imaginaries within the country. Here I will again argue that the New Religions, while obviously not representative of the Japanese population as a whole, nevertheless form an important conduit for new imaginaries to emerge, ones which moreover give insights into emerging forms of cultural nationalism forged out of the interaction between elements in Japanese society and globalisation.

The internal imaginaries of the members of most contemporary nation-states, and Japan is certainly no exception, are increasingly made out of the intersection between the internal and the external. The "imaginary community" so tellingly described by Benedict Anderson a decade ago, is no longer confined to the boundaries of individual territories. Of course in reality they never were and patterns of colonialism, trade, the expansion of the missionary religions, migrations and wars have long ensured that cultures mix and that hybridity, even if a new term, is not a new reality. Globalisation however has intensified this process and speeded it up to an unprecedented degree, and has accelerated mutual flows of influence. As the Japanese religions have set about expanding into the world, so the world has flowed back through the same channels, but do not leave their source unchanged. This chapter however is not a study of the ways in which globalisation has changed the New Religions per se, but of the ways in which that interaction with an international environment has provided the soil for new imaginaries to emerge.

But are the New Religions the best route to uncover this? An argument could certainly be made that fixing upon the older *nihonjinron* debates or taking up issues of citizenship and gender (e.g. LeBlanc 1999) would provide more suitable avenues to approach Japanese identity politics. Certainly they are equally valid approaches, but here I wish to build on the observations of Iida Yumiko that the appearance of Aum Shinrikyo, and by implication other JNRs, of which Aum was an extreme and violent exemplar, was of central significance. She argues that "In the Japan of the late 1990s, the spectre of an inarticulate, free-floating desire for identity seeking a concrete foundation upon which to fix ideal meaning appears to be intensely present. Put differently, modern Japan suffers from a seriously troubled state of intersubjective meaning in which the "superstructure" is no longer capable of bonding the Japanese subject to a vision of collective unity. By promising its followers an identity and goals and an appealing collective imaginary where life was filled with meaning, the cult was able to establish a sub-nation within Japanese society" (Iida 2002: 244). This provides us with a clue that will be unpacked in the following pages. It also should alert us to the fact that different levels or aspects of identity—citizenship, gender, political affiliation, economic status and so on are intertwined in complex ways, of which in modern Japan religious identity is an important but neglected part, and that there is a pluralism of identity politics strategies in Japan in which there can well be alternative expressions of collective membership and relationships with the outside world, and certainly not only one.

Furthermore the imaginaries and constructs of "Japan" or of Japanese identity today draw on a variety of eclectic sources—old elements revitalised, as in recent attempts to refurbish Shinto as a modern and ecologically sound religious alternative (International Shinto Federation 1994), and newer forms of popular culture such as *anime* which have been highly successful in spreading Japanese culture abroad and have an immense impact at home. The JNRs additionally play an important role in a society in which there is a paucity of NGOs and civil society organisations (Pharr and Schwartz 2003), and so in which they in fact constitute important social movements, often embodying a very different ideology from that of the Statist central authorities. Finally, they lead us to question dominant existing models of nationalism and cultural nationalism in Japan as their internationalism opens up new channels of dialogue, and to reopen Japan's long standing debate with modernity on rather different terms than the largely political ones in which that issue has previously been framed.

The Peace Paradigm

In his study of pacifism amongst the Japanese NRs, Robert Kisala notes that a common platform of many of them, regardless of the specific underlying religious tradition out of which they have emerged, is a common preoccupation with peace promoting activities. While a level of social welfare and civic volunteerism is found in many of the NRs, it is, he argues, in peace activities that a major expression of their social concern is found (Kisala 1555: 4). He also correctly points out, without pursuing its implications, that the social ethics of the JNRs points to their role in

Japanese identity politics, since not only does their membership encompass a substantial number of Japanese citizens, but they effectively act as social movements, whether or not they identify themselves as such. In his sample of five JNRs of varying sizes and histories (*Nipponzan Myohoji*, *Rissho Koseikai* and *Soka Gakkai* representing the Buddhist camp, *Shuyodan Hoseikai* and *Shoroku Shinto Yamatoyama* in what he terms the "folk-religions" or essentially Shinto category, and *Byakko Shinkokai* as an exemplar of the "spiritist" groups) all place peace promoting activities at the centre of their missions. Byakko Shinkokai is well known internationally for its main activity of erecting "peace poles" and distributing stickers inscribed with the "peace prayer" beginning with the phrase "May peace prevail on earth," Myohoji for its erection of Peace Pagodas in Japan and around the world, Rissho Koseikai and Shoroku Shinto Yamatoyama for the pursuit of a specifically religious approach to world peace through inter-religious dialogue and cooperation and Soka Gakkai through its peace teachings and development and education work overseas.

While in each case there is a link between the religious doctrines of each religion and its peace activities, there are also good sociological reasons to stress this particular approach. As noted briefly above, in relatively conformist Japan, social activism does not have a strong pedigree, and the civil society or NGO sector is weak compared with many other democratic nations. A peace agenda as a basis for a social platform however has two major strengths in Japan—on the one hand, as Michael Pye notes in his study of Byakko Shinkokai (Pye 1994), the peace agenda allows JNRs to both develop an international identity by linking themselves to a central world issue, and to pursue a legitimate local identity by drawing upon what some have argued is the central historical trauma of modern Japan—the Atomic Bombing of Hiroshima and Nagasaki, events burnt deeply into the Japanese national psyche—which has allowed indigenous peace activists to place themselves at the symbolic centre of both international and domestic peace promotion activities. In representing themselves as victims of the world's only use of atomic bombs in warfare, activists can both claim an international legitimacy and play upon a major trope of postwar Japanese life, a sentiment still alive and well as signalled by the massive public protests against the Japanese government's support for the US led invasion of Iraq in March 2003. It turns out then that the JNRs are mostly two-faceted entities—on the one hand directing much of their attention to their natural constituency of supporters or potential supporters—the domestic Japanese population—and on the other seeing themselves as having a world mission, centred on the promotion of peace. Even the smaller groups such as Shuyodan Hoseikai with a largely domestic base and little of the international reach of large organisations such as Soka Gakkai have devoted themselves to the establishment of world peace as their primary objective, while significantly falling back on such prewar terms as *hakko ichiu* (the whole world under one roof) to describe their mission of making Japan the centre of world civilisation, not this time through colonialism and conquest, but through peace and a universal brother-and sisterhood led by Japan with its war-renouncing constitution (Kisala 1999: 13). It is to this new agenda and its implications for new Japanese imaginaries under globalisation that we must now turn in greater detail.

In his study of Byakko Shinkokai, Michael Pye notes that "Much of the interest in the study of major religious traditions lies in the relationship or tension between universalist claims and local, particularist identity-creating forms" (Pye 1994: 78). While the world religions have all of course made universalist claims (while always in practice being expressed in concrete, particularist local forms), this is true of new religious movements too. In fact their late appearance on the stage makes it even more imperative that they demonstrate themselves to be something more than a syncretic blending of the already existing, and one major way of doing this is to promote a universalist agenda. As religions have attempted to recommend themselves beyond their original geographical or ethnic base, there is a strong tendency for even very old established religions to be pushed in this direction. As Tibetan Buddhism has spread through the post-Chinese occupation Tibetan diaspora and has begun to attract a substantial following in the West, so its paramount leader, the Dalai Lama, has moved from being a particularistic primate to a world figure, actively lecturing and publishing around the world not on the technicalities of his brand of Buddhism, but rather on issues facing the members of modern industrial consumer societies and on world problems of war, peace, conflict resolution and ecology (e.g. Tenzin Gyatso 2000). The local becomes legitimised through its ability to relate itself to the global, something as true of NRMs as it is of ethnic and minority groups and social movements attempting to establish their very local claims through appeal to the universal declaration of human rights.

The Byakko Shinokai, like many of the other more recent manifestations of JNRs, came into existence in the context of its founder's (Goi Masahisa) experience of prewar ultra-nationalism and militarism, war, defeat and postwar reconstruction and reflection on Japan's responsibilities and of its relationship to the rest of the world, especially its Asian neighbours. As Pye suggests "Thus the question of Japanese identity in the world arises naturally in the movement which he [Goi] founded. Indeed…the Byakko Shinkokai may be taken as a paradigm for the structure of this whole problem. My thesis is that the religious dimension provides both a dramatisation and stabilisation of this structure in Japanese consciousness" (Pye 1994: 79). In the Byakko Shinkokai the prayer for world peace is central, and the liturgy of meetings involves the recitation of the prayer directed specifically at each country listed in the Foreign Ministry's *Sekai no kuni ichiranhyo* or official list of foreign countries, continent by continent, a large map of the world being hung at the front of the prayer hall. This conscious identification with the world is however linked to communication with the spirit of the founder who, through the medium who channels his presence, is the link between the believer and the wider spirit world. The Byakko is a fascinating blend of a highly local guru-centred spiritist movement taking on itself a universal mission of world-salvation, in which the prayer for peace is itself a gate to spiritual experience and meditative states. But the desire for universalisation does not necessarily bring about its realisation, and those JNRs that have stayed closest to their Japanese roots (Byakko Shinkokai, Omotokyo, PL Kyodan and Tenrikyo for example) have been the least successful in going global. Soka Gakkai on the other hand, by stressing its Buddhist universalism while simultaneously downplaying its specifically Japanese characteristics, has been very successful in its internationalisation efforts. Studies of Soka Gakkai and Tenrikyo in Singapore for example show clearly how one has flourished and rapidly gained members, while the other languishes as a small minority religion with few local adherents despite quite a long history of missionary and cultural work in a small society quite used to high levels of religious pluralism (see chapter 5 and 6 above). In the case of the Byakko ("The White Light Association") we see an essentially spiritist movement centred on the figure of its late founder Goi Masahisa to whom believers direct petitions and receive help, and who continues to write letters from the other side and to reply to those addressed to him and the title of whose biography (*Ten to chi o tsunagu mono* or "The man linking heaven and earth") suggests his role as a karmic mediator. The syncretic nature of Byakko theology and its concern with purification rites demonstrates its continuity with many other JNRs. But its emphasis on the peace prayer rather sets it aside, or at least locates it within those JNRs that have made peace activities an essential aspect of their larger identity on the world stage. For the prayer is accompanied by no political action to actually promote such peace, but it is, in Pye's interpretation that "...the search for world identity in the form of the prayer for peace of the world may be understood as a ritualised means of coping with the fact, bitterly experienced, that Japan is not alone in the world" (Pye 1994: 85). The peace prayer then operates at two levels—as a route to meditation (and no doubt a genuinely meant and felt sentiment for world harmony), and as a vehicle of collective identity in which Japan is located centrally, or even first amongst, the family of nations. Universalism can thus be expressed from within the comfort of a very Japanese religious setting, one which moreover contains few if any actual foreign members. A strongly local identity can then be reconciled both with a genuine desire for world peace, and a reassurance that through the divine interventions of Goi-sensei, Japan is at the centre of a new, but this time spiritually-led, world order.

While the Byakko represents a small movement in terms of its numerical strength, and with none of the missionary thrust in local languages, or even in Esperanto, of Soka Gakkai and Omotokyo or the inter-religious harmony activities of Rissho Koseikai, it is structurally similar to these larger JNRs in its basing a universalist vision of a peaceful and religiously led world community, with Japan as the country of peace as the leader, in very particularistic local Japanese religious practices, something that can also be seen very clearly in the teachings and practices of the Shoroku Shinto Yamatoyama amongst others. It is just this conflation of Confucian based ideas of benevolence and moral self-cultivation with Shinto ones of ethnic superiority that Kisala dubs a "civilisational" approach to peace and to Japan's place in the world order. In Nipponzan Myohoji for example the founder Fujii Nichidatsu, whose later ideas on peace were decisively influenced by two meetings with Gandhi, began from a position with three main elements—Japanese ethnic and cultural superiority, the national mission of spreading the benefits of (Japanese) civilisation, and Buddhism (of which Japan had the purest examples of the Mahayana tradition) as the basis of peace. Internationalism in the JNRs has consequently been largely focused on the promotion of essentially this programme, although in publications designed for external consumption, these aims are not made so explicit, but are disguised in the language of peace. Historically indeed the JNRs have been associated with right-wing, or at least right of centre, politics (Komeito, the party currently part of the ruling LDP led coalition, having its origins in Soka Gakkai), despite the strong initial influence of the forms of Christian Socialism that were evident in the late Meiji period, but which themselves tended to be rapidly assimilated to a nationalistic Japan-centric world view—for example in the writings of the late Tokugawa and Meiji ideologist Okumi Takamasa (Breen 1996) who never personally became a Christian, or even in the voluminous writings of Uchimura Kanzo, who of course did.

What emerges, as Kisala fully documents, is a cultural complex with a set of interestingly interconnected facets: a rightwing political stance (or totally apolitical), an anti-Americanism fuelled by fears of the erosion of Japanese cultural identity by Hollywoodisation and a view of globalisation as constituting essentially US cultural hegemony, a strong internationalism centring on the promotion of world peace, a distinctively Japanese concept of peace consisting of an amalgam of moral cultivation, a "civilisational" approach to international stability, a strong dose of post A-Bomb victimology and a spiritual view of world salvation, based for example in the case of Byakko Shinkokai on the peace prayer that links the individual to spiritual forces that enable the overcoming of karma and hence the spiritualisation/salvation of all mankind (Kisala 1999, pp. 126ff). The structure of this complex is then made up of Occidentalism or "reverse Orientalism" (Kisala 1999: 159) in which the spiritual East is contrasted with the materialistic West, an appeal to the Atomic bombings as conferring on Japan a unique moral status as the centre of world peace in the postwar era, a strong continuity with traditional Japanese nativism, a strong element of religious syncretism combined with a basically spiritual view of humanity's salvation and remaking. These views of a national mission can be found not only in the smaller JNRs, but as Kisala shows, also in the larger examples such as Soka Gakkai and Rissho Koseikai, in which the view of Japan's uniqueness and unique role in the world represent a kind of globalisation of the *nihonjinron*, or its translation into a higher register. And if we were to stop at this point this is what we would be essentially left with, and this is the fundamental weakness of both Pye's and Kisala's otherwise ethnographically detailed and insightful pieces. In fact the analysis needs to be taken much further, and while accepting the claims of both Pye and Kisala that the JNRs do indeed provide a unique path into the understanding of contemporary Japanese identity, their basic paradigm needs to be transformed if the subject of emergent Japanese imaginaries is to be pursued in depth.

Imagination, Memory, Identity

In the broader sociology of Japanese society, religion plays an ambiguous role. In a society that rather proudly announces itself as far-gone in secularisation, very large numbers of people quietly participate in Buddhist or Shinto rituals, a large if indeterminate number of people belongs to the JNRs, Christians, while statistically a very small minority have a major impact through their educational, medical, and social welfare activities and have historically had substantial influence on Japanese thinking and politics, especially in relation to the origins of socialism in Japan (Clammer 1997a). The temples and shrines that abound in Japan's historic cities (Kyoto, Nara and Kamakura especially) are sites of pilgrimage as well as tourism (and the two are in practice often mixed), the *matsuri* of virtually every Japanese neighbourhood are well attended and supported, the building of a house requires the intervention of Shinto priests and amulets and charms are bought in large numbers from the little shops that are to be found in every major shrine. But while religions form this deep substratum of Japanese society, they are rarely very visible or socially activist. Helen Hardacre has argued that "For the most part, religions have shunned the limelight and maintained a self-imposed media blackout. As organisations, all sectors of religion share a need to hold together people affiliated by various ties of variable strength, all of whom are extremely sensitive to criticism. Christianity is sometimes the exception to the rule, but just as they generally counsel their believers to accommodate themselves to circumstances rather than attempt to change society, the first and second sectors of Japanese religions tend to regard public protest as unbecoming" (Hardacre 2003). This is true insofar as it goes, but it occludes another important aspect of Japanese religion—its identity creating capacities. The eschewing of obvious activism by religious organisations in a country in which the state has historically tended to aggrandise social and political intervention and policy to itself (hence the weak NGO sector) makes sense, but it obscures the other and more subtle ways in which religion works in Japanese society. In the post-bubble economy and society the JNRs especially are repositioning themselves around a set of agendas which, I will argue, operate essentially through a politics of identity, rather than through a politics of activism.

These agendas have a number of common elements, all drawing on cultural imaginaries that relocate Japan as central to the emerging world order. The first of these elements is ecology. Even as Shinto is attempting to reinvent itself as the new ecological religion (International Shinto Federation 1995), so too both the JNRs and established sects of Buddhism are stressing not only their own ecological relevance, but also the organic links between this position and what are seen as traditional elements of Japanese culture, a culture seen as being uniquely nature-oriented in its inspiration and expression (Clammer 1995 pp. 59-81). So even as the peace paradigm provides one vehicle for JNRs to promote a quietly non-controversial social platform, so too does the ecology paradigm, and like its peace counterpart, allows the representation of Japan as a centre of the new thinking, uniquely qualified by its nature-centred culture on the one hand and its post Atomic bombing peace-centred culture on the other. And indeed this is not simply wishful thinking: Japanese Buddhism has long promoted the idea of the potential Buddhahood of all things, including what anthropocentric humans rather arrogantly refer to as "nature" (LaFleur 1974), and while the atomic bombings have promoted a fairly extensive victimology, they also act as a kind of memory-base, a primal trauma, since when Japanese society really has been in many respects different. The "memoryscapes" of Hiroshima and Nagasaki do indeed provide a kind of founding-myth for a new self image of Japan. Even as many self images of Israel are founded on memories or representations of memories of the Holocaust, so too are many aspects of postwar Japanese identity emerge from the memories or representations of the bombings. While there is always the danger of such "memories" being co-opted by the state, those very memories also possess subversive power. As Lisa Yoneyama phrases it "Insofar as nation-states continue to exist as institutional entities, and their apparatuses of knowledge continue to interpellate their subjects, nationalisation remains a powerful force in shaping our memories, knowledge and representations. Residues of Hiroshima's catastrophe are constantly in danger of being recuperated for the establishment of coherent national narratives and identities. Nevertheless, these shards of memory, as traces, also carry the power to obstruct that same process" (Yoneyama 1999: 217). The peace paradigm that Kisala identifies is not itself simply nationalistic. It also represents a negotiation with the traces of memory that subvert that very nationalism, and which from the experience of a particular locality becomes the basis for a new internationalism. The apparently apolitical nature of most JNRs then needs to be interpreted with some subtlety, and their seemingly right-wing orientation in fact is a mixture of reversion to a contemporary form of the "national learning" of the 18th Century, the current expression of "overcoming modernity," and a subversion of the conventional materialistic politics that dominates Japanese society both by replacing it with a spiritualised mirror of itself and by relocating Japan at the centre of a kind of emergent "new age" world culture. Japan in this view becomes a kind of Tibet—not necessarily politically or militarily strong on the world stage (the power of the Japanese global economy tending to be forgotten at this point)—but as a spiritual centre, a source of peace-teachings, pacifism, ecological awareness and new internationalism. While Yoneyama speaks of the "feminization of memory" in the contemporary Japanese culture, here we might talk of the "aestheticisation of politics" on a global scale as being the social project pf the JNRs. The idea of a "cultural turn" recently so trendy amongst avant-garde social theorists in the West, is old-hat in Japan, and here we see its latest incarnation as Japanese identity being rooted in culture, but with the added twist of that culture (understood in a very traditional sense, rather than as contemporary pop-culture) becoming a world-saving export.

Interestingly parallel trends can be seen elsewhere in East Asia, especially in China and Taiwan, where moral critique of consumerism, individualism and money-politics is coming from religious circles which consequently have a tradition-defending or creating role, and where ecological movements have strong roots in religion. The result is not the absence of civil society, but, as in Japan, civil society of an alternative configuration from that visible in the West (Weller 1999). The "anonymous religion" of Japan conceals and embodies an "anonymous civil society" in which the seeming quietism of the average citizen disguises an substantial level of activism aimed more at subverting conventional politics than trying to gain access to it (LeBlanc 1999). The programmes of peace and ecology then, while they may reflect a Japan-as-promised-land thinking at one level, deeply subvert the isolationism, materialism and ethnocentrism of mainstream Japanese politics. There is a strong tendency in Japanese studies to see all expressions of Japan-centeredness (as with the whole *nihonjinron* debate) as expressions of nationalism (an attitude rarely applied however to let us say US, French or Irish patriotism or cultural pride). In fact a much more nuanced approach needs to be taken in which the idea of imaginaries needs to be given a more central theoretical place in the creation of identities.

As I have argued elsewhere in a study of Japanese anti and philo-semitism (Clammer 2001c, pp. 189-216), a deep theme in Japanese religious/political thought (although often at the fringes) is the redemptive role of Japan in the world order. In this particular version the Jews are either the obstacle to Japan achieving its status as world-saviour by their domination of global economic and political structures, or, as in the Christian Zionism propagated by some of the indigenous Christian denominations (Mullins 1998), that while Christians should strive for the conversion of the Jews, Japan and Israel are somehow linked in a mystic bond in which the divine mission of the two are intimately connected, with some even going as far as to argue for parallels between the Bible and the Japanese classics, or that the Japanese themselves are, or are the descendants of, the lost tribes of ancient Israel. Furthermore, in the writings of the postwar revisionist Mimura Saburo (who himself worked closely with the JNR Omotokyo, itself a source of the Mahikari NR and a fascinating blending of syncretic and spiritist beliefs and a mission of world transformation through peace), the recognition of the common divine mission of the Jews and the Japanese is the route to world peace (Goodman and Miyazawa 1995: 158). For others at the JNRs/peace/world redemption interface such as the NR theologian Okusho Kazuo, the atomic bombings of Hiroshima and Nagasaki were expiatory events that are figures of the opening of the heavenly cave from which in Japanese mythology the Sun Goddess emerged and which herald the unification of the world under Japan's benevolent tutelage (Okusho 1972).

Buddhism, World Peace and Japan

Despite claims to being a secular society, the Japanese psyche has been deeply moulded by Buddhism. Art, architecture, music, calligraphy, ethics, attitudes to nature, conceptions of death, foods and many other aspects of aesthetics and culture find their deepest roots in Buddhism. And while there are many schools of Buddhist "theology" and practice, it is interesting that a number of the most prominent JNRs—Soka Gakkai, Rissho Koseikai and Nipponzan Myohoji especially, as well as long established Buddhist sects such as the Tendai school—draw their inspiration primarily from the Lotus Sutra (the *Saddharma-pundarika-sutra* or *Myoho-renge-kyo*) in Japanese. The Lotus Sutra, to simplify a rich and complex text, expounds the doctrine of an eternal Buddha working for the enlightenment of all beings over aeons of time and interpretations of the sutra have since the 8th and 9th centuries stressed its connections to the welfare of society and the establishment of universal peace (Stone 2003). In one sense then the universalising mission of JNRs is simply the expression of a Buddhist teaching, revered in China and Korea as well, that has existed for centuries. What has given it a new salience is globalisation.

The question of globalisation in relationship to Japan is a complex one with many dimensions, and while Pye sees it primarily as a source of anxiety leading to the questioning of identity, it can also be seen as an opportunity for Japan to draw on its past and to represent it in a new and very different light. The problems of memory and coming to terms with the past that preoccupy the major revisionist thinkers such as Kato Norihiro (Kato 1997) are here recast. The atomic bombings in particular become expiatory events, transforming Japan from belligerence to victim, from warmonger to peace promoter and from a remote closed country on the periphery of the world system to its new centre. There are structural similarities here between Japan's assimilation of postmodernism by claiming essentially that it is nothing new and that Japan has always been postmodern (Miyoshi and Harootunian 1989; Clammer 1995) and the rereading of the history of religion in Japan. As Stone suggests "In claiming that faith in the *Lotus Sutra* would realise the Buddha land in the present world, Nichiren drew both on perceptions of the *Lotus's* magical power as a "nation-protecting sutra" and on traditional tendai doctrine, which asserts the non-duality of subjective and objective realms (*esho funi*) and the identity of the present, *saba* world with the Buddha's Land of Tranquil Light (*shaba soka jakkodo*). Nichiren made clear that the nonduality of the self and its environment, or the immanence of the Buddha in the present world, was not a mere matter of metaphysical assertion or even of subjective, personal insight: where people embraced the *Lotus Sutra*, the outer world would actually be transformed" (Stone 2003: 65). Indeed this argument is taken very seriously in Rissho Koseikai and its teaching that the *Lotus Sutra* embodies an ideology of peace. In Nipponzan Myohoji the doctrine of absolute pacifism in which Japan would stand as a moral exemplar even if attacked carries this idea even further and includes the idea that while the evil of the atomic bombings, like all aggression, somehow rebounds upon its perpetrators, it is also a sacrifice accepted by the Japanese people who by demonstrating the horror of atomic warfare have saved humanity as a whole from destruction. But whereas most scholarship (Stone's own excellent essay for example) discuss the ways in which such teachings can lead to a socially engaged Buddhism with a form of activism however rather different from that of its secular counterparts or other religions, little attention has been paid to how these teachings might relate to the issue of identity. We are now in a position to draw these out and to relate them to the double context of globalisation and the symbolic management of the past, which equally constitute the framework within which identity issues are being worked out and in which new imaginaries flourish. While religion is only one element of this (the economy, popular culture and environmental issues are clearly others) it does, I believe, provide us with an especially useful key to exploring identity issues in contemporary Japan.

The Dialectics of Globalisation

In his book on the relationships between religion and globalisation (Beyer 1997), Peter Beyer notes that religion itself is an valuable index of globalisation—as religions themselves become globalised in new ways, as they change their means of communication in this new context and how while at one level pursuing universalistic agendas, at others religions become a means of expressing what he terms "socio-cultural particularism," not necessarily in opposition to globalisation but in a complex interplay with it (Beyer 1997: 45). In particular with the salience of ethnicity as an organising principle of the modern nation-state, religion (as in the Balkans, Northern Ireland, the southern Sudan, Indonesia) becomes a way of asserting local identities while exploiting a more universalistic language of identity categories or labels which allows the definition of in and out groups. But while ethnicity is the basis of the self-definition of many modern nation-states (Japan itself being a prime example), ethnicities "are not simply identical with nationalisms" since they leave "room for group culture to enter the globalisation picture in other ways than as the legitimating identities of states" (Beyer 1997: 51). This is important for the analysis of JNRs since it allows them to pursue both universalistic and localistic agendas simultaneously, while remaining outside of the state. The common tendency to see their Japan-centeredness as simply crude nationalism (either political or cultural) is inadequate. It would be more accurate to see them as trying to define a new sense of identity out of culturally appropriate raw materials in a dialectical relationship with the necessary conditions of globalisation. Drawing on a vocabulary of peace and environmentalism then is not deception—it represents a genuine attempt to renegotiate the relationship of Japan to the world that both transcends the psychic-spiritual Westernisation that many Japanese quite rightly feel they should defend themselves against, while refusing to equate globalisation simply with political-economy. A different model of the world is being proposed in other words and while it is true that many of its proponents are struggling to detach themselves from a language of ethnocentrism derived from the past, the issues posed are real ones to large numbers of Japanese, for whom, today, any concept of citizenship must include their relationship to the wider world.

Beyer indeed argues that (based on an analysis derived from Wallerstein and Niklaus Luhmann) globalisation itself, especially in relation to religion, contains a central ambiguity: "The structural sources of inclusion thereby favours the equai legitimacy of exclusivities and identities based on them, along with the efforts to express this legitimacy in greater access to the functional systems for their members. But the functional rationalities of the various instrumental systems also often bring about discrimination against or in favour of certain groups in spite of inclusion ... religion and religious movements can under circumstances respond to this ambiguity in modern globalised structures" (Beyer 1997: 61). In an impersonal globalised world in which structural forces appear as oppressive and non-deflectable, ethnicity and religion provide a haven. This I think we already knew, but what is important at this juncture to remember is that these havens themselves are globalised—the universal penetrates the particular even as the particular flavours the universal. Interestingly in his study of religion and globalisation Beyer does not discuss Buddhism—the new Christian Right, Liberation Theology, new religious Zionism and the Islamic revolution in Iran comprise his empirical case studies—but interestingly he does discuss what he terms "religious environmentalism," although largely from the perspective of Christianity. In that discussion he notes both that ecology has become a central concern for religious movements and that there are close links between religion/ecology and "peace and justice" movements and that in fact under the regime of globalisation they are likely to be intimately connected. Beyer suggests that environmental issues concretise the effects of globalisation more clearly than other less visible and more diffuse effects. Furthermore "Translated into the terms of the globalisation debate used here, the continued elaboration of the global system depends on pursuing the cultural values that resonate with that system. The liberal religious concepts of peace and justice are not, however, simply an accommodating confirmation of emerging global social order. Contained within both notions is the assertion that the injustices are to a significant degree the result of the operation of the globalising, instrumental systems" (Beyer 1997: 210). While their goals are not identical, environmental and justice/peace movements are linked, not only by their own internal logics, but also by globalisation which provides their common ground of critique. It is not surprising then in the JNRs too that peace/ecology issues are closely related. What is less apparent however is an emphasis on justice, an uncomfortable question given Japan's vast economic power and the way that it is being used. The transnationalism of many of the JNRs then reflects not only their access to globalised communication structures, but also the fact that they are simultaneously located within globalisation, are in many respects opposed to it while drawing on its communicative advantages, and are actually engaged in attempting to define or create a new version of globalisation. As George Monbiot has cogently argued (Monbiot 2003), the challenge for the global justice movement is not to overthrow globalisation, but to capture it and turn it to humanitarian ends. This too would seem to be the agenda of the JNRs.

At this point we should return to the argument of Yumiko Iida which was referred to earlier. Iida, in a sensitive and articulate analysis of postwar Japanese identity (Iida 2002) is nevertheless fixated on the idea of nationalism as the primary trope with which to explore modern and contemporary Japanese imaginaries of belonging (the subtitle of her book is "Nationalism as Aesthetics"). Iida certainly wishes to move beyond a conventional understanding of nationalism, but the political issue for her is still the basis of identity, as the choice of the authors that she chooses to examine reveals—she is concerned with the ways in which Japanese intellectuals have thought about identity, not how the actual producers of culture (amongst I would include the founders and theologians of the JNRs) have actually attempted to negotiate it. She is engaged in other words in a second order debate about what are actually primary existential issues for the actual population. Many of her arguments are nevertheless important, and here I want to briefly enter into a conversation with those arguments in order to further deepen the understanding of the issues of imaginaries and identities that we are both discussing.

While rejecting what we might call a "crude nationalism" model, Iida attempts to situate both *nihonjinron* and historical revisionism in the context of the socio economic, political and cultural contexts that have shaped those practices and ideologies in the postwar period. A similar model can be applied to the JNRs, for while I have argued that they cannot for the most part be seen as crude nationalism, they too are situated at the intersection of new political, economic and cultural forces and likewise form the interface between what Iida terms the political, economic and the aesthetic-symbolic realms. While Iida rightly sees the Aum Shinrikyo movement as reactionary and anachronistic, she does also note that, in attracting a substantial number of members, "*Aum Shinrikyo* promised two things contemporary Japanese society could not: a collective imaginary where life was filled with meaning, and a vision of an ideal worth living, and indeed, dying for. In a society where the ever intensifying penetration of the structuring forces of technology and rationalism into the remotest corners of life has jeopardised the subject's access to the empirical realm of life outside consciousness, the subject is left...with 'no place to hide'" (Iida 2002: 244). This malaise Iida ultimately traces to a breakdown (or hypersuccess) of capitalism, and its dissolution of political and economic structures, and with them both socio-cultural ones and states of subjectivity. In her view what the revisionists "seek in the knowledge they create is, consciously or not, the reconstitution of a national community in order to 'repair' the diffusion of the intersubjective meaning of the Japanese nation, a repair that would, they believe, restore the damaged link between the subject and the society as a whole" (Iida 2002: 245). In a sense the project of the JNRs is similar, but with the very important difference that their vision, even if Japan is at the centre of it, is international and universalistic. Whereas many of the prescriptions of the revisionists are nationalistic, paternalistic and authoritarian, those of the JNRs link themselves to a language which in another context might almost be called "New Age"—a spiritualist universalism drawing on ideas of peace, ecology and anti-materialism, certainly with deep roots in Japanese culture, especially its Shinto and Buddhist strands, but yet also deeply subversive of both the national project of the main-stream politicians, and that of the revisionists with which it most certainly should not be confused despite its structural similarities. An ethical universalism enters the space formerly occupied by what Iida terms the "national/cultural contingency" (Iida 2002; 251). This space is no longer the "native space" of former expressions of *nihonjinron*, but is an attempt to conserve a cultural heritage not by further localising it, but on the contrary by universalising it, and in so doing moving beyond either the nihilistic solution of Aum on the one hand, or the resentment driven solutions of the revisionists on the other. In making such a move, the older language of Japanology is also transcended—no longer should debate be focussed on the tired categories of nationalism, *nihonjinron* and particularism, but on a new identity discourse that sees the "salvation" of Japan and of Japanese subjectivities as intimately linked to the global, but in a fresh way—a way that builds on a vocabulary of non-materialism, peace and nature, not as a screen for sinister right-wing machinations, but as a genuine attempt to draw on cultural resources as a basis for an interlinked sense of identity in which the Buddhist idea of "dependent arising" takes on a new and sociological meaning.

Rethinking Imaginaries

For these reasons I think that Winston Davis is profoundly wrong, mainly because he is working from within the old Japanological paradigm, when he argues that "In spite of their obvious differences, Japan Theory and the country's New Religions have several things in common. Both are keenly interested in questions of identity ... Both Theorist and Messiah are enthralled by virtually the same eschatology—the same vision, incidentally, that captivates Japanese politicians, bureaucrats and intellectuals—namely, the beatific vision of the coming twenty-first century as the 'Age of the Pacific Rim,' or more explicitly, the 'Century of Japan'" (Davis 1998: 180). Like Iida, Davis sees the malaise of modern Japanese society stemming from a lack of meaning and identity brought about by, presumably, late capitalism, in which the "Theorists" (i.e. writers in the *nihonjinron* mode) provide the place of priests—they are the purveyors of meaning and identities. But he appears to imagine, that the solutions are essentially homogeneous, even as his subjects (the Japanese) are often alleged to be. In fact such a view is I think empirically wrong and is an ideological rejection of the possibility that Japanese society can contain within itself alternatives, widely differing images of Japanese identity and counter-cultures. In fact it contains all these things, and the JNRs can be understood as social movements proposing just such an alternative vision, which if nationalistic, cannot be seen in terms of the old debates about Japanese nationalism, despite the continuities with prewar ideas of a world centred on Japan, but in terms of a new discourse in which the local and the global are indeed linked in a complex and dynamic dance, the outcome of which can never be fully predicted.

"Japan" itself is not a fixed entity, but is a construct, the outcome of past imaginaries and subject to revision as new ones and new senses of identity come into play. But to fully grasp this some quite old mental habits need to be overthrown. When Kisala argues for example that "Fujii

Nichidatsu and Nipponzan Myohoji make use of the rhetoric of occidentalism to describe their mission of spreading peace: the spiritual East will save the scientific West from destruction" (Kisala 1999: 162), this is not only something of a caricature of a subtle body of teachings, but overlooks the fact that debates within Western social theory have also involved bitter attacks on the scientism of Western world-views and the deleterious effects these have had there on values and subjectivities, and have even, in the view of Zygmunt Bauman led to the Holocaust, something totally unknown within the context of Japanese society (Bauman 1989). The idea that the Enlightenment and its associated modernity have led to the implosion of the societies that invented them, is not a Japanese idea and having that very idea expressed back to the West from Japan does not necessarily make the idea an example of "occidentalism." The Japanese have tended to see themselves, and a whole mass of Western scholarship especially during the "Bubble" days, was devoted to reinforcing the impression, of being the odd-man-out of modernity, the one successfully industrialising but noncolonised nation in Asia, the unglobalised globaliser. The problem for Japan is not the desire to reinsert itself into the world, but how to do this, since every attempt is rebuffed as yet another example of neo-nationalism, exceptionalism or disguised superiority. As anyone who has lived for any period of time in Japan will know, the Japanese are characterised by an odd sense of superiority at home, combined with a serious sense of inadequacy when managing the "outside" world, a world that under the regime of globalisation however is now very much "inside" too. Japan is certainly a society in which cultural identity is central to any sense of belonging and it is through the realm of culture then that new subjectivities are constructed and with them larger communal imaginaries.

Japan has long been a society engaged on a utopian project—of making itself a land of harmony and peace. In many ways this project has succeeded remarkably well, but there are deep contradictions between the vision of the politicians and business bosses and those of many "ordinary" Japanese. By no means all have been captured by the blandishments of consumer capitalism, although it is on those who have, usually in the guise of "popular culture" studies that western scholarship of Japan has concentrated. There is another dimension altogether, represented both by the JNRs and by the many small communal and educational experiments that dot the landscape. William Kelly has suggested that postwar Japanese society should be read as simultaneously "increasingly homogeneous" and "persistently diverse" (Kelly 1995), a position substantiated in many ways by the discussion here. What is missing is a model of how this logic works itself out in Japanese society. Part of the answer suggested here takes us back to Iida's notion of resentment. In relation to the revisionists she sees this as a purely negative concept, but it can be read in other ways. As Eric Gans suggests "Resentment may be defined as the scandal of the peripheral self at the centrality of the other which transforms the equality of the original scene of representation into an absolute polarity of significance. It differs from envy in being directed not at contingent but at communally significant and hence ethically necessary differences. It is thus a necessary evil" (Gans 1985: 174). The crisis of subjectivity that Iida announces then can be addressed in many ways—through consumerism, revisionism, *nihonjinron*, or, as suggested here, through new imaginaries drawing on cultural resources that can be turned to unexpectedly good use when confronting the challenges of globalisation, with resentment as a significant medicting psychological mechanism. As Kevin Hetherington suggests, while new social movements (amongst which I here include the JNRs) are almost always about identity and are themselves an important form of identity-politics, what is often ignored is their relationship to space (Hetherington 1998: 101). If Jean Baudrillard a decade earlier characterised or caricatured Japan as a "satellite of the planet earth" (Baudrillard 1988: 79), while it might be going too far to suggest that now the earth is a satellite of the planet Japan, it is certainly true that Japan, or at least many segments of its population, are redefining their relationship to the world. The JNRs are one of the important ways in which they are doing this, for while arguably containing nationalist or ethnocentric sentiments, they also contain one of the few universalistic discourses available in Japanese society. One of the positive moves in recent social theory has been to emphasise the importance of agency: things don't just happen to people, they also make things happen. In discussing Benedict Anderson's now classic view of the nation as "imagined community," the Southeast Asianist Anthony Milner has argued that "conceptualised" rather than "imagined" was a better term for the emerging states of Asia: "the concept of imagination tends to disguise the anxiety, the experimentation, the contest and the sheer intellectual difficulty faced by those who relinquished loyalty to their older forms of community and constructed a new form" (Milner 1997: 89). Many Japanese are now in the same position—but not this time of constructing the nation out of the local identities of feudalism, but of constructing the post-nation out of the failures of nationalism in the face of the overwhelming reality of globalisation. A religious discourse reflecting the particularities of the local and the universal issues of human survival is one of the major ways in which these new imaginaries are being constructed out of the very subjectivities already deconstructed by capitalism and postmodernism.

8

Globalisation and Citizenship in Japan

New Identity Politics in a Post-Bubble Economy

The nature of citizenship has been a contested theme in postwar Japanese history, and with Japan's increasing if reluctant involvement in global politics (in addition to global economics), the question has taken on fresh salience. The Japanese term for citizen (*shimin*) means literally a town dweller, civilian or even a "commoner." In pre-modern Japan, at least up to the end of the Tokugawa Shogunate (1603-1868), political authority was highly centralised and society was stratified into ranks, with the lowest two—the peasants and the townspeople/merchants having few political resources and being confined to their status by sumptuary laws and other restrictions, despite the townspeople in particular often having far more wealth than the not uncommonly impoverished rural samurai and having developed the vibrant urban culture of the Edo and early Tokyo periods (Seidensticker 1983). The relative opening of Japan after the Meiji Restoration of 1868 (with the collapse of the Shogunate and the reestablishment of the political authority of the Emperor), while it saw the appearance of a modern and modernising state apparatus, including a professional bureaucracy and an army, largely modelled on contemporary European forms, did little to extend real political freedoms. The new Meiji Constitution was far from liberal in intent (having been in large part framed by Prussian constitutional lawyers) and established an oligarchic political structure rather than anything approaching a true democracy. The subsequent periods of industrialisation, colonial adventures and militarisation culminating in Japan's involvement in the Pacific war saw the continuing reluctance of the state to extend liberties or responsibilities to its population, looked upon in any case rather more as subjects than as citizens.

The defeat of 1945, the abdication of the Emperor from his divine status to that of constitutional monarch and the imposition of the postwar constitution by the Allied occupation forces (and still in force, if increasingly contested, today), had the effect of throwing open the doors to democratising forces. Some of the seedbeds for citizen activism had indeed existed in the prewar years in the form of the Left, cognitive minorities such as the small Christian community, the feminist movements of the Taisho period, and other liberal tendencies especially amongst independent intellectuals (Hoston 1986). But they had been unable to make much impact on the repressive apparatus of an increasingly centralised, bureaucratised and control obsessed state. Postwar extension of the franchise, legalisation of the political opposition and the lifting of restrictions on a whole range of social movements, including religious ones, transformed this landscape. But it did not do so entirely. The re-emergence of big business, especially the large combines that were supposed to have been broken up after the war (the zaibatsu) and of a very cosy relationship between business and government during the postwar high-growth years, together with the historical effects and bureaucratic culture of the prewar period, have ensured continuities that still make the issue of citizenship a contested one in contemporary Japan (Matsumoto 1991).

There are many potentially interesting issues here, including that of the nature of Japanese political culture, of the power of certain institutional forms in creating or distorting patterns of political and social access, or of the behavioural expectations of Japanese culture (or of stereotypes of that culture). Similarly a detailed study of postwar social movements—against the US-Japan security treaty, the construction and expansion of Narita airport, the siting of nuclear power plants and many other issues, notably pollution (Broadbent 1998)—demonstrates at least a vocal minority of citizen activists mobilised around current issues, even if formal political participation (as measured for example by voter turnout in national and local elections or active party membership) is weak. But here my focus will be on one of the most profound forces impacting Japanese society—globalisation—and the effects that it is having the understanding and practice of citizenship.

But before turning to that issue, it is necessary first to devote some space to examining the concept of citizenship in Japanese society and its substantial differences from Western ones. Although some sociologists of globalisation such as John Meyer have argued for international institutional convergence especially in such areas as political and legal cultures and in education (Meyer 1980), in fact major, if often subtle, variations exist deriving from cultural, historical and philosophical factors between conceptions of rights, duties and political identities between different societies coexisting in the world system. The presence of structurally similar institutions can mask big differences in the practices and procedures that animate those institutions. This I will argue is very much the case in Japan.

A good place to begin in discussing conceptions of citizenship is an investigation of the procedures that one must go through to become a citizen of a given society if one is not but desires to become one. In Japan in principle a foreigner with sufficient residence time (at least a decade), who has a good reason to remain in the country (for example by reason of intermarriage or professional activities) and who can pass a Japanese language requirement, is eligible to apply. In fact few do and less are accepted. Very few amongst its very small refugee population (mostly of Vietnamese or other Indo-Chinese origins) have succeeded in gaining citizenship, and neither have the majority of the very large Korean population (over 800,000) most of whom continue to be resident aliens despite decades of residence originating in Japan's colonial occupation of Korea up until 1945, although the most recent literature on the Koreans by Ryang and others suggest that the rate of naturalization has speeded up dramatically. In fact without being of Japanese descent, obtaining citizenship is rare and difficult, and despite cosmetic changes in other immigration regulations (making it easier to obtain the much less stringent permanent residency which confers no political rights, and allowing resident aliens to re-enter Japanese airports through the Japanese passports channel, for example) obtaining political rights by a non-citizen is a very rocky path. Even a child born in Japan is not guaranteed citizenship as recent controversies surrounding the status of children born out of wedlock to Filipina entertainment workers and unknown but indisputably Japanese fathers, or the recent case of the twin "test-tube" children of a Japanese couple born to a non-Japanese surrogate mother, but refused recognition as citizens by the state. The whole issue of invitrio fertilisation has in fact thrown open fierce debates about the status of children born by such methods when there is the possibility that the donor or surrogate mother may not be Japanese (Deguchi 1999). Ethnicity and citizenship are intimately linked notions in Japan (as indeed they are in Germany and a number of other places) and this notion of ethnicity involves at least two elements—race and culture—often conflated. Notions of being Japanese (genetically) are in other words commonly associated or identified with possession of a distinctive culture. The problem for a foreigner who wishes to become Japanese is not only that of race, but the assumption that the culture is somehow impossible to acquire except by birth. The constant exclamations of amazement or dismay that greet a culturally correct "performance" (and one often senses that it is literally regarded as such) on the part of a foreigner (for example by actually speaking intelligible Japanese) is indicative of this. The difficulty of separating citizenship from ethnicity in Japan is thus a crucial one, and helps to explain why current forms of nationalism in Japan frequently take a cultural form rather than an overtly political one (Yoshino 1997).

But where does this conflation come from? Some would argue (that as in England) it arises from the relative sense of isolation of a smallish island country that (unlike England) has been the recipient of very little in-migration and has been the source of relatively little out migration. The two and a half centuries of isolation under the Tokugawa Shogunate and Japan's subsequent imperial history up until 1945 were largely devoted to building up a sense of nation, not undermining it (Gluck 1985), and Appadurai's argument that the world is now composed of deterritorialised "post-national formations" with "translocal solidarities, cross-border mobilisations, and post-national identities" (Appadurai 1996: 424) constituting a new form of "transnation," a diasporic identity, while romantic even when applied to most of the world, is hollow when applied to Japan. The project of "nation-building," or perhaps nation-maintaining, is far from over in Japan and while certainly Japan exports itself vastly through its technology and to a lesser extent through its popular culture, this is not at the expense of keeping a very strong sense of boundaries, ethnically, culturally and geographically explored by (McVeigh 2004).

But the sources of differing conceptions of citizenship cannot be only traced to ethno-geography. Space does not allow a discussion of the extensive debates that have surrounded the concept of citizenship in the West, its sources in liberal and republican thinking, its connections to a whole discourse of rights and duties, and its connection to associated debates about civic society and civil society (the literature is vast: for a brief sampling see Stevenson 2000, Isin and Wood 1999, Kymlicka 1995 and Kymlicka and Norman 2000). What does need to be said however is that this whole bundle of conceptions arises out of a particular philosophical tradition, a specific religious history, an expansionist political and economic (capitalist) dynamic, and views of the self rooted in a complex interplay of all these factors. In Japan however notions of identity, including political identity, are rooted in Buddhism and Confucianism, the former certainly leading to a decentred notion of the self, and the resulting legal culture and associated views of rights, while certainly influenced by ideas coming from the West, have maintained an independent philosophical position and operating procedures quite at variance with those of Europe or North America. Recent debates about rights and citizenship in Asia have strongly suggested that China and Japan in particular possess an alternative tradition that not only contests Western notions of citizenship, but is in many ways a better model that the West itself should learn from, given the manifest failures of the liberal project (e.g. Solinger 1999; De Bary and Tu 1998; Bauer and Bell 1999).

Many of the shifts allegedly occurring in conceptions of citizenship in the West—for example the blurring of the equation between citizenship and nationality, increasing tension between the rights of individuals and emerging group rights, the emergence of global/transnational forms of citizenship and the dilution of birth (as opposed to residence) as the primary criterion of citizenship—have simply not appeared in Japan. In a society where the sense of individualism is weak for example, group rights have always taken priority over personal ones. In Japan what we find is a complex formation which includes the idea of Japan as an ethno-cultural nation (in which citizenship can be legitimately denied to those who do not satisfy these requirements), as a Durkheimian society perceiving itself as an organic whole and closer to the communitarian ideal than practically any other society (except perhaps Singapore) in which individualism is weak and hierarchy is strong (Clammer 1995) and in which the state is still a profound force restricting the emergence of a strong civil society (Schwartz and Pharr 2003–and also McVeigh passim) by representing itself as a moral entity in which (again as in Singapore) the necessity for debate is muted because the state is the people and is the political embodiment of their identity. The absence of any history of liberalism and the weakness of the sources of individualism such as the Judeo-Christian tradition and the notions of self and personhood that historically emerged from this (Dumont 1986 or 1985?) have led to a decentred notion of citizenship—one attached more to ethno-cultural identity than to any clear conception of rights. Of course this picture is contested, especially by groups and individuals that have contact with the wider world, the source of discourses of rights and empowerments, but which, and this is crucial, are largely deployed in the Japanese context not to promote the internationalisation of the society, but on the contrary, as a mechanism for the pursuit of localism and particularism in the face of the global (Clammer 2002).

Globalisation and Japanese Society

Japan has long been an isolated society in comparison for example with Southeast Asia, constantly transformed by migrations of peoples, cultures and religions and for a long period under varieties of Western colonial domination, or with the great continental neighbour, China. During the two centuries of Tokugawa rule, intercourse with the outside world was limited, being largely confined to cultural exchanges with China and Korea and with the West being kept very much at arm's length. Even since the opening of Japan in the later Nineteenth Century, Japan has continued to attract the reputation of being a closed society—one that exports its own products and technology while not welcoming too much from the outside, and one into which integration by a foreigner is impossible or severely limited by cultural, linguistic and attitudinal barriers. This paradoxical positioning of Japan as economically central, but as culturally and politically peripheral to the world system has led Jean Baudrillard to characterise Japan as a "satellite of the planet earth" (cf. Clammer 2000a). While this image is by no means completely true (Japan imports a huge amount from the rest of the world for example), it has led to a whole discourse of difference, in which Japan being outside of the rest of the world is seen as a positive advantage, insulating Japan from the worst effects of globalisation (including Hollywoodisation) and allowing a distinctive form of society and culture to flourish without being subject to the homogenising influences so powerfully at work in the world (Clammer 1995, 2001).

This problem of the relationship of Japan to the wider world is not a new one, and has not only been a constant theme in Japanese discourse, from the remoter (e.g. Pollack 1986) to the recent pasts, where in the 1970s-80s a language of "internationalisation" (*kokusaika*) was the dominant way of linking Japan to the bigger universe of societies at a time when the concept of globalisation had not yet become common currency. The term as it was used at that time, while it implied an opening of Japan to outside influences, turned out to mean for most Japanese little more than making some foreign friends, travelling abroad more and perhaps studying (although rarely mastering) a foreign language (Mouer and Sugimoto 1986). A major difference however between the 80s use of the term "internationalisation" and the slightly later concept of globalisation is that the while the former was in a sense inner directed—managed that is by Japan and by Japanese people who could essentially decide how far to go, how much to learn or to admit into Japan, and how porous the boundaries between Japanese culture and the rest of the world should be allowed to become, the latter implies much less voluntarism and suggests forces that impinge on Japan like it or not.

Given that many of these forces (especially in the rest of Asia) have been unleashed by Japan itself—economic penetration, off-shore manufacturing, the spread of Japanese popular culture (especially *manga* or comic books, *anime* or animated movies and made for TV cartoon series, and music), Japanese fashion and technology—it is not so surprising that many of the same forces have to be accepted when they rebound on Japan, even if reluctantly accepted (Befu 1998; Ching 1996; Miyoshi and Harootunian 1993). How the forces of globalisation rebound specifically on notions of citizenship is the issue to which I will now turn, having placed it hopefully in the larger historical and social context within which it needs to be understood.

Globalisation has both made the average Japanese aware of the complex interdependencies of the contemporary world and of the fact that such interdependence cannot leave Japan untouched in terms of its social organisation and cultural forms. While many have resisted this inevitable implication, others have embraced it as providing exactly the lever that is needed to transform Japanese society in more open, equitable and creative directions suitable for meeting the challenges of the new century, one of which of course is managing globalisation itself (Eades, Gill and Befu 2000). Globalisation of course effects subjectivities, it transforms notions of the self by bringing that self into contact with the Other. Japan's exporting of itself through economic penetration, aid and popular culture has not surprisingly triggered both cultural interest in Japan and the desire in many cases to go there to take advantage of the high wage economy on the part of those on the receiving end of those exports. This has brought the world quite literally into Japan, in the form of cultural influences (food being a main one) and people—foreign workers, both legal and illegal, spouses of Japanese, increasing numbers of foreign students and tourists. The 2002 FIFA World Cup was a remarkable case of a sudden upsurge in numbers of visitors, an effect which may well translate into the desire on the part of at least some of those who came to Japan for football to return for work or study. In return Japan had for the first time since the end of the war to manage such a huge foreign influx (and to manage relations with co-host South Korea), something which had profound effects on perceptions of the outside world (Whang 2002).

These issues would be significant enough for Japan if all else was normal in the society, which, however, it manifestly is not. In less than a decade Japan has gone from an overconfident booming "bubble" economy with all the cultural pride and willingness to export itself that that implied (corporations pouring money into foreign universities for example to establish or expand programmes in Japanese studies) to a society deeply unsure of itself. Not only has the bubble economy imploded leaving vast uncollectible debts on the books of financial institutions, a declining stockmarket and plummeting property prices, but the last decade has also seen almost unthinkable events in postwar Japanese society. These have included the atrocities of the Aum Shinrikyo religious cult, and murders (including of children), rising crime, the collapse of guaranteed lifetime employment, a rapidly ageing society, and natural disasters, most conspicuously the great Hanshin earthquake which revealed amongst other things the total unpreparedness and lack of coordination in the government and bureaucracy for managing the most predictable kind of crisis in highly volcanic Japan. A seemingly endless string of scandals have involved not only big business, but also prominent politicians and even such august institutions as the Foreign Ministry and most recently the Self Defence Agency (the defence ministry). Intermittent conflict with Japan's immediate neighbours over apologies for war crimes, unacceptable revisions to history textbooks and visits by prime ministers to the notorious Yasukuni Shrine in Tokyo which enshrines amongst others A class war criminals has again escalated. It is the confluence of globalisation and these internal crises that pose the biggest challenge for contemporary Japanese identity.

Dimensions of the Citizenship Debate

What then is the state of that citizenship/identity? I would argue that it stands at a crucial crossroads, one path leading back into a closed and conservative society, the other leading to creative openings built on the foundations of citizen activism that have extensive postwar roots. Japan does not of course face the situation of some societies in which the majority of its population are attempting to obtain citizenship. With a largely ethnic Japanese population fully enfranchised by the postwar constitution, basic human rights, political access and freedom of expression is guaranteed. Except that is for those minorities who do not qualify for Japanese citizenship or for whom attaining that citizenship is difficult. Japan, while priding itself on its ethnic homogeneity in fact contains large minorities of Korean and Chinese origin, many of whom do not have Japanese citizenship despite periods of residence in some cases extending over two or more generations (Weiner 1997). Japan likewise has substantial numbers of foreign workers and residents, many perfectly legal (business executives with foreign companies, diplomats, language teachers, legitimate refugees, students and spouses, or Latin American workers of Japanese descent), but many also who are illegals working in construction, catering, dry-cleaning, scrapyards and other less desirable occupations shunned by Japanese. Japan (unlike say Singapore) has yet to evolve a consistent policy on foreign unskilled labour despite substantial academic and some political debate (e.g. Shimoda 1994).

But despite the falling birthrate and fears of a declining work force in the near future, no serious initiatives have come from the government to address this issue or to expand the ease with which legitimate foreign residents (including refugees) might obtain citizenship. At the formal level debate circulates around access to citizenship in the legal sense and the stories of those who have made this difficult transition—a former foreigner of Finnish origin for example having finally made it to political office—and of still unresolved controversies about allowing permanent residents (many of whom are Chinese or Koreans ethnically) to vote in local elections and to be employed in government service at the city or prefectural levels of administration. At another level altogether citizens' groups are active in seeking the human rights of foreign workers (including illegals) and in providing counselling, language training and medical care to such workers. The foreign worker issue in other words has been a catalyst at both governmental and local levels for reopening debate about the meaning of citizenship in this globalised environment, because it is an inescapable issue that reframes the question of identity for the first time (in Japan) in transnational terms.

The key question has become that of detaching a notion of citizenship from its association with ethnicity: the situation (totally familiar say in Britain) where I recognise you as a fellow citizen if you fulfil the standard qualifications of residence, taxpaying, subjective identification and contribution to the society, regardless of your race or place of historical origin. In his classic book on nations and nationalism, Benedict Anderson introduced the idea of the "imagined community" as defining the nation as a collective of individuals who do not and cannot actually know each other, yet become bound into a sense of commonality (Anderson 1991). The problem for Japan is no longer the creation of this primary nationalism (something largely accomplished by the beginning of the last century both ideologically through the creation of a common statehood reinforced both through symbols—the Emperor in particular), a common standard language, colonial adventures, and geographically with the establishment of stable boundaries of the national territory with the incorporation of Okinawa and Hokkaido. Rather it is the expansion of the imaginary community to encompass those not part of the dominant ethnic group (something that applies to Ainu and Okinawans to some degree as well as to Koreans, Chinese and other Asians and non-Asians) and challenging the received versions of the actual or mythical history of the dominant group and the official versions of its own ethnogenesis. Paradoxically this is harder in a society that sees itself as ethnically homogeneous than it is in highly plural ones and the psychological challenge to restrictive Japanese notions of citizenship is to break through this barrier.

The unstable nature of concepts of citizenship and their dependence on particular histories can been seen refracted in one of the major contemporary intellectual debates in Japan at the moment—that of school history textbook revision and the associated issue of the "Comfort Women." School textbook revision has long been a subject of controversy within Japan (especially between the left-leaning teacher's union and the very conservative Ministry of Education) and between Japan and its Asian neighbours. The debate however has been given new currency recently by the emergence of a movement known as the Jiyushugi Shikan Renkyukai or "Liberal Historiography Research Group" offering a revisionist view of Japanese history aimed precisely against the teaching of the "history of shame" symbolised by such subjects as the Nanjing Massacre and the question of the "Comfort Women" or women forced into sexual slavery for the wartime Japanese armed forces. This movement, which has garnered considerable local support as well as attracted a storm of criticism, has many dimensions, all of which cannot concern us here. But one important feature of the debate is exactly that of postwar and in particular contemporary Japanese citizenship and what it means to be a citizen in relation to responsibility for the past, and the particular subjectivities and distorted cultural identities that lack of reconciliation with that past imposes on individual Japanese and the national psyche (for commentaries on the controversy and its implications for identity see Morris-Suzuki 1998 and Ueno 1999).

In a way parallel with that of attempting to come to terms with the foreign worker issue, the textbook controversy forces the question of cultural politics into the limelight. But it does so in a new way. Until recently renegotiation of political and cultural identity could take place within the more familiar boundaries of the older discourse of cultural nationalism. There Japanese identity was understood as not only membership in a particular geographically circumscribed political entity, but also as membership of a very specific (read "unique") culture, one not understood by outsiders, but into which the Japanese young should be systematically socialised and which is packaged and propagated by intellectual and business elites as the "Japanese Mind, the Japanese way of business" and so forth (Yoshino 1992). But this more comfortable sense of self-identity is called into serious question by globalisation and its magnifying of Japan's links with the wider world, its emphasis on the recognition of pluralism within and its impact on Japanese subjectivities including gender, since globalisation has revealed to many Japanese women many alternative conceptions of femininity outside of classical or conventional Japanese ones. (Rosenberger 1993, Iwamura 1996, Fujimura-Fanselow 1995). So while the ongoing renegotiation of identity is reflected in arenas such as the textbook controversy, made vivid by the recognition of the fact that Japan's history cannot be understood as only that which went on within its own borders, globalisation, while challenging received notions also opens up many new possibilities for the redefinition of citizenship.

Some commentators indeed even go so far as to see contemporary Japan caught up in a struggle between older and minimal conceptions of citizenship represented by traditional identity politics, the almost unbroken conservative postwar rule of the Liberal Democratic Party and the domination of corporate interests on the one hand and emerging social forces embodied in new social movements and citizen's initiatives on the other. Whereas the old "social contract" was negotiated largely between government and a small range of civil society organisations—in particular trades unions and small business associations (Garon and Mochizuki 1993)—in which a largely agreed social framework was assumed, this implicit agreement on basic social goals has evaporated in the post-bubble years. With the result that a rather static view of citizenship represented as political participation reflected in the right to vote while subscribing to the consensus view of postwar Japanese cultural identity, has been replaced, at least for a substantial minority, by a much more dynamic, contested and internally diversified understanding.

This is apparent in a number of ways—the huge expansion of a discourse (if not a reality) of civil society (Ichikawa and Clammer 2002), the emergence of very large numbers of NGOs addressing both local and international issues, the increasingly social and global role being taken by the legitimate Shin Shukyo or "new religions" (such as Soka Gakkai) which collectively have a membership of many millions, the increasing political visibility of previously ignored groups such as housewives and their involvement in local politics and in social movements, the consumers' movement and in consumer cooperatives (LeBlanc 1999). It is also apparent in rising levels of volunteerism [that became a big movement after Kobe], and in the proliferation of local level citizen's groups organised around specific issues (road safety, security of school-children in and on their way to school, recycling, the needs and rights of the aged). This is in addition to older movements such as the Buraku Liberation League struggling for the rights of one of Japan's own excluded communities, feminist groups and groups representing the interests of Japan's ethnic minorities. While unions and similar formal organisations continue to play a role, their significance has declined relative to these newer organisational forms, new social movements and the redefinition of older ones (such as the new religions) as seeing themselves as involved in a much wider range of social issues (Pharr and Schwartz 2003).

The impact of globalisation is also apparent here in a number of ways—the formation of international alliances on the part of NGOs and minority rights groups such as those movements active amongst the Ainu people of northern Japan and the Okinawans of the deep south, the appropriation of a universalising language of human rights in the pursuit of local interests, and the participation in international forums such as the UN sponsored conferences on the rights of indigenous peoples and in anticorporate and anti-globalisation struggles and very conspicuously in the international environmental movement (Clammer 2002). Globalisation, while challenging local and particularistic conceptions of citizenship, has also and equally expanded opportunities for discovering resources internationally, for expanding and redefining the scope of local citizenship to encompass much broader issues and responsibilities and for expanding the range of democratic participation quite outside of traditional or institutional political categories. Let me elaborate on some significant dimensions of this in the Japanese context.

Globalisation and Democratisation

To its critics globalisation is usually seen as an anti-democratic force (e.g. Greider 1997) that removes sovereignty from legitimate national governments and concentrates it instead in the hands of unelected and unrepresentative organisations such as MNCs, the WTO and the World Bank. While it clearly has these characteristics, together with its tendency to cultural homogenisation, media imperialism and the erosion of job security and workers' rights internationally, it also creates opportunities for alternatives to emerge. The very information technology that may be used to control and to promote "flexible accumulation" can also be used to organise and promote alternatives, to create networks of international solidarity and to mobilise information and criticism of political or corporate mismanagement (Starr 2000). The expansion of international civil society and of new social movements promotes forms of political and social participation beyond or outside of conventional political channels. Networks of international solidarity are thus born that prevent any hegemonic form of globalisation from ever fully establishing itself.

In the same way that earlier attempts to negotiate social contracts in Japan and to keep broad democratic freedoms alive through unions, business associations and special interest groups in the context of a general ideology of accommodation leading to the decline in militant politics and confrontational tactics need to be placed in the context of twentieth-century Japanese history (Gordon 1993), so do later and post-bubble attempts. Just as the high growth policies of the 1960s-80s brought with them social costs—urbanisation, social displacement, disappearance of older industries, internal migration, a changing class structure—so has globalisation in the 1990s and since. Many of the debates within Japanese cultural studies—preoccupation with the self, massification of society and culture (*taishu shakai/faishu bunka*), the new social configuration of "tribes" (*zoku*) as comprising the fluid organisation of the new consumer society—can be traced to the effects of globalisation and the enhanced risks and uncertainties that it has engendered. (Clammer 1997b). Shifting patterns of politics and political opposition (for example the profound effects of urbanisation and the effects of the emergence of "world cities" in Japan (See Fujita and Hill 1993, Sassen 1990) are intimately connected to these bigger international shifts, linkages between the Japanese economy and the world economy and the dialectical interplay between Japanese culture and world cultures. This is of course also taking place in a society with almost universal literacy in which newspaper reading is amongst the highest in the world and in which information on almost any subject is easily and abundantly accessible. Just as in the past there were struggles to find new definitions of democracy and social justice, so these are occurring again, but in this globalised context, and in the context of mass access to information, a situation that Japan has never experienced before in this form (but then neither have most of us).

These global forces of course operate or reproduce themselves at the most local levels, and it at such levels in Japan that some of the most interesting responses are occurring. Robin LeBlanc's study of housewives in Tokyo for example demonstrates not only the rich and complex political lives of her subjects, expressed in local level politics, PTAs, volunteerism, and consumer cooperatives as well as in voting in national elections. But also very explicit in LeBlanc's study is the women's critique of liberalism in general and their situation of themselves as non-party voters and as "non-political" citizens. As LeBlanc summarises this:

> "As a 'bicycle citizen,' the housewife acts as if she were a citizen, but she believes that extending the reach of her actions to what she conceives of as political spheres would be defeating. The constraints of politics would strip her actions of their real meaning for the community. The housewife might be said to see herself as a citizen, but with a citizenship that is not viable in the contemporary political world. Through the eyes of political theory, we might see this housewife as a citizen without a polis. We might conclude that the problem of citizenship for a Japanese housewife results from unique characteristics of the Japanese political system—that the Japanese political system is simply not open enough to the representation of a variety of interests, that Japan has failed to have a fully liberal democratic system." (LeBlanc 1999: 65).

What LeBlanc has to say about housewives can be extended to other politically underrepresented groups in Japanese society, a society in which in any case distrust in the political system and of politicians in general (noted for their corruption and the seemingly interminable string of scandals that fills the media) is very high. It is also noteworthy that LeBlanc's summary refers to the housewives relationship to her *community*; to a vision of citizenship in other words that extends well beyond individualism or the self-centred demands of "lifestyle politics" (Giddens 1991) to encompass collectively defined social issues.

Such an attitude can also be seen in many of the more coherently organised new social movements in Japan (Muto 1999) and in the new religions, many of which have adopted peace, development and creative citizenship platforms, even as many of them have begun to internationalise themselves (Kisala 1999). The notion of a "political culture," although it originated in an older, Western "civic society" discourse, is as a result, by no means defunct. Recognising this has drawn attention back to the cultural basis of political behaviour, including on the part of anthropologists, amongst whom there is a reviving interest in the nature of the contemporary state (Ong 2000). While I would hesitate to agree with Aihwa Ong that Japan represents a form of Asian liberalism similar to the kind she sees as prevailing in Malaysia and Singapore (indeed in LeBlanc's informants terms it is a form of Asian illiberalism), Ong's discussion of new forms of "bio-politics," of the possibility of other concepts of political agency than Western individualism, of alternative modernities and hence of different concepts of citizenship, not all of them congruent with Western understandings, and of the priority of communalist forms, or what she calls "cultural notions of sociality, rather than laws" (Ong 2000: 59), both opens up the prospect for alternative discourses on citizenship, and potentially for linking such discourses with others that are now expanding in the region on Asian conceptions of human rights and of freedoms (Bauer and Bell 1999, Kelly and Reid 1998).

While the contemporary and historical situation of Japan differs from that of Southeast Asia, globalisation has focussed these questions once again and put them once more at the forefront of public debate in Asia's largest economy. Debates about the postmodern subject, the sinister exercise of corporate and bureaucratic power against the interests of the citizens (as revealed most recently in scores of cases of corporations misusing public funds or of the Defence Agency illegally creating dossiers on citizens who had legitimately requested information under the Freedom of Information Act cf. Japan Times 2002) have surfaced not only because of the growing recognition of pluralism within Japanese society and the sense of crisis created by the implosion of the bubble economy and the social and physical calamities of the last several years, but most significantly because of the impact of globalisation, the larger frame within which all these events are located, and which while calling into serious question older notions of political identity and responsibility, have also opened Japan again to influences that are having a transformative, even revolutionary effect, on notions of citizenship. [NB similar debates about state surveillance in the US–this may be a global trend, not limited to Japan, provoking similar backlashes in different countries?] Both the resources and the challenges to expanded notions of citizenship come from the same directions—a slowly changing legal culture in which recent legislative changes have made it possible for interested citizens to be involved as participants in the courts and dispute resolution and in which resort to legal remedies (e.g. women suing companies for wrongful dismissal or lack of promotion on the basis of gender under the Equal Employment Opportunities Act) (Upham 1987) have greatly increased. Japan's increasing international involvement in UN led PKO (peace keeping operations) and most recently in reconstruction activities in Iraq (Mori 1993), a growing language of human rights, utopian and communal experiments, the enormous expansion of civil society organisations despite the legal and legitimacy issues that such organisations still face (Schwartz and Pharr 2003) and the problems of maintaining or transmitting responsible citizenship in a highly consumeristic society further expand this list. This latter problem and its obvious connections to globalisation (Clammer 2000b) is the frame within which most contemporary Japanese social life and politics takes place.

Reframing Japanese Citizenship

Many of the issues now confronting Japan are shared by other parts of the world as effectively all societies are drawn into the vortex of globalisation. But there are nevertheless significant variations in the ways in which citizenship is being redefined around the globe. In central and eastern Europe the issue of postsocialist transition still looms large and with it the problems of renegotiating identity as within a little over a decade whole populations have moved from a protected if authoritarian political and economic environment to one in which the acids of global capitalism have dissolved virtually all the social bonds that kept society secure and predictable, even if in a condition of stasis. In western Europe with the advent of the European Union, with the incorporation of a large swath of the formerly socialist East and with the Turks knocking on the door, both new conceptions of what constitutes "Europe" are emerging and new understandings of belonging in a transnational entity now sharing, with a few exceptions, a common currency and a borderless interior political geography, are now in the process of being forged (Soysal 1994). Japan has had a very different history, is located in a very different religious environment and has long been in socio-cultural terms, an isolationist society. Globalisation has radically called into question the identity certainties that history has bequeathed to Japan, or which the Japanese have so industriously constructed for themselves (including the whole vast body of the *Nihonjinron* or "theories of Japaneseness" that fill the shelves of any library or bookshop).

This has necessitated a (not always welcome) re-evaluation of what it is to be Japanese that has many facets, all linked to each other in complex ways. In confronting globalisation, Japan has had to address the Other without (the larger world in its totality and menace) and within (the expanding foreign population with no political rights), the past, subjectivities and understandings of gender, and the non-human world in the form of the environment and the effects of Japanese industrial activity, consumption patterns, and government commitment to nuclear energy on that environment. Such external challenges have had huge internal effects, issuing in increasing challenges to the postwar conservative hegemony and the subtle forms of authoritarianism through which it operates even in ostensibly democratic Japan. If the crises of the past decade have had any good effects, it has been to shatter the sense of unquestioned "harmony" on which Japanese society is allegedly based, and to expose the underside of the postwar Japanese "miracle," bringing with it the new questionings of political and social identity that now animate debates about citizenship in Japan.

The result is an interesting model from a comparative point of view. Japan is characterised by some as being an example (perhaps formally like Singapore) of "soft authoritarianism"—a strongly statist society with a weak civil society and with the institutions of a democracy without their full content. In part this is true, but it is also the case that Japan can be seen as a depoliticised society with a high level of citizen activism and a strong sense of cultural participation, even if that activism is largely directed to local issues (local environments, organic foods, security for local school-children etc), rather than to national/political ones. It is in fact a society where civil society is struggling to be born and which, despite its appearance of social harmony, contains conflict, something which the occlusion of class analysis in Japanese sociological work has concealed. For comparative analysis then Japan poses a number of interesting questions: can a society be modern but non-western? How are rights and duties philosophically rooted in a Buddhist/Shinto religious environment rather than a Judeo-Christian one? What forms might cultural citizenship take in a society in which identity has always been framed in cultural as much as political terms? Can one be cosmopolitan is a society with a very strong sense of its own homogeneity? And finally, although in western discourses citizenship is often posed as a set of rights and duties, it also contains its own subjectivities, something taken very seriously in Japanese discourses of citizenship, in which some prominent commentators have argued that the key issue goes beyond such formalism to the creation of a new and gender-neutral sense of *shutaisei* or "new citizen's subjectivity" that will provide the basis for other transformations of identity society wide (Iwane 1993).

As we began with Jean Baudrillard, perhaps we should end with him too. In one of his accounts (Baudrillard 1983) of what he understands to be postmodern society (an example of which Japan often claims to be) he suggests that in a society dominated by "simulacra"—media generated representations of such volume and apparent authority—it becomes impossible to any longer know reality from these representations, and that in such a situation, society or the public sphere "implodes" and any sense of citizenship evaporates with it. Politicians still exist, but they largely talk only to each other since no one else is listening, being involved primarily with their private lifestyle issues. This gulf between those pretending to govern (although in fact mostly caught up themselves in global forces that they do not understand or control) and the governed (who no longer feel themselves to be governed since they regard politics as irrelevant to their lives), is seen by some commentators on Japan as existing very visibly in the society that Roland Barthes characterised as the "empire of the sign" (Barthes 1970). Yumiko Iida for example argues that

> "On the political terrain, Japan as a nation has become uncertain of what it should represent, while the Japanese population has largely lost confidence in the ability and the will of political parties to represent their interests. Together, the phenomena have exacerbated the rift between the 'nation' (people) and the 'state' (government). Perhaps the most extreme allegorical gap—if it can be described as a 'gap' when the correspondence between content and form has all but lost its meaning—has been in the sphere of popular image production where a virtually infinite number of images can be produced without historical referents. While each of these spheres has been embroiled in its own crisis, the temporal coincidence of these inter locked forms of representational crises is no mere accident, but rather reflects the greater structural breakdown that Jameson and others have called the crisis of late capitalism" (Iida 2002: 253).

This is all true, and many of these crises stem directly from globalisation. However, this is also not the whole story. Baudrillard's gulf continues in fact to be crossed in both directions, by new political initiatives on the part of the established parties and especially by the opposition and the splinter groups that constantly appear, merge and disappear again, and most significantly and increasingly by citizens seeking new routes to empowerment, democratisation, a safe and healthy environment and a future in which higher standards of access, transparency and values will prevail.

Part Three

Postcolonial Reconstruction of Religion

9

The Politics of Religious Memory

Confucianism and Reinvention of Patriarchy

All Chinese societies, whether on the mainland of Asia, in Taiwan, Hong Kong or throughout the world-wide diaspora, have had to struggle with their past, to recall it, to edit it, and, where necessary, to invent it. The intensity of this historical remembering, in contrast to the societal amnesia of much of the West and of contemporary Japan, comes from three sources: the need to remember because individual and cultural identity lies primarily in continuity (best expressed anthropologically in the concern with descent and the role of ancestors); because present political legitimacy derives from the patterns and fractures of the past; and because of the constant pressure to assimilate, express and reinterpret the fuzzy body of practices, sentiments and ideologies known collectively as "Confucianism." Much of the history of the Chinese speaking world in the last half-century can be seen in these terms: the struggle against, and subsequent reincorporation, even redeification, of Confucius in the People's Republic, in the struggles for legitimacy, autonomy and democracy in Taiwan and in the identity politics of Southeast Asian Chinese, most of them ethnic and linguistic minorities in societies now their own, but in which to varying degrees they are still considered outsiders.

The society in Asia which is in many ways the clearest exemplar of these preoccupations is Singapore: the one state in Southeast Asia with a substantial Chinese majority, the one in which identity anxiety seems to be most keenly felt, but also the one that at its origin as an independent state in1965 committed itself to a model of perpetual multiracialism, a model from which it is now in some significant ways retreating. Chinese dominance in this society of many ethnicities has begun to reassert itself in some obvious and many subtle ways. It is also of great interest because it represents the attempt to sociologically as well as culturally achieve the "resinification" of a population already ethnically Chinese. To attempt resinification culturally is one process—to reintroduce language, art, architecture, literature, music and even philosophy, and is one to which has to some extent occurred spontaneously, individually, or through the efforts of community associations and religious and educational bodies in may Southeast Asian Chinese societies over a considerable period of time (e.g. Clammer 1975b). But for the state to attempt a deliberate policy of sociological resinification requiring the creation or adaptation of social forms—family organisation, descent systems, community organisations, the management of the microeconomics of everyday life, religious practices and patterns of reproduction and socialisation—which had previously not existed or had fallen into disuse, is a rare and interesting phenomenon.

And indeed this has happened and is continuing to happen in contemporary Singapore and can be analysed from a number of points of view—in terms of ethnic relations for example, or through the study of the political sociology of the society. While these and a number of other dimensions are involved and will be discussed, I will argue here that the phenomenon of resinification is best approached through the exploration of a group of social policies involving population, education, the creation of ideology and the refurbishment of Confucianism and which collectively but hiddenly focus on the re-establishment of patriarchy. In a world in which patriarchy is under fairly general attack, the attempt to reassert patriarchal practices and values is a somewhat audacious move and one worthy of deeper commentary. In order to do this some context needs to be established which makes sense of the framework in which these policies have arisen.

The Context of Policy

The movement towards the establishment or invention of patriarchy reflects the end point of four characteristics of social change in Singapore over the last decade. The first of these is the slow shift from genuine pluralism or multiracialism—the original "founding charter" of postcolonial Singapore society (Benjamin 1976)—towards a distinctive Sinocentrism in language policy, political culture, promotion of high culture and siting of Singapore within the geo-politics of the wider region The second is the increasingly politically driven nature of change. As far back as the 1970s some commentators (e.g. Chan 1975) were arguing that Singapore was an "administrative state," one in which bureaucratic management had replaced genuine politics. What this argument overlooked was that plenty of politics in fact existed, but was elite politics committed to a form of "guided democracy" which involved the suppression of political alternatives other than those sanctioned by the government coexisting with the intense politicisation of virtually every level of Singapore life—housing, education, culture, language, reproduction and family life, religion, car ownership, the keeping of pets, the chewing of gum. Social change has, as a consequence, arisen almost entirely not from spontaneous sources, but from political intervention designed to create, direct or prevent the evolution of social practices and values.

The third is the progressive racialisation of identity. At its inception independent Singapore opted for a primary ordering of the social structure in terms of race. Every permanent member of the population is required to "have" a "race," the title of which is inscribed on his or her identity card and which determines many aspects of social life—the languages of education, possible religious identities and position in relation to privileges, quotas and access to cultural resources (from issues as significant as entitlement to scholarships or entry to the civil service or indeed to political life to those as minor as the amount of television or radio air-time available in one's native language and reflecting one's cultural interests or the public holidays and religious festivals that symbolically mark, or do not mark, the political visibility of one's ethnic group. The rhetoric of meritocracy in Singapore in fact masks unequal ethnic distribution of national resources. The result has been the enshrining of a classificatory system which allocates every individual to a racial category (Chinese, May, Indian or "Other") which is regarded as permanent, essentialist and non-negotiable. This system has been both reinforced in its fundamental characteristics—immutable, creating a social organisation based on vertical loyalties rather than horizontal class lines, and in which race, ethnicity and culture are conflated—and slowly distorted in a pro-Chinese direction—by other social policies. These include education, the establishment of quotas for ethnic minorities (i.e. non-Chinese) in public housing estates, and very much in the area of language with the active and very public (using taxpayer's money) promotion of Mandarin, not only as a way of unifying the "dialect" (i.e. South Chinese regional languages) speakers who form the majority of Chinese Singaporeans, but also to assert Singapore's primarily Chinese identity and to establish closer cultural and business links with the People's Republic of China.

Shifts in regional geo-politics have made this "Chinese" identification possible. Almost surrounded by Malaysia to the north and Indonesia to the west and south, stressing a Chinese identity was not such a healthy idea until the establishment of the Association of Southeast Asian Nations (ASEAN) created a relatively stable regional grouping within which Singapore was contained, and until diplomatic relations had been established between the individual nation states comprising ASEAN and the PRC. While sensitivities to China's long term political and economic objectives in Southeast Asia still remain these are to some extent deflected by even greater fears of Japan's large and ever increasing presence in the region [this is based on data from the 1990s–is it still true??] (Ben-Ari and Clammer 1997), by the increasing significance of Overseas Chinese investment in China and of the links that these are creating and of the interest that this is generating regionally and internationally (e.g. Seagrave 1996), and by the sheer business opportunities that the Chinese market or use of cheap Chinese labour offers to entrepreneurs familiar with the language and culture of that most populous of countries.

Public policy and geo-politics have both found an ally in the spread, especially in Singapore and Malaysia of ideas derived from socio-biology which seem to suggest to their supporters not only the basically racial nature of identity (i.e. discrete groups each with distinct physical characteristics and with culture, intelligence and even entrepreneurial skills) derivable from this primary identity, but also of course the irreducible character of these elements (Chee and Chan 1984). The appeal to socio-biology, which we will shortly return to in its direct connection to patriarchy (for a broader discussion see Clammer 1996) relates closely to the fourth aspect of social change: the attempt to legislate values. This is interesting for several reasons—the attempt itself in a world in which the effectiveness of such propagandist methods has been called severely into question; the attempt to create a "national ideology" in a society of disparate ethnicities and cultures; and the attempt to base this ideology on a but faintly veiled version of Confucianism (Clammer 1993a). Where an essentialist view of identity exists the easiest way to derive values is not from open debate about what kind of world people want and how their religious and cultural histories might contribute to this, but from a view of racially defined "givens" of an ultimately genetic nature. Taken together these four aspects of social change in Singapore have great significance for the organisation of the family and the situation of women, a theme which takes us to the next level of analysis.

Women, Biology and Race

The most conspicuous and best known example of these elements coming together and being expressed in policy is undoubtedly to be found in the "graduate wives' controversy that broke out in 1983 when the then Prime Minister Lee Kuan Yew announced figures that showed that women who were university graduates were not marrying to anything like the same extent as non-graduate women and that those who did were having fewer children. These bald statistics however were placed in an interpretative framework deriving from some of the most dubious examples of writing in socio-biology, an interpretation which led Lee to the conclusion that intelligence is 80 per cent genetic and only 20 per cent environmental in origin, that intelligence is genetically transmitted and that consequently declining fertility rates amongst the well educated would lead to a progressive diminution of the intelligence of the nation as a whole (Lee 1983). Policies, including substantial tax advantages for graduates with children, the setting up of an agency called the "Social Development Unit" to encourage marriage between graduates, and cash grants for lower educated couples who agreed to voluntary sterilisation, were instituted. The whole issue is significant not only for its basing of social policy on the flimsiest of scientific bases, but equally for its racialist overtones.

The blame for this sorry state of affairs significantly was laid at the feet of Singaporean Chinese women, especially the well educated ones: they were selfish and career-oriented, were refusing to get married and were failing in their duty to expand the number of intelligent consumers in Singapore. The social inadequacies of Singapore Chinese men (a constant source of local humour and satire), their careerism, materialism and self-centred attitudes were not discussed or considered publicly to be part of the "problem." The difficultly facing the government in 1983-4 was how to address the issues raised by Lee in order to quietly offset the ethnic erosion that he was clearly referring to, while not making it too obvious that the policies introduced were actually racial ones, an important difficulty given that the ideology of multiracialism cannot be publicly questioned, even if it is being undermined in practice. Two possibilities emerged—the financial and social incentives mentioned above, and a broader set of policies intended to create a world view, a sense of reality, in which certain behaviours would be seen as naturally acceptable and so people, and in particular Chinese women, would adjust their attitudes and practices accordingly. Normalisation, the creation of an acceptance of "reality" where there is really only ideology, is standard Singapore political practice. In this case however the adjustment of population coincided with what in the mid 1980s was beginning to emerge as the major underlying domestic political agenda: the enhancement of Chinese superiority not only in educational, occupational and material terms (goals already achieved), but also in cultural and symbolic term—as creators and arbitrators of values—something which had as yet been imperfectly achieved and which was by its very nature a contested realm.

To create this shift was not entirely easy, even in controlled Singapore, for two major reasons. The first of these of course was the status of multiculturalism as the formal foundation of the society, and the fact that in the light of this the ethnic minorities would oppose any signs of the erosion of their position or opportunities. The second was that the new population policy—encouraging larger families for the educated—was a complete reversal of its preceding policy with its slogans (posted on bus shelters throughout the island and even projected at night onto the end walls of public housing blocks) of "Boy or girl—two is enough" and its dire warnings of overcrowding, pressure on social facilities and resources and the economic non-sustainability of a large population in a small country. At that time a different set of incentives and disincentives had been offered (including tax measures, access to preferred schools and access to public housing) to promote limitation of family size, and many women had undergone sterilisation to gain these benefits, especially Chinese women who are particularly hard-headed about economic realities. The same women (many of them no longer able to have children) suddenly found themselves castigated for bringing about a long term population decline, both in terms of numbers and intelligence. Now suddenly the emphasis was on more people to swell the ranks of consumers (to stimulate the domestic economy) and to maintain Singapore's economic competitiveness internationally. But how were these new ideas to be made to take root and to achieve their desired effect, especially on a population that is well educated and which is increasingly sceptical of ever changing campaigns of exhortation and bullying. Clearly the best plan was to make the shift seem "natural," to place it in a framework where policy seems pat of a social cosmology. And the place to begin, given that the "problem" was seen as arising from the behaviour and attitudes of Chinese women, was quite logically the family.

Since independence the Singapore government has had a strong but fluctuating interest in the family (Salaff 1988). Initially concern with the family focused on sense creating families in an immigrant society with a large percentage of single person households. Many of the numerous social problems of colonial and postcolonial Singapore, especially as they applied to the Chinese population, hinged on crime, drugs, unemployment and secret society involvement of single men, and on prostitution, servitude and ageing amongst single immigrant women (for case studies see Koh 1994 and Chiang 1994). The early policy of developing extensive public housing projects had three objectives: to generate employment and economic activity; to root people in Singapore and to generate political loyalty by giving them a stake in the country through home ownership; and to create more stable family units by providing the physical infrastructure for the emergence of more "normal" patterns of marriage and care of the aged. The Women's Charter of 1961 was designed both to protect women and girls from economic abuse and to encourage the regularisation of marriage, through, for example, the banning of further polygamous marriages except amongst Muslims. With the growth of the economy, the widespread provision of education and the stabilisation of marriage, the family had not been of primary political concern between the late 1960s and the late 1980s. Suddenly however, with the revised population policy, it moved back to centre-stage, but in an interestingly different way which has not so far received any detailed analysis.

In Chinese society it is not an exaggeration to say that the family has always been the central sociological feature: it (at least in its ideal-typical form) organises descent, is the focus of socialisation, the locus of religious activities, the agency for structuring memory and identity. It is also, as a host of commentators have pointed out, a highly gendered organisation, strongly patriarchal in nature and in which historically marriage was not a free union of equals, but a relation of subservience for a wife to her husband, eventually to her sons and certainly to her in-laws (Watson and Ebrey 1991). Yet in practice many Chinese Singaporeans came from backgrounds in China in which their families did not possess lineages, in which many "irregular" patterns of marriage and residence were common (Jashok and Miers 1994), and in which poverty was a normal experience. Nevertheless, the family as an ideal remains at the very centre of Chinese self images world wide, it is the fundamental element in what Barbara Ward, in discussing the ethnography of a very "deviant" group—the Tanka boat people of Hong Kong's harbours and inlets—has called the "conscious model" of Chinese social organisation (Ward 1965). Basic to this model in other words is not only an image of culture (language, food and everyday practices for instance), but also one of race (understood as lineal descent from ancestors of common stock and the phenotypical representation of that ancestry) and one of social structure. To be Chinese is not only to be a member of a "race," it is also an equally to be a member of a distinctive form of social organisation To resinify Chinese Singaporeans then necessarily requires not only the recreation of culture, but also the recreation of that distinctive social organisation.

The need for such fundamental social intervention indicates the limits of conventional social policies that are bringing about structural change. And there is no shortage of such policies, which have been applied at three levels. The first of these is most easily recognisable as a zone of "normal" policy intervention, which has encompassed a range of strategies including the aggressive promotion of Mandarin, the encouraging of interest in Chinese art not only through private or semi-private agencies such as the Chinese Chamber of Commerce, but also through the creation of an officially sponsored gallery of Chinese art in the old Immigration Department building at Empress Place in the heart of the colonial district and within minutes walk of the Parliament House and the Supreme Court.

Other social plans include the encouragement of immigration from "traditional" source areas, which turns out in practice to mean the Chinese speaking world, including members of north American Chinese communities, but, significantly, not India; the restriction of non-Chinese minorities settling in large numbers in individual public housing estates (officially to prevent "ghettoisation" but in practice because minorities tend to vote against the government); and the population policy noted above.

The second level has been in the promotion, since 1983, of socio-biological theories of genetic determinism. This essentially takes the form of the identification of race with biology (i.e. genetically determined hereditary characteristics), of the equation of intelligence with such inherited characteristics and the assumption that certain races have a specific distribution of such qualities. In reality this is an argument for Chinese superiority as it is the Chinese who are assumed to have (inherited) qualities of entrepreneurship, intelligence and cultural development and to be unusually (by the standards of other local ethnic groups) hard working. It is also an argument against ethnic intermarriage (except presumably amongst the non-dominant races) and against any "melting pot" model of ethnic integration: it strongly supports in fact the official four race classificatory model of permanent racial difference. The allegedly "scientific" nature of this theory makes it difficult for the average layperson in Singapore to argue with it, particularly as it accords so well with widely held local folk models of racial stereotypes.

The third level has been the attempt to out-Weber Weber himself, by assuming and building into policy the belief that values determine practice, and not the other way around. This is seen most clearly in two policies, one that ran throughout the 1980s and was then quietly abandoned, the other which began in 1988/89 and which is officially still in place. The former was the attempt to introduce the teaching of values into Singapore schools via the introduction of religious education. This was a considerable innovation given the secular nature of the state in Singapore, but makes sense when seen as an attempt to offset the situation that the government's own social and economic policies had brought about—a highly materialistic, individualistic society in which public levels of participation in voluntary and political affairs was declining; and as an outcome of the assumption that religion is potentially dangerous (its prophetic dimension could and has led it into opposition to government policies) and is best handled through control—by teaching sanitised and approved versions which stress socially "positive" moral values such as thrift, honesty and hardwork. The policy was designed in other words to compensate for the government's own destruction of the tender shoots of civil society in Singapore and took the form of compulsory religious education, pupils being however taught their own religion (or in practice that of their parents). Muslim children were thus to be taught Islam, Protestant or Catholic ones Christianity, Hindu ones Hinduism and only ones who could not claim any religious affiliation were taught comparative religion. Chinese students however, who form the bulk of the school population were taught not Buddhism, the religion to which, mostly in its Mahayana form and substantially mixed with elements of Chinese "folk" religion (mainly Taoism and spirit-mediumship) they or their parents adhere, but rather Confucianism. Confucianism as a religion has almost no followers in Singapore (there was at the time only one, small, Confucian temple) although Confucius appears as a deity (usually of education) on the altars of many syncretic Mahayanist temples. There occurred in Singapore late in the Twentieth Century a process parallel to that which had taken place in Japan almost a century earlier when the modernising government of the Meiji Restoration set about the systematic suppression of both Buddhism and folk Shinto in an attempt to replace them both with state Shinto—a bureaucratised, non-critical religion closely watched and controlled from the centre.

Significantly however this policy was quietly abandoned after a decade (and great public expense in the training of teachers, preparation of teaching materials and so on) because it had not delivered the political goods, because religion itself was becoming more visible with both the revival of traditional forms of religiosity, the substantial expansion of Christianity, the spread of fundamentalism in just about all religious communities, the rapid spread of the Japanese "New Religion" Soka Gakkai, the appearance of numerous sects (for example that of Sai Baba amongst Hindus) and the migration of large numbers of both Indians and educated Chinese to Theravada Buddhism (Clammer 1991). Many of these forms of religious expression were beyond government control or understanding and as such were very anxiety provoking in a government that values control above all else. The consequence was the abandonment of religious education in schools, the passage of an act of parliament (the quaintly named "Maintenance of Religious Harmony" Act) designed to restrict the expression and practice of religion except in approved forms and to absolutely ban any political expression of religion, and the decision to formulate and promulgate a "National Ideology." This latter policy, which I have analyzed in detail elsewhere (Clammer 1993a), has many elements and strategies within it. Amongst its key elements relevant to the present discussion are two: the decision to officially define the family as the basic unit of society and to rather rapidly replace the vaguely Marxist sounding notion of ideology with one of "Shared Values," based however not upon any empirical attempt to actually discover whether such values exist in Singapore, and if so, what they are, but on the a priori decision to base these values on or derive them from, Confucianism.

This idea in itself conceals two others: Firstly, the idea that Confucianism is based on something called "consensus" (i.e. no debate), is the fundamental expression of something called "Asian values" which are mainly defined by what they are not—i.e. Westernised, which means in the words of Lee Kuan Yew "individualistic and self-centred." Quite apart from the extreme unlikeliness of there being any genuine pan-Asian values, Lee seems to have overlooked the fact that the National Ideology was introduced not to prevent the emergence of such "Westernised" values in Singapore, but precisely because they are already rampant in what must be the most Westernised society anywhere in Asia and derives its distinctive culture from exactly that fact. Secondly, the idea that essential to Confucianism is not only a set of fairly vague "values," but also its sociological expression: Confucianism means a particular ideology of the family and a particular practice which embodies that ideology.

The Problem and Practice of Confucianism

The difficulty with introducing Confucianism in an approved and bureaucratised way into Singapore, whether as something taught in the schools or as the basis of the "Shared Values" or National Ideology, was that nobody in Singapore appeared to have a clear idea of what it was. Paradoxically and without the least sense of irony (for this was after all supposed to be a national ideology) "experts" on Confucianism were flown in from the United States and elsewhere to advise the government on exactly what it was that they were supposed to be talking about. The local intellectual and academic community leapt as usual on to the bandwagon and began to produce instant books on the subject (e.g. Lu 1983; Lim 1992). And parallel to all this mental activity was a quasi-sociological one, which must be understood against the background of a very specific form of local cultural politics.

David Brown has argued (Brown 1993) that the status of ethnicity has evolved since independence from the original multiracialism seen as a delicate structure requiring a strong state to keep it all together, through a series of intermediate transformations each one of which has redefined the relationship between race, politics and culture, to the current model, one that he dubs "corporatist." Here, as in all the earlier models, the primacy of the state is not questioned, but two innovations have occurred: the definition of a national community based on the allegedly shared values, and the reconceptualisation of ethnic groups as interest associations. This last idea means that, without diminishing the priority of the state, responsibility for the welfare of individual ethnic communities' members is transferred from the state apparatus to those individual communities themselves. Such a move has occurred within the context of large scale "privatisation" in Singapore (meaning that the state keeps ultimate control while increasingly transferring responsibility, problems and costs to the public)—in housing, medicine, education and other key area. In a sense "corporatism" means the "privatisation" of ethnicity—the transfer of responsibility for management and the provision of social services from the state to those communities themselves. But to do this requires the creation of institutions and structures to make the delivery of any such services effective.

The problem has been however that the modern history of Singapore has been one of the suppression of pre-existing social networks and social movements and their replacement by a government created set of local level as well as liaisonal institutions—community centres and resident's associations being the main ones. Community associations, of which one is to be found in every constituency, provide recreational and cultural facilities, often including Mandarin lessons and are often part of the same complex housing government run kindergartens and the local Area Office which has amongst its many functions the registration and monitoring of all the inhabitants of its district. Political, educational and cultural functions are thus often run together and become effectively indistinguishable, as the few constituencies that have gone over to the opposition have found to their cost, it being very easy for the government to step up monitoring activities while simultaneously reducing social and cultural resources in such places. The destruction of civil society however has not been complete, and each community retains at least residual institutions reflecting its culture of origin and very frequently its religious practices. In the case of the Chinese community, these have been the remains of the once dense network of clan, dialect and other associations which once animated the immigrant Chinese community from its earliest days (Hsieh 1978; Mak 1992).

At its inception, Singapore Chinese society was made up of a disparate mass of migrants, mostly male but with a slowly increasing number of women, from a number of areas in China, mostly along the southern seacoasts. Each of these areas spoke different languages—Cantonese, Hokkien, Teochew, Hakka, Hainanese, and in a few cases more easternly languages such as the Shanghai dialect. Very rarely were northern dialects such as Mandarin spoken at all amongst the migrants to Singapore. Very little sense of ethnic or class identity united the first generation of migrants and reports from as late as the 1960s still speak of the rivalry between language communities, clashes between Secret Societies and the need for social workers on the island to speak several of the many dialects since there was no lingua franca spoken amongst the Chinese community, except possibly varieties of bazaar Malay. Even after independence this situation continued to prevail for years until military service for men, imposition of common political institutions, the spread of Mandarin through the school system and participation in the common economy and public housing schemes began to forge an increasing sense of unity, or at least of being Singaporean, amongst the local Chinese population. At least up until independence, the numerous associations of the Chinese community, some based on dialect, some on place of origin in China, others on occupations or trades and yet others on religion, made up the basic social structure of that community and provided many of the few welfare facilities as then existed—hospitals and hospices, schools and homes for the elderly.

Very importantly they also provided what might be termed quasi-kinship functions. Many Chinese migrants to Singapore were single or, if married, had left their spouse in China. And although most did originally intend to return to China, many never did, which meant of course that they grew old and died far from their native villages. Essential to Chinese familialism is what is often called Ancestralism or sometimes, and inaccurately, "Ancestor Worship." What this term actually refers to is the centrality of patrilineal descent and the necessity for the dead, especially the recent dead, to be memorialised (for elaboration of this see Hsu 1975; Baker 1979). Failure to do this meant a kind of cosmic loneliness for the dead—not being remembered, without offerings being made to them—or at worst (for both the living and the dead) becoming a wandering ghost Normally the functions of memorialisation (the enshrining of the soul-tablet of the deceased, the cleaning and maintenance of graves and the making of offerings to the spirits of the ancestors) would be performed in the clan temple in China. For those dying alone in Southeast Asia, without kin and far from their native soil, the prospect of death was even more of an existential crisis than it would anyway be. Community associations overseas took on these functions and often provided a variety of services under the same roof, oddly disparate to members of many other cultures, but very acceptably combinable to the overseas Chinese. Thus an association, formally based on dialect and/or district or even village of origin, would provide a shrine for the display and memorialisation of the soul tablets of its members (who would pay a subscription to the association while they were alive and economically active), a recreation area and space for elderly members to relax, drink tea and read newspapers, would sometimes provide a free or very cheap clinic on certain days or evenings of the week, and might well provide space for a *wayang* of Chinese opera performance for the dead (and the living) during the Hungry Ghosts month. Some would provide retirement spaces for elderly individuals such as single women and might provide loans or welfare payments from the capital accumulated from member's subscriptions. Religious, social and recreational functions would thus often be combined in the same association.

Two issues stand out here: the production, amongst such associations, of quasi-kinship relations between people not genetically or agnatically related, and the fact that, in order to reproduce a system of Chinese kinship, a form of patrilineal descent had to be created. In practice some associations fudged on this second requirement. In theory the spiritual status (i.e. the disposition after death) of an unmarried Chinese female was extremely marginal and dangerous. Not incorporated into a husband's lineage and without access to patrilineal status in her father's lineage, the death of a female of marriageable age was an extremely anxiety provoking event for all parties—for the woman herself and for living relatives and neighbours, since she too was liable to become a wandering ghost, resentful and revengeful in the way that such Chinese ghosts are often expected to be. The sociologically unincorporated individual is spiritually dangerous in Chinese religious culture. But there were always such women in Singapore—female labourers, domestic servants, prostitutes and others—often unaware of what legal protection was available to them and until 1961 with no clear code governing Chinese customary marriage (Chiang 1994). Some such women married and their names were inscribed on their husband's soul tablet; others took the option of never marrying (many indeed had fled from China precisely to avoid marriage (Topley 1975) or became members of women's vegetarian houses, to which they paid a subscription during their working life and where they could spend their days off and could eventually retire, sometimes even going through a form of marriage with another woman and adopting a female child to care for them in their old age (Topley 1954). In such cases the house took care of their post-death status. For those who took neither of these options, associations would sometimes enshrine a soul tablet on their own behalf. But generally in ideology and in practice a patrilineal world view prevailed,

Although they had retained some residual functions (mainly of a cultural and religious nature) this once extensive network of associations had steadily lost ground as their position was eroded by the expansion of government activity, by conversion of members to Christianity and other religions and by the maw alternative attractions that an expanding consumer economy could offer younger people. By the early 1990s many still existed (many others had entirety disappeared), but as shadows of their former wealth and influence, a far cry indeed from the days when they had essentially composed the social structure of the Singapore Chinese community. However two things had now suddenly occurred which once again reversed previous government policy, which had been deliberately to diminish the strength of "natural" organisations and to closely regulate and monitor them through an agency set up specifically for this purpose—the Registry of Societies. The first was that with the invention of the "corporatist" conception of ethnicity, clan associations were suddenly once again needed to carry out the new "privatised" policy. The second was that the parallel reinvention of Confucianism as the ideological basis of the social order required the sociological embodying of Confucian principles. The nuclear family in its modern form had hardly existed in China where smaller kinship units were always in principle incorporated into larger kin groups—lineages where these existed (and they were far from universal, even in south China from whence most migrants came) and certainly surname or clan temples necessary to properly memorialise the dead (Watson and Rauski 1988).

The reinvention of Confucianism then did not only mean the imposition of a set of "values." It also meant the invention of a tradition to which many or most Singaporean Chinese did not belong and the stimulation or fabrication of "memories" of Chinese culture and descent patterns where they did not in fact exist (Clammer 1993b), a tradition which incorporated patriarchy as its fundamental principle. The problems that this might create in a modern Singapore in which many women worked and in which very many (those recalcitrant graduate brides or non-brides) were highly educated, did indeed occur to the engineers of these new policies and the visiting experts were asked to address the problem of producing an acceptable version of Confucianism when the whole system was well known to be sexist, hierarchical and not at all liberal in respect of social change or political development except in a very statist direction. How then was Confucianism to be made digestible to a modern, well travelled and materialistic contemporary Chinese population?

Several factors (apart from the government propaganda machine and the tame press) suggested that this could be done. The first was the emergence of China as a force to be reckoned with economically and politically in the region and, with its own rapid progress (or regression) towards capitalism, as a market and trading partner, no more the communist ogre. This major shift in regional geopolitics made a looking-towards-China policy possible and indeed culturally desirable. The second was the emergence of what might be termed Overseas-Chinese triumphalism. Sometime in the late 1980s many diaspora Chinese and many non-Chinese commentators on the Asia-Pacific region, as East Asia was now becoming called, had begun to note the extensive economic and social networks of the overseas Chinese and their role in promoting investment, trade and industrialisation throughout the region Many of the emerging multinational companies in Asia were overseas Chinese ones. From being a somewhat neglected minority, both envied and despised as entrepreneurial enclave dwellers amidst much larger Muslim (in Malaysia, Indonesia and Brunei), Theravada Buddhist (in Thailand, Cambodia and Burma), Catholic (in the Philippines) or historically hostile (in Vietnam) host populations, the Chinese suddenly have become visible. With the rapid expansion of economies like that of Vietnam, in which both indigenous Chinese and overseas Chinese have played a major, if not *the* major, role this marginal community has become a central one, a fad which has promoted an upsurge of pride and publications. And naturally the question has arisen as to what has made both the economic resurgence of China (or at least or rather of south coastal China) and of the overseas Chinese possible. Predictably the answer is Confucianism, although a Confucianism that the Sage himself would probably not recognise. This neo-Confucianism has two main characteristics: it does for the Chinese what, according to Weber, the Protestant ethic did for the British—it allegedly provides the value system that makes capitalism possible; and it constitutes a system which not only links Chinese to one another through language and culture (making business relations easy), but which is also based on the primacy of the family. At the basis of Chinese economic success in China, Taiwan, Hong Kong and throughout Southeast Asia is the patriarchal family, the descent system and pattern of domestic relationships which, in the last analysis, is what Confucianism represents. Patterns of saving, capital accumulation, long working hours, socialisation into an entrepreneurial life style, all, on this theory, are ultimately related to Confucianism (the literature on this question is now large and confused and extends even beyond the Chinese to encompass the neo-Confucianism of Korea and Japan. For a good sampler of this genre, by one of the experts much consulted by the Singapore government, see Tu 1996).

Familialism (of the patriarchal variety), while the fundamental plank in this explanation of entrepreneurial success, especially as contrasted with the Malay peoples of the region (the vast majority from southern Thailand through Malaysia and Indonesia and on to the Philippines) with their bilateral kinship patterns, matriarchal families and even in some cases (the famous Minangkabau people of Sumatra are a conspicuous case) with matrilineal descent, is not the only factor at play. For there is also an internal link between the promotion of Confucianism on the one hand and the promotion of ideas derived from socio-biology on the other. We have already suggested that "race" in Singapore parlance is understood or is represented officially as a set of biological qualities transmitted over time within a fairly discrete breeding population. Descent in this model has two meanings: it is firstly a purely biological concept of genetic continuity, and it is secondly a notion of sociological descent—a notion that is of lineal continuity ensured by marriage and inheritance practices. Significantly it is only the Chinese who have an (in theory—there are exceptions such as the *chin choe* or in marrying or adoptive son-in-law, or the *san po tsai* system of transferring young girls from their natal households to those of their future husbands) patrilineal descent system of great depth reinforced by a patriarchal authority system within the family. Malays as we have said practice bilateral or matrilineal kinship, for Indians the primary focus of kinship is caste rather than the descent group in the institutionalised Chinese sense, and Eurasians tend to have simple nuclear families with shallow notions of descent closer to those of the modern European or North American family system. Furthermore, for Malays and Indians, ethnicity is not primarily a matter of race, but of culture, and it is possible for a person not born Malay to become one through adoption (particularly of Chinese girls at one time), marriage or religious conversion for example.

For the Chinese however ethnicity is primarily racial and so one can neither become nor cease to be Chinese in the way that potentially Malays or Eurasians can. One is Chinese by descent understood in the twofold sense (biological/sociological) mentioned above. This helps to explain two things. Firstly why the Baba or Peranakan Chinese, arguably the most genuinely Singaporean culture in the country with their unique combination of Chinese descent, Malay culture and language and European political attitudes, never became the model for the society as a whole: they are too Malayanised, probably with intermarriage in the distant past and they too frequently practise *chin choe* patterns of marriage. And secondly why inter-ethnic marriage amongst the Chinese is largely confined to marriage between Chinese women and men of other races, especially Europeans. Women, by definition in a patrilineal system, marry out and are lost to the patrilineage: sociologically they do not count, and the children of an ethnically outmarried woman will not be Chinese. Indeed it is official policy in Singapore that children of mixed marriages follow the "race" of the father and cannot themselves either choose which race to identify with or to choose an alternative identity. Subtly hidden in the Singaporean raw and socio-biology model is the assumption that, while formally a child of course inherits genetic material from each parent equally, in reality it is the male genes that somehow predominate.

The resulting policies are perhaps not surprisingly rife with ambiguities. Women are encouraged to enter the workforce, and to hire maids to look after their children while they are at work, but are then criticised for turning over the upbringing of their children to foreigners (most maids being Filipinos, and sometimes Indonesian or from the PRC). The educated ones are criticised for not marrying and breeding enough (intelligence being, as we have seen, officially transmitted genetically), yet it is subtly insinuated that it is the male genes that are really important (in families with "too many" female children, it is the husband who will be blamed in the local folk model for having "weak sperm"). Confucian "ethics" has to promote seemingly universal values while actually arguing for the subordination of women and the primacy of "the" family—which has never actually been defined in Singapore public discourse, it of course being both axiomatic and unspoken that it is the "Confucian" one. What the population policy, with its roots in socio-biology, actually says about women is hardly encouraging: they are for breeding intelligent consumers. Indeed Lee Kuan Yew is on record as saying that he regrets the social policies that made education so widely available to women, a remarkable statement given that it is internationally thought that one of the most positive aspects of Singapore's development policies has been to equally educate both genders (in many departments of the two main universities women indeed predominate; the medical faculty at the National University, under government direction established a quota system to deliberately keep down the number of female medical students as they were becoming a majority; in most fields female students do better than males academically).

Singapore women of course are not unaware of what is going on and even as their Chinese sisters in the past resisted patriarchy through a variety of strategies, so they do today; through not marrying at all, through education and independent careers, through ethnic out marriage, through consumption, migration and conversion to Christianity with its egalitarian ethos (and significantly there are far more Chinese Christian women than men in the Singapore churches, and a high percentage of those women are well educated: it is not only graduate women who are not marrying, but graduate Christian women), a factor that may well have influenced the government's relative turning against Christianity—which it had previously looked upon benignly as promoting desirable family and moral values—and its quiet but visible encouragement of much more "Asian" varieties of religion such as Soka Gakkai. Many women even choose their own personal names, usually ones of a European or European derivation by which they are known amongst their friends although they do not always inform their fathers of the de facto abandoning of their Chinese given names, especially if those names are derived from the hanyu pinyin syllabary now used in the PRC for Romanising the script rather than from the traditional dialect names. There has in fact been a quiet "feminisation" of culture in Singapore as women have begun to dominate religion, such social movements as exist, teaching, wide areas of medicine and some key areas of the bureaucracy.

One of the inadequacies of the Singapore government's own analysis of what it has itself created is its failure to understand the nature of capitalism. There is rather strong resistance to any such analysis, not only because it smacks of Marxism, but also because the government has committed itself to a form of state capitalism in which in theory the market governs (it does not of course: the state does, except when the economy is doing badly, as it did during the recession of the mid 1980s, significantly the period from which many of these latter day social policies also stem). In reality the social policies of the last two decades have caught women constantly on the wrong sides not of trends of their own making, but of shifts in official policy. In the late 1970s and mid 1980s population was to be kept down and women were strongly encouraged not to have children. By the late 1980s this policy was reversed and (Chinese) women blamed for not having sufficient children. Women were encouraged to enter the work force in large numbers during the same period as the first phase of the population policy; then they were criticised for displacing domestic responsibilities onto maids, from neglecting their (Confucian) responsibilities to the aged, and, during the economic downturn, from taking jobs from men, who were the "natural" breadwinners, or rather, fillers of ricebowls. Encouraged to consume and thus to promote the expansion of the domestic economy, women were then accused, by the very architects of high growth, of materialism and of loosing their "Asian" values. While many of these fluctuations were simply the outcome of flip-flopping policies (known in Singapore polit-speech as "pragmatism"), they were actually the result of the modes of social relationships habitually unleashed by capitalism. The government, sensing that it could not have its cake and eat it, and unable to think of a way forward that would not seriously compromise its own political vision and techniques, fell back into the past: it reinvented Confucianism with a dash of socio-biology for extra flavour.

Race, descent and patriarchy are thus conflated, a distinctively gendered view of history is generated and until very recently (e.g. Chiang 1994, Warren 1994) the experience and contribution of female migrants to Singapore was discounted. Within this male-biased world view Chinese descent itself was seen as male dominated and its paradigm—the patrilineage—seen as the essence of a Confucian social order, despite the absence of empirical lineages in the social backgrounds of many Singaporeans and the extensive evidence of variations in actual marriage practices throughout south China (Jaschok 1984, Watson 1991). As suggested elsewhere (Clammer 1996) the "Confucian" model requires, and where it is successful produces, docile bodies. Women in this view are essentially bodies: reproductive organisms whose emotions, if recognised at all, are entirely secondary. Women are to be presented and packaged according to patriarchal expectations of propriety, to be concealed or exposed according to whims not of their own making and to be controlled through the establishment of norms, in some cases enforceable by law, about acceptable dress, gesture, habits and public comportment. There is a whole sociology of the body waiting to be written from the perspective of the ideology and practice of Confucianism (for some hints about how this might proceed see Zito and Barlow 1994). The memories, experiences and expectations of women—the possible roles, the preset limits of careers and responsibilities, the position and duties within the family—are consequently set, not by the expanding dynamics of a naturally evolving society, but by the constraining influence of a politically generated Confucianism, designed to limit the very gains that Singaporean Chinese women had made in the years since independence.

The earlier mention of Soka Gakkai, in origin a Buddhist-based Japanese "New Religion" which grew very rapidly in Singapore in the late 1980s and 1990s, should alert us to the extent that Japan and Japanese Confucianism as well as the Chinese variety were used as models in Singapore. Japan was seen during the 1980s as a model not only of economic growth, but also of social order—peaceful labour relations, politics dominated by a single party and a hierarchical social structure (Stanley 1988). Here however a somewhat a historical and confused sociological approach prevailed, since the Confucian virtues extolled (obedience, service to the state, duties to parents), were rather more characteristic of prewar Japan than of the contemporary situation, particularly since if there is any one institution that is in a state of quiet crisis in Japan, it is the family. But then the emotions and quality of relationships within the family are not the primary concern of Singapore's policy makers: what they are concerned with is structural attributes. The modern Confucian family is understood as being led by a male, with responsibility for child socialisation residing in the wife, and with what is called in Singapore a "three tiered family" structure in which parents, children and grandparents comprise a single-residential unit. New public housing units were built to accommodate this extended family type and priority in allocation of public housing units was given to three-tier rather than nuclear families. Conversely, the ranking of single person or single parent households, especially those headed by a woman, was made so low as to make it extremely difficult for such cases to gain access to public housing at all. So while current legislation, while making divorce possible and relatively simple, also makes it very difficult for women who initiate divorce proceedings (as an increasing number do) to subsequently form a viable economic or residential unit with their children or even some other woman in the same situation.

So today television advertisements promote the delights of having children, pre-university students are taught the desirability of marriage, a Social Development Unit has been set up to promote romantic meetings between unmarried graduates and very material incentives, particularly through the tax system (paradoxically given that real Confucianism teaches disdain for materialism) are given to graduate couples who have more children. But then the whole policy is riddled with ambiguities and Confucianism in Singapore is fundamentally paradoxical in its promotion of patriarchy and the hierarchical family on the one hand, while leaving untouched the individualism and materialism that characterises the actual operation of the society. As W.J.F. Jenner has argued, Confucius in reality was a person who could not even accept the changes taking place in his own (somewhat pre-capitalist) times, but set his face towards the distant past as the model for contemporary relationships. In fact the "plastic Confucianism" (as Jenner aptly calls the Singapore variety) invented by the visiting experts is actually a highly selective culling of elements taken out of context and repackaged as an apparently coherent set, while leaving the actual operation of capitalism (which the Sage would have abhorred) untouched. But then the family, not the economy is the target, and in theoretical terms correctly so, since there is no historical evidence of any positive connection between Confucianism and rapid economic growth (Jenner 1994).

Patriarchy and the Narratives of Culture

Chinese society has long had profound difficulties with women and with women's sexuality. Women as wives and mothers is one thing, but powerful women, free women, or women who begin to determine how reality is to be conceptualised is another matter altogether. Despite legislative changes in marriage, divorce and custody laws throughout the Chinese speaking world, practice has been for the most part different from theory, especially in a cultural universe where the pull of the past (often encapsulated in the idea of Confucianism) is so strong (Croll 1995). The struggle, rather than the accommodation, between women and Confucianism appears in many forms and is reflected perhaps most clearly in modern and contemporary Chinese fiction in which Hu Ying sees a narrative trajectory in the following terms; "Metaphorically, then, the ability to sire sons is similar to the ability to tell a story, the authority to narrate. Even more than the siring of sons, the telling of stories confirms the patrilineage retrospectively...one might even say that it is an act of paying homage to one's forebears, an act of filial piety" (Hu 1996:5556). What fiction (and film also) illustrates and should alert the anthropologist to is the construction of patriarchal narratives-stories which through their emphases, selections and suppressions edit out the history of women. We have already suggested that the writing of Singapore history already does this and as such is not only ideological politically, but also in respect of gender (e.g. see the recent history of Singapore edited by Chew and Lee 1991). Neo-Confucianism has the same effect: it imposes on reality a reading of history and of social causation which privileges patrilineality and places patriarchal narratives in the foreground.

Interestingly this observation needs to be placed in a rather special context: that of the virtual absence of either feminism or of a movement for homosexual rights. There is a small women's movement dominated by educated upper class women and by no means a voice for the average Singaporean female and which, despite its undoubted positive effect, has done nothing to challenge the political suppression of feminist discourse. But one might suppose that patriarchy would be very compatible with male homosexuality, which would after all remove women from the arena entirely. But in Singapore this is not the case at all and at the 1993 United Nations Human Rights conference in Vienna Wong Kan Seng, the Singapore foreign minister, publicly stated that "Homosexual rights are a Western issue, and are not relevant to this conference" (cited with commentary in Berry 1996:159). The problem for the Singaporeans is a complex one which appears to encompass the suppression of the concept of human rights, their replacement by the "shared values" (which emphatically do not include either women's or homosexual rights) and a politics of regional difference: the West is Other/the East is Us, and the belief that this "East" is unified by its adherence to "Asian" values. The foreign minister's statement is also interesting for its characteristic ignorance of or suppression of alternative, non-statist histories, for there is ample evidence of extensive homosexuality in Chinese culture (Hinsch 1990). What it fundamentally seems to reflect, consistent with the ruling party's deep puritanism, is a fear of sexuality, especially any "deviant" form which challenges the order of the patriarchal family. Indeed speaking of Singapore, two well known local critics and writers argue that "women and all signs of the feminine are by definition always and already antinational" (Heng and Devan 1993:354). State fatherhood and the empowerment of women are not compatible and the Confucian family (as in prewar Japan) is the means to ensure the reproduction at the microlevel of the macrolevel of the state itself.

The discourse of Confucianism becomes both the mechanism to link the political to the personal, but also to justify a particular collectivist conception (or non-conception) of human rights (Berry 1996:175).

All this points to levels of analysis not always attained in intellectual discourse within Singapore with its positivist assumptions and modernist mentality, which has prevented for example debates about patriarchal familialism such as have occurred in Japan in the context of postmodernity from occurring, or possibly even being conceivable (for example see Heine 1995) despite the fact that both are seen as being rooted in Confucianism. One of these levels involves the management of the body and the constitution of the self. It was suggested above that Confucianism at least in its Singapore version, promotes a particular view (or non view) of the female body. Similarly it carries with it certain images of the self, not only those based on the achievement of righteousness and nobility, but of such virtues encapsulated entirely within a system of hierarchical relationships. They are not in fact abstract virtues at all, but highly contextualised ones, set within the five fundamental relationships of ruler/subject, parent/child, older sibling/younger sibling, husband/wife and older friend/younger friend and traditionally underscored by the mourning grades and by the extensive ramifications and extreme hierarchalisation of kin-terms in classical Chinese. The "humanism" of Confucianism is by no means universal, but is set within a pattern of relationships in which male precedes female, older precedes younger and ruler precedes subject. Significantly, Singapore's policy makers have never in any way drawn on the other major traditions of Chinese thought—Taoism for example, or the egalitarian philosophy of Mo Di who lived only a century after Confucius.

What has emerged in modern Singapore then is a fascinating contemporary example of bio-politics in the setting of a rapidly developing Asian economy and one moreover which is attempting to practise and to keep alive ancient Chinese statecraft, historiography and kinship at the turn of the Millenium. Singapore is in this sense, despite its putative multiracialism, a deeply Chinese polity, and many of the things that can be said about modernising China, for example the equation of race *(zhongzhu)* and culture *(wenhua),* the selective use of western ideas of eugenics, the attempt to create authoritarian modernisation or "capitalism with Chinese characteristics" and the suppression of both democracy and feminism, can equally be said about Singapore, to the extent that it is no longer clear which state is borrowing ideas from which (Ong 1996).

If woman is the "primitive"—the bearer both of (non-political) wisdom and of chaos—then her position is dangerous to the state, whether in China or in Singapore.

As Rey Chow puts it:

> "If the conception of 'woman' was in the past mediated by women's well defined roles within the Chinese family, the modern promotion of the nation throws into instability all those traditional roles, how are women's sexuality, social function, economic function, contribution to cultural reproduction, and biological reproduction to be conceived of outside of the family and in terms of the nation? This is the historical juncture when, in what appeared to be a sudden 'liberation' of the traditional constraints on women's identity, romantic love became a leading social issue. For what is 'romantic' about romantic love is not sex, but the apparent freedom in which men and women could choose their sexual partners, in a way that differed from arranged marriage. And since the traditional family system was paternalistic—that is resting on the sexual stability, chastity, and fidelity of women while men were openly promiscuous or polygamous—the new freedom meant first and foremost the production of a new female sexuality. In other words, because the conception of the nation sought to unify the culture regardless of sexual and class difference, it left open many questions as to how women's sexual identities, which were carefully differentiated and monitored within the kinship system, should be reformulated. This is why, one could say, the Chinese woman suddenly became a newly discovered 'primitive'—a body adrift between the stagnant waters of the family, whose oppressiveness it seeks to escape, and the open sea of the nation, whose attention to 'woman' is only such that her sexual difference and history become primarily *its* support i.e. become erased." (Chow 1995:67-68).

In Singapore we see the attempt to recover those traditional roles, and to force even romantic love to submit to the requirements of the state in the interests of its own brand of control and its own version of Chinese capitalism.

Indeed Chow goes on to argue, in a passage that exactly fits Singapore if one substitutes the word "capitalism" for "communism" and if one replaces the phrase "cultural revolution" with "post 1983 developments" (that year being the one in which Lee announced his new eugenics policy in the light of falling graduate birth rates):

> "In the aftermath of the Cultural Revolution, the affirmation of traditional family values comes as an attempt to mask the lack created by the bankruptcy of communism *and* nationalism, even though nationalism may persist by reinscribing itself in traditional forms. The

> main point is that the central roles played by the family and village community are here signs of the *dismantling* of the modernist revolution from 'family' to 'nation.' 'Woman' is now caught between the bankruptcy of nationalism and communism, in which the sexes are 'equal' and women's problems do not exist, *and* the resurgence of older patriarchal forms of community, in which female sexuality is strictly managed for purposes of kinship reproduction." (Chow 1995:70)

This is not only true of Chinese societies (witness the profamily and procapitalist rhetoric of the New Right in Europe and the Moral Majority in the United States), but it does indicate an important sociological and theoretical point: that modernity unleashes forces that it itself cannot fully comprehend which, once they become visible are managed by treating them as the Other within, as stigmatised and marginalised outsiders to the "real" processes and purposes of the masculine state—thus women, ethnic or sexual minorities, artists, the handicapped—all who threaten order not through what they do, but by what they are (e.g. Bauman 1995:143-148 especially), who threaten degeneracy by their very being. They are as it were ontologically unsound unless co-opted and reincorporated into the patriarchal state. When Deng Xiaoping sends a delegation to Singapore (as he did in 1993) to study its state capitalism and state Confucianism something interesting is clearly happening, especially when it is conceded that this new Confucianism, when actually explored historically, is, if not the product of the Jesuits in China, at least in part the brain-child of such Western scholars as Peter Berger and Herman Kahn (Dirlik 1996).

Singapore represents one of the many strategies of nationalism, and particularly of cultural nationalism, in the modern world, and is an interesting variation on the issues of public culture and state hegemony. But while Gellner in his major work on nationalism (Gellner 1983) has argued that nation-building must be forward looking in nature, Singapore demonstrates the coexistence of forward-lookingness in technology and economy and a decidedly backward looking stance in many aspects of social policy. In attempting to overcome ethnicity as primordial sentiments, and to replace it with "corporatism" and a notion of shared values, social policy has attempted to resurrect a patriarchal and largely mythical version of the Chinese past, and to create an identity out of a reinvented Confucianism (Chun 1996) and a dash of socio-biology. What is particularly revealing about recent Singapore cultural discourse is that as element after element of policy was seen not to work: only 17.8 per cent of students enrolled for Confucian ethics, less than the number enrolled for Bible Knowledge, during the decade of moral education in schools; there was fierce opposition from many quarters to the incentives for graduate women; the National Ideology concept was received with less than total enthusiasm) and as its electoral base was slowly but surely eroding, the strategies changed, but not the basic theme. Quietly the new Confucianism has been maintained; what is significant is the way in which it has been refocused from the realm of public values to private ones, from politics to patriarchy. But patriarchy proves to be politics by other means, the point at which the politics of gender, culture, history and the state finally come together.

10

The Crisis of Asian Modernity

Buddhism, Development and Postcolonial Theory in the Thought of Sulak Sivaraksa

Western sociology has long been subject to cycles of universalism and self-doubt. In the first of these cycles the assumption is that the theoretical models of North Atlantic sociology, and the methodologies, often positivist and quantitative in nature, to which these models give rise, are applicable globally. Such a view underlies many of the metanarratives of the social sciences—ideas of modernity, of progress, of development, and in many cases even ideas about the constitution of the self and definitions of religion. Periodically however this grand cycle is interrupted, although so far never derailed, by sub-cycles of critique, which, while critical of the totalising schemas of the grand narrative, usually operate in terms of the same language and underlying epistemology. Such critiques include the "critical theory" of the Frankfurt school, the large self-reflexive literature on the "crisis of representation" in anthropology (e.g. Marcus and Fischer 1986), postcolonial theory, and in particular and very relevant to the analysis of contemporary Asia, the even more recent attacks on the whole notion of "development" and the homogenising, unilineal and materialistic assumptions on which its conventional versions are based (for example Sachs 1995, Esteva and Prakash 1998, Munck and O'Hearn 1999).

Largely outside of the mainstream social sciences however, and challenging rather than simply reproducing their standard conceptual language, are a number of other contenders, reflecting very different visions of the good society and the means of reaching it. Some of these take the form of attempts to create an alternative indigenous social science (Alatas 2000), some build on work in postcolonial theory either to develop a deeper understanding of the violation of subjectivities engendered by the experience of domination (Nandy 1983, Mannoni 1990) as something going far beyond the simply economic and political effects of colonialism, or to suggest what, in a new era of globalisation, might be called "post-post colonial theory" (e.g. Nandy 1998), some, such as the work of the early Japanese ethnographer Yanagita Kunio (Kawada 1993) or in the broad tradition of indigenous Japanese social thought collectively referred to as the "Nihonjinron," seek to revive or promote a nativist discourse (Sugimoto 1999), while yet others seek the sources of renewal of social vision in religion. In the latter case, while certainly technical social and economic analysis is involved, for example in the search for an Islamic economics (Jomo 1993), the broader motivation appears to be a search for social justice, and the development of methodologies rooted in indigenous knowledge, culture, values and spiritualities, whether these are expressed as Muslim economics in Malaysia and Indonesia, varieties of Catholic liberation theology in the Philippines and Sri Lanka (Pieris 1992) or its indigenous offspring such as *Minjung* theology in Korea (Abelmann 1993), forms of Gandhian socialism (Rao 1970) and Hindu based but caste transcending social/economic transformation movements such as Swadhyaya in India (Srivastava 1998), or social, ecological and peace movements based on Shinto (in Japan) or on Buddhism (in Japan, Thailand and Sri Lanka in particular: cf. Kisala 1999).

In practice many of these forms of alternative (alternative that is to mainstream Western paradigms and their associated methodologies) forms of social science/practice/thought inform each other in creative ways. Much of the impetus behind the religion-based varieties comes from a discontent with the nature of modernity as it has been experienced by many Southeast Asian societies and with the failure of "development" to eradicate poverty and other major social problems, while simultaneously promoting the hedonism, individualism and materialism of consumerism as its most obvious by-product. In this respect it dialogues extensively with secular critiques of the same phenomena, and often draws widely upon empirical research carried out by local or foreign scholars who do not necessarily share the same faith presuppositions. Although sometimes they do, and one of the movements or alliances that religious practitioners and social scientists cooperate within is the one that has become known as "Engaged Buddhism" (Queen and King 1996).

It sometimes appears that such movements (and it is important to note that sociologically many such initiatives in Southeast Asia they are just that, and not simply or only networks of intellectuals talking to each other) are new. While some indeed are, many have evolved out of thinking decades old, although their intellectual sources are often forgotten. With the major turn to the study of "indigenous knowledge" in/by the social sciences it is important to recover these sources. For it may turn out that at least some of the local thinkers responsible for providing the theoretical basis of such movements might qualify as significant contributors to social science discourse, not only in their achievement of praxis (a unity of theory and practice) and their building of distinctive local traditions, but also because their reposing of many of the basic questions of sociology from fresh and surprising alternative cultural premises throws down a major challenge to the supposed universality of the mainstream (largely Western or Western derived) discourses and paradigms of the social sciences.

One such thinker/activist is the Thai (or Siamese as he would no doubt insist) writer, speaker, organiser and general gadfly Sulak Sivaraksa. Although now increasingly well known in the West as an initiator and theorist of "Engaged Buddhism" (a chapter of Queen and King's 1996 volume by Donald Swearer is devoted to him), he is not for the most part taken seriously as a social theorist: not so much forgotten as ignored. I shall argue in this chapter that, despite shortcomings in his work and issues that he has neglected to address, he does indeed qualify as a major Southeast Asian social thinker whose work implicitly engages some of the fundamental questions of the mainstream social sciences and forces upon them a serious rethinking of many of their premises about selfhood, agency, power, social order, and their own origins and location within a particular and peculiarly Western version of modernity, one that appears to be now hegemonic until one looks closely for the cracks and chinks in its armour.

A Brief Life and Times

I will not attempt here to give a detailed account of Sulak's life, particularly as he has recently published extensive autobiographies in Thai and, more recently, in English (Sulak 1998). Some key details however are important to locate the more theoretical discussion that follows and I will simply briefly sketch these in. Born in Bangkok in March 1933 into a reasonably well off Sino-Thai family, Sulak was educated at a series of both Protestant and Catholic missionary schools, including the well known Assumption College, interspersed with a period as a novice monk in a Theravada Buddhist temple. After preparations to enter Bangkok's prestigious Chulalongkorn University, it was decided that instead he should study in England. After a period of language and academic preparation, he entered St. David's College, Lampeter (now part of the University of Wales) and on graduation from there moved to London to study law at the Inns of Court. After his admittance to the Bar he worked for the BBC Thai service while active in Buddhist activities and other work with Thai students in the UK. In 1962, feeling the urge to contribute something more direct to his homeland he returned to Bangkok where, after various part-time jobs he launched on the course that has carried him up to the present.

This began essentially with his appointment as the founding director of the Social Science Association Press of Thailand and his launching in 1963 of the innovative Thai language journal *Social Science Review*. This journal, which soon became a quarterly, published works of social analysis (rare under the conditions of military dictatorship that had prevailed since 1947 under which independent intellectual life had suffered severely), poetry, essays, illustrations by interesting young Thai artists and translations of significant foreign work pertinent to the Thai situation. Book publishing (the main official activity of the Social Science Association), teaching and increasingly work with the *Sangha* (Thai Buddhist monks) on raising social awareness and linking Buddhism to social issues began by the mid-1960s to make Sulak increasingly visible both in Thailand and internationally.

This expanding reputation was consolidated by a period (that has never really ended) of intensive organisation building—creating links with the American Friends Service Committee (Quakers) in Southeast Asia (the Indochina war was escalating and Thailand was becoming a major centre of US bases and "rest and recreation" activities), the International House of Japan through its Southeast Asian intellectual exchange programme, the Cultural Relations for the Future committee, and the Pacific Ashram, amongst others. Prom this time on, if Sulak were a businessman, he would be seen as a highly successful entrepreneur, establishing one enterprise after another. Rather than businesses, for the most part (with the major exception of his founding of the Suksit Siam bookshop specialising in books on Buddhism, Southeast Asia and of course specifically Siam, and a subsequent book distribution company) he was establishing what would now be called NGOs, each one in a slightly different way linking Buddhism and social issues. These included the Paritat Sevana (a Buddhist youth organisation modelled on the Student Christian Centre), the Sathirakoses-Nagapradipa Foundation which among its other activities published an "alternative" journal, *Pajarayasara*, blending ecological, Buddhist and social-critical themes, the Komol Keemthong Foundation (another youth related movement) and a conservation movement designed to oppose the destruction of many of the most beautiful buildings and canals in Bangkok in the name of "development."

Sulak's unwavering attention to social issues, corruption, militarisation, cultural destruction masquerading as progress and modernisation and his youth work in the Thai countryside brought him to the attention of the government and the successive coups of 1971, 1973 and 1976 made work difficult, since any kind of social activism was likely to be labelled communist, and Sulak did spend a brief spell stranded abroad in effective exile. However he did return and went on organising, restarting his book distribution network, founding the still extant Thai Interreligious Commission for Development and the Asian Cultural Forum on Development, both of which have been and continue to be important alternative voices on development questions in Thailand and Southeast Asia. The years following his arrest and trial (and acquittal) in 1984 on charges of lèse-majesté were spent in publishing, book distribution, travelling (including to China and Tibet after Thailand normalised relations with the PRC), meeting with the Dalai Lama, youth work with the Pacific Youth forum, the establishment of a permanent ashram (Wongsanit Ashram) and the foundation of the International Network of Engaged Buddhists. A second charge of lese-majeste in the wake of the 1991 coup forced Sulak into exile and a period of wandering in Europe, Japan and North America. Returning home a year later after the collapse of the Suchinda government and with a guarantee of safety from the incoming civilian Prime Minister Chuan Leekpai to face trial again, Sulak was once more acquitted. In December 1995 he received from the Swedish parliament the Right Livelihood Award (sometimes called the "alternative Nobel prize") and since then has continued his work on engaged Buddhism, interreligious dialogue and, most recently, critiques of and alternatives to, consumerism. Interestingly although he has often given short courses or individual lectures, Sulak has never had a full time university post, but has remained throughout his life an independent, but very much "public" intellectual.

The Critique of Modernity

Despite all this intensive organisational activity, travel, political engagement and self-supporting business activities, Sulak has been since the 1960s a prolific writer. While he has never written a systematic book in English (even his autobiography was transcribed and integrated by others from a collection of audiotapes and notes) his collected essays and transcriptions of his speeches fill at least three volumes in English and several more in Thai, and many more are scattered in journals, collections and conference proceedings in several languages (although mostly in Thai and English). One is reminded somewhat of Gandhi whose equally intense, although more overtly political, career not only did not prevent him from writing, but actually spurred the production of many volumes of speeches and essays, and also a well known autobiography. Unlike Gandhi however, Sulak's work has as yet attracted little commentary, an omission that this chapter is designed in part to rectify.

The unsystematic and scattered (and indeed in some cases repetitive) nature of Sulak's *oeuvre* (hardly surprising when they have emerged from such an activist life) requires that the commentator mine it for the themes that are implicit in it, but which are rarely theorised or grouped into coherent patterns. The following body of the essay is consequently my reading or interpretation of a large body of work. I hope that this does not render it inaccurate, and indeed I hope that Khun Sulak may find things here that he did not fully realise were contained in his own nearly forty years of output.

Thailand (or Siam to use our subject's preferred usage) has undergone profound changes and disrupting experiences during Sulak's own lifetime. The establishment of constitutional monarchy and the introduction of de facto military rule more or less coincide with his birth. Until the introduction of civilian control with the Chuan Leekpai cabinet in 1992-5 and again post 1997, Siam experienced a series of military administrations punctuated with coups and periodic democratic uprisings against whoever was running the current junta. While remaining theoretically independent, the country became embroiled in the Second World War and was occupied by the Japanese, and then, with the outbreak of the second Indochina war became a major staging post for US forces fighting in Vietnam, Cambodia and Laos and was the site of huge American airbases from which bombing raids were launched over the neighbouring countries. With the cessation of the war Thailand launched on an aggressive period of "development" and industrialisation that has become a paradigm case of the problems of "progress"—massive urbanisation, pollution, the decline of the rural economy, tourist enclaves cheek-by-jowl with slums, massive corruption, non-compliance with basic standards of industrial safety, erosion of worker's rights and extensive social problems including prostitution, child labour and a massive AIDS/HIV problem, mounting debt, and deforestation (Bello, Cunningham and Li 1998), all of which came to a head with the currency crisis and implosion of the economy in 1997 a crisis which triggered by the huge structural and fiscal problems of Thailand, rapidly spread to the rest of Southeast Asia (Arndt and Hill 1999).

Spreading social inequalities, materialism and consumerism, corruption in the Sangha and the loss of the spiritual values underlying Siamese civilisation, have become in the view of many social critics, including Sulak, the reality behind the facade of the "Land of Smiles" promoted in the tourist brochures. Modernity in other words has failed, because it has only delivered a one sided (materialist) version of progress while ignoring deeper existential human needs. In fact, in its Asian varieties, it has often proved to be anti-democratic, committed to growth rather than rounded well-being and has eroded the religious and traditional cultural values upon which Asian civilisations are themselves founded. Its latest phase—globalisation—has if anything intensified these tendencies, and while Siam was never formally colonised, in reality it has experienced as a result of development, what Ashis Nandy (another major and relatively neglected Asian social thinker) has described as the psychic traumatisation of cultural invasion and value loss resulting in severe damage to the sense of self and its integrity (Nandy 1983).

In Sulak's view the solution to these traumas of development, and indeed the creation of a new form of civilisation that transcends them and speaks instead to genuine human needs rather than ephemeral ones, lies essentially in the recovery of the religious/cultural roots of the socio-cultural entities now known as nations (Theravada Buddhism in the case of Siam), the rediscovery of the social teachings and ethical systems implicit in these foundational value systems/cosmologies, and in ecumenical dialogue between the different religio-cultural configurations that make up the social geography of Asia, a view which again interestingly converges with that of Nandy (Nandy 1998). Stated thus, Sulak would appear as just one more voice in the chorus of postcolonial, antidevelopment or anti-modernist voices that constitute the various levels of alternative discourse in Asia, a significant Siamese member of the chorus, but otherwise not particularly distinctive. I will suggest however that his originality lies not mainly in his broad message, but in the particular methodology for social analysis and practice implicit in his thought.

This methodology is based on Buddhist principles. A claim could certainly be made that of all the possible challenges to the epistemology of the mainstream tradition in the social sciences, Buddhism represents the most radical. The originally Western if now internationally hegemonic social sciences are largely based on a particular view of the human individual as a permanent and essential self, a Cartesian view of the relation between body and mind, and a resulting model of how the individual acts upon or relates to reality (Morris 1991). A certain view of the basic elements of social analysis in the Western tradition—agents, agency, structure and causality—naturally leads to specific methodologies for exploring society (including positivist and statistical ones) and creates a distinctive theoretical field within which sociological discourse operates. Anthony Giddens has argued for example that the central theoretical problem of sociology is that of relating agency and structure (Giddens 1983). While the foundational view of selfhood in the Western sociological tradition has been challenged empirically (for Japan for example see Kondo 1990, Clammer 1995 and for Thailand see Mulder 1979), the radical methodological consequences of a shift to a "Buddhist" model of epistemology and ontology has not yet been systematically explored. I use "Buddhist" here in inverted commas, both because some would argue that there is some move in this direction in French deconstructionism with its Derridian notions of the decentred self which in some ways parallel say Japanese notions of the subject (Odin 1995, and because Sulak himself argues for what he calls "Buddhism with a small b" (Sulak 1992: 62), a vision of reality with its roots in Buddhism, but which has universal features that: can be shared and utilised by members of other religious/cultural traditions without their becoming in some confessional sense Buddhists. Sulak is implicitly (he does not theorise his own position) a major agent in forcing on social theory the necessity of confronting Buddhism and its huge implications for social practice and methodological shifts as well as for conceptual innovation. As one commentator has argued, Buddhism represents an "Enlightenment project" (pun very much intended!) radically at variance with that of the Western version and one which urgently needs to be considered in a shrinking and globalising world still fragmented by primordial ethnic and religious disputes, exacerbated by the very "development" that globalisation is supposed to deliver (Batchelor 1998). Its decentred view of the self, its inherently "ecological" cosmology implied by its theory of causality ("dependent arising"), its non-Cartesian view of the body/mind relationship and its view of the inherent relationship between desire and suffering pose fundamental challenges to mainstream sociology, and to applied ideas, including that of development, that have emerged from the Western project of modernity.

Buddhism and Methodology

What then are the basic elements in Sulak's methodology? They essentially derive from a blending of Theravada Buddhist practices and social analysis, the foundational components of which begin with the notion of Mindfulness. Recognition of the "suchness" of things is a key component of all schools of Buddhism, but is especially stressed in the *Vipassana* practices of the Southeast Asian Theravadan variety. Sometimes called or based on what is termed "insight meditation" (Goldstein 1994), mindfulness is the grasping of the true nature of the reality that presents itself to the observer/experiencer. When walking, walk; when sitting, sit; when eating, be aware of the food that one is ingesting—its texture, colours, flavours, its origins and the processes of rain and sun, human labour and skills, that have brought it eventually onto one's plate, in some ways parallel to the non-conceptual seeing recommended by some forms of Western phenomenological philosophy, mindfulness brings together an actual clear perception of reality as it is, together with a kind of cosmic gratefulness for the processes that have come together in that particular experience, event or object of contemplation. Sulak recounts how at a very tender age, during his monastic novitiate, the importance of such mindfulness was conveyed to him by the daily practices of the temple (Sulak 1998: 20). The actual attainment of mindfulness is difficult—the "monkey mind" is endlessly introducing distractions, memories, concepts, anxieties and so forth into our clear perception of what is actually around us, and its full achievement is indeed akin to enlightenment itself: the recognition of the true nature of reality. But while many Buddhist practitioners see mindfulness as a kind of interior discipline achieved through meditation, Sulak takes it one step further. Mindfulness in his version also gives us insight into the nature of social reality and in doing so makes us aware that our apparent "individuality" is actually the outcome of a huge number of forces. An awareness of our *interconnection* both to other people and to nature is the result. This has two theoretical consequences—one being that the "individual" does not really exist in any monadic sense, and autonomy is an illusion since we are acted upon by numerous complex interrelated forces rather than act independently or upon those forces. The recognition that we are all part of one another, and of the natural processes that ultimately sustain us, clearly shifts our understanding of society from one of active individual agents to a much more "communitarian" one often described in Buddhist influenced Japanese social theory where this idea is well developed, as a "relational", "situational" or "inter-personal" image of social relationships (cf. Hamaguchi 1982).

In much the same way that Louis Dumont has argued that Western individualism has its roots in Christianity and that the consequences of this individualism are profound for the arrangement of society and assumptions about how relationships within it work (Dumont 1986), so Sulak is arguing for a "trans-individualism" that arises from Buddhist roots, and which has equally profound implications for the ordering of society. It distinguishes for example between ego and the true self "which has a cosmic dimension and functions in synergy with the negation of the empirical self" (Dumoulin 1994: 138), and as such promotes an attitude of mutual gratitude and forgiveness between people (Sulak 1998: 22).

This view of the relationship between mindfulness and truth has a number of rather practical implications as well as philosophical ones. It promotes an "ecological" view of both social and social-nature relationships, is non-violent, suggests that (unlike in Western postmodernism) there are "metanarratives" in that cultures are based on foundations, these foundations being primarily religious in nature and as such are the source of social ethics and as political/social practice implies some form of what Sulak calls "Dhammic socialism," different from both Marxist varieties of socialism and Western social democracy (Sulak 1998: 201). Sulak sees the failure of democracy in Siam as a result of the (mis)copying of Western models and transplanting them to a soil where very different assumptions about social relationships actually prevail. It is the gap between the Western and Siamese models that has been the cause of the huge political instability that the country has experienced since 1932. Yet the material for achieving the same universal values as espoused by the European "Enlightenment Project" are available in Buddhism—notably democracy, fraternity, equality and liberty, values that were incarnated in the original Sangha founded by the Buddha himself (Sulak 1998: 201).

Such a view of an intimate relationship between culture and religion naturally points to a concept of alternative development—one rooted in those values rather than overriding and violating them. "Unmindful development" in fact becomes the very thing to oppose as it strews social and ecological chaos in its wake and fails to address fundamental human problems. Much of Sulak's energy has been invested in attempts to concretise alternative strategies, for example in his work with the Asian Cultural Forum on Development and the creation of an ashram blending contemplation and action (the Wongsanit Ashram), an idea emerging both out of his own Buddhist practice and his admiration of figures both within Buddhism who have attempted this (in particular the Dalai Lama who contributed the foreword to Sulak's autobiography, and the Vietnamese monk Thich Nhat Hanh), and from Catholicism, such as Thomas Merton, Dorothy Day and Paulo Freire.

Buddhism, to some extent rather like Christianity, has long had something of a problem in defining its social ethics. Individual ethics have not been such a problem, but unlike Judaism with its intensely social prophetic tradition and Islam with its dissolution of the boundaries between the sacred and the secular, the metaphysics of Buddhism make it much less clear how, or even why, individuals should intervene in society or engage with issues of social justice. While not entirely successful attempts have been made to define a Buddhist social ethic (for example Butr-Indr 1979), Sulak, in tandem with Thich Nhat Hanh, has attempted to provide the basis for such an ethic by showing how the principles of Buddhism in fact do translate into a particular understanding of human relationships, and how violation of those relationships, by unmindful development for example, or by militarism, violence or capital punishment to cite other examples used by Sulak, in fact and as a result violate Buddhism itself. The notion of "Engaged Buddhism," influenced in particular by Asian forms of Catholic liberation theology, was the natural result. In many ways since at least the mid-1980s, Sulak's work has been the attempt to articulate and deepen this vision of engaged Buddhism (Sulak 1998: 186-190), through the promotion of seminars, publications and activities aimed at linking Buddhism and social justice issues (partly through the Santi Pracha Dhamma ("Peace, People, Righteousness") Foundation that Sulak founded in 1988) especially by focussing on questions of peace, democracy, non-violent social and political engagement and the promotion of the writings of significant Thai intellectuals such as Dr Puey Ungphakorn, the title of one of whose books provided the name of the Foundation itself. This work by the mid 1990s had expanded to include the need to seek for alternatives to consumerism, by then becoming one of the most visible products of unmindful development in Siam, and the search for educational alternatives (in the form of the Spirit in Education Movement started by Sulak in the late 1990s) designed to overcome the dysfunctionality of conventional education in a country like Thailand and to relate education to political alternatives and to the critique of consumerism by way of a methodology that includes meditation and in general tries to "link the heart and the head" (Sulak 1998: 209).

Culture and Development

The sociology of development, hamstrung by its own overly economistic approach which it largely shares with those it criticises, has begun in recent years to cast around for a fresh direction. With a world beset by the problems created by globalisation and the world-wide expansion of consumer capitalism and recognising perhaps that their own modest attempts to understand this complex reality have not been totally successful, sociologists have begun to look for "new directions" (Schuurman 1996) which have included a sudden interest in "indigenous knowledge," a concern with participatory methodologies, sustainable development, engagement with the political, ecological and gender issues implicit in development, concern with the local social effects of such macro issues as the debt crisis faced by many developing nations, and, rather belatedly, an interest in the ethics of development. Many of these questions have come together under the general rubric of "culture and development" (for instance Schech and Haggis 2000). Oddly though, this fresh interest in culture (fuelled in part no doubt by the general "cultural turn" in the social sciences in the last decade and the strong emergence of cultural studies as a discipline in its own right) mostly does not talk about culture at all. Rather it talks about social structures: gender, class, social groupings (e.g. peasants or urban migrants), social units (e.g. farms, villages), networks (of knowledge, people or power), or, at its more anthropological end, of the conventional entities of social analysis—families, clans, tribes or ethnic groups. Culture itself is mostly missing, and amongst the factors that clearly make up culture, certainly in its Asian settings, most conspicuously absent is religion. This is true both of development sociology and of cultural studies in the region. While there are plenty of social science treatments of religion, they tend to be studied as something apart from other social processes, especially those implicated in so-called development (Clammer 2000d). A major aspect of Sulak's contribution is in the bringing together of culture and development, and specifically the religious aspects of culture, into a dialogue, specifically in the Thai situation, but with much wider regional and theoretical implications.

The first of his concerns is with the problem of identity. Historically Siamese identity has emerged out of cultural interchange with and a sense of distinction from the Chinese to the north, the Khmer civilisation to the east and the Burmese to the west. With the advent of contact with Europe and subsequently north America, this negotiation became even more complex with not only culture seeping in from the West, but also ideas of political organisation, space and boundaries, nationalism and new forms of economic practice (Thongchai 1994). It is in reaction to these that Sulak expresses a strong form of cultural nationalism—the need to learn from the West (and from Japan, China and other places) while keeping it at arm's length. His formula—avoid Western intellectual domination, learn from the past mistakes of earlier generations in their attempts to manage identity or of the spoiled identities resulting from excessive westernisation and development, build self-reliance and safeguards against the inroads of consumerism and the multinational corporations, revitalise the countryside, take the local spiritual tradition seriously and try to promote it actively, and to think ecologically. What saves this very view from its apparent conservatism or even reactionary nature are the two additional factors that Sulak also requires: that a critical stance be taken towards local cultures, towards history and in particular the political institutions that have evolved from it, and the belief that it is through the spiritual tradition that liberation, spiritual, cultural and ecological, will be achieved. His is not simply a call to "return to religion" as espoused by many of the Sangha in Thailand, but to discover the liberatory potential inherent in Buddhism and to apply it (Sulak 1991a). Elsewhere in the same volume, in a dialogue with the Filipino novelist and Magsaysay award winner F. Sionil Jose, he goes on to elaborate on the idea of non-violent change as a mechanism of social transformation rooted in Buddhist principles and distinguished from conventional concepts of revolution (Sulak 1991b: 166-215).

These views are actually the elaboration of ideas that go back to his earlier collections of essays *Siam in Crisis* (1979), *A Buddhist Vision for Renewing Society* (1981), a lecture in Thai published in English also in 1981 as *Religion and Development* and a substantial compendium issued in

1985 entitled *Siamese Resurgence*. As his ideas to a great extent repeat themselves, I will illustrate Sulak's ideas largely from the latter (Sulak 1985).

Sulak divides his book into a number of sections, three of which deal with historical figures in Thai society, with specific small issues (notes on Angkor Wat and suggestions for the reform of Thai universities, and appendices relating to his own political vicissitudes, respectively). The main body of the book however deals with the three central themes of Sulak's thought—Buddhism and society, Buddhism and development and issues of culture in the Asian context. In the first of these sections (each one of which consists of a series of short essays), Sulak suggests that the modernisation model of development is essentially Western and as such does not permit the flowering of indigenous identities and destinies in Asia. Seeing the identification of suffering and a solution to that suffering as being the key insight of Buddhism, Sulak expounds, in the essay "Buddhism and a World of Change," both the key doctrinal ideas of the Theravada school and the suggestion that these, especially as embodied in the Four Noble Truths and the resulting Eightfold Path, constitute a more reasonable approach to the basic existential problems of humanity (at least in Asia) than does the pursuit of materialist "progress" and foreign models of development, which actually promote more suffering rather than alleviate it. In the subsequent essay ("Buddhism as a Catalyst of Social Unity and Progress") Sulak extends these ideas by attempting to show through examples and case studies, particularly of the contribution of monks to positive social change, that if the image of Buddhism as a quietist religion can be overcome then it can make great contributions to the quality of human life. This he goes on to further elaborate in an argument that religion, far from being the opium of the people, is the source of the most significant values, values which in his view are to be contrasted with those of the materialism, competitiveness and consumerism of the secular modernisation or development models. In an essay concluding the first section of his book, he addresses the question of Buddhist women and produces a basically feminist critique of ideas of the subordination of women ("Buddhist Women: Past and Present").

In the second section of the book Sulak turns more specifically to articulating the relationship between Buddhism and development. But this he does in an unconventional way, by suggesting essentially (in "Buddhism from a Thai Perspective") that self-consciously searching for a "social message" in Buddhism (as many Christians have also been tempted to do with their faith) is unnecessary. It is in the fundamental teachings of Buddhism itself that a radically "alternative" vision is to be found. If one begins to trace the implications of the ideas of egolessness (the non-permanent self), of dependent arising, of the cessation of suffering, they lead to an ethical framework (the Five Precepts and the Noble Eightfold Path) the application of which to wider social issues provides in principle a non-violent and ecologically sound basis for "development" practice. The identification of humans and nature (the potential Buddhahood of all things taught in some schools of Japanese Buddhism for example), renders violations of nature violations of oneself. Sharing, equality, friendship, and constructive action then become the basis on which human scale development can be pursued ("A Buddhist Perspective on Asian Development"). This view however involves Sulak in a strong critique of many aspects of contemporary Thai Buddhism (and especially the Sangha), which he sees (perhaps not entirely fairly—cf. Somboon 1977), as non-activist, uninvolved with the real social problems of either rural or urban Thai society, and as having been bought over by the corrupt and undemocratic political powers. While he is also critical of the quietism of the Western Buddhism that he encountered during his own sojourn in Europe, he reserves his strongest criticisms for the Buddhism of his own society. He is fighting in fact on two fronts simultaneously—for the reform of Thai Buddhism and its separation from corrupting political influences on the one hand, and the critique of conventional development on the other. What links the two is the belief that it is a purified Buddhist vision that will provide the basis for humane development in Thailand and elsewhere in Asia. Given that Sulak sees the basic problems for development thinking as poverty and social injustice (Sulak 1985: 97), this is not an argument for a spiritualised idea of development detached from material realities, but an attempt to redefine priorities in a way that brings values and political economy symbiotically together rather than detaching them and letting them exist in different spheres in which, in practice, the political economy colonises, in Habermas's term, the "life world" not the other way around.

Sulak's argument is indeed that the bottom line for assessing any programme of development, is whether it contributes to or degrades the quality of life ("Quality of Life: A Buddhist Perspective"). Since "Social growth in Buddhist terminology does not mean social recognition or socialisation, but it means that one cares about social justice—that one does not want to exploit oneself or others" (Sulak 1985: 107). The key to Sulak's thought then really lies in the idea that genuine outer development is impossible without inner development—cultivation achieved through meditation, ethical conduct and the sincere practice of a religious discipline (which need not be Buddhism). "Facts" are not simply those propositions or empirical entities generated by the methodologies of positivist science, but are those discerned through wisdom. In the light of this, Sulak summarises his view of development as follows:

> "True development will arrange for the rhythm of life and movement to be in accordance with the facts, while maintaining an awareness that man is but a part of the universe, and that ways must be found to integrate mankind with the laws of nature. There must be no boasting, no proud self-centred attempts to master nature, no emphasis placed on the creation of material things to the point where people become slaves to things and have no time left for themselves to search after the truth which is out beyond the realm of material things." (Sulak 1985: 113)

Respect for the environment, which Sulak takes to mean not just prevention of pollution and resource depletion, but also demilitarisation and the use of appropriate and non-intrusive technology ("Southeast Asia and the Environment") and a "think small" approach to development planning avoiding capital intensive style investments and planning (Sulak 1985: 165) complete the picture.

These views have been refined and summarised in one of Sulak's most recent publications (Sulak 1992), demonstrating the continuity of his ideas. His intellectual and most of his practical work have been less a linear progression than a constant elaboration of a small group of fundamental themes. There, setting out once again his basic themes—the corrosive dangers of consumerism, the failures of the "think big" approach to development, the necessity of making the quality of life the basic criterion of successful development, the links between personal and social transformation and the contributions of Buddhism to both defining moral and social values and providing a "methodology" for their realisation—Sulak also enters more fully into dialogue with contemporary critical work on development issues. In discussing the idea of sustainability for example, he poses the very crucial question of whether unsustainable lifestyles can be considered moral (Sulak 1992: 43).

In the chapter of the book which summarises his approach ("A Buddhist model of society"), Sulak surveys firstly the traditional teachings of Theravada Buddhism, something that he has done often in the past, but then takes the step of more analytically relating them to contemporary social issues. In earlier publications he rarely if ever made fully explicit the passage from his view of Buddhism to his social analysis. Here he finally attempts to remedy this lack. Essentially he suggests that the insight and mindfulness coming from Buddhism translate into the following contemporary precepts: a transnational response to the transnationalisation of capital; political and economic solidarity of the South in dealing with the

North; the need for strict arms control, conflict resolution agencies and mechanisms for the maintenance of security, curbing consumerism, the promotion of democracy, egalitarianism, and international organisations (including a global disarmament administration, an effective international judiciary and a permanent international peacekeeping force); and a universal Bill of Rights (Sulak 1992: 113-115). The extent of suffering in the world compels action, and "To alleviate suffering we must go back to our own spiritual depths—to retreat, meditation and prayer. it is nearly impossible to sustain the work otherwise. It is easy to hate our enemies—the industrialists who exploit us and pollute our atmosphere. But we must come to see that there is no 'other.' We are all one human family. It is greed, hatred and delusion that we need to overcome" (Sulak 1992: 116).

Locating Sulak

Several strands then run through Sulak's work: critiques of Thai political culture and of a non-socially activist "establishment" Sangha which has entered into cosy relationships with rather than speaking truth to the political power brokers; an understanding of development as meaning the eradication of poverty, social inequality and injustice without falling into the contrary evils of greed, materialism and consumerism; an argument for the vitality of (purified forms of) religion as providing the value basis for human centred development and genuine realisation and liberation, an argument that has led him not only to stress the importance of a Buddhist approach to reality, but also to a deeply ecumenical appreciation of other religions (especially Christianity with which he seems to have the greatest affinity); and an analysis of the epistemological basis of Western science and technology and of the imperialisms that carried it to Asia, which, in Sulak's view, have set most of the world on a course of modernisation that has created more problems than it has solved.

The simplest way to locate Sulak would be to place him on the one hand in the tradition of a succession of Asian social thinkers from Gandhi on, and including such individuals as the Indian economist J.C. Kumarappa (1984), Pandurang Vaijinath Athavale (the founder of the Swadhyaya movement) and a host of lesser known figures who have stressed the connections between spirituality and social transformation and the need for people-centred development, and who like Rabindranath Tagore, were also nationalist and anti-Western to varying degrees. Many of the social movements, communes, ashrams, NGOs and new religious movements that have sprung up in Asia, despite their variety and geographical spread, do share many of the same formal features, including a self-conscious rooting in some kind of spiritual soil, whether it be Buddhist, Muslim, Shinto,

Catholic, or representative of some kind of indigenous nativist or syncretic tendency such as Tonghak in Korea. On the other hand Sulak clearly has affinities with (and acknowledges his debt to) what might be called the "critical communitarian" school of Western thinking that has its roots in England in such figures as Ruskin and in North America in Emerson, and which shares an anti-industrial and often anti-urban ideology, while favouring small scale craft production, anarchist politics and a rural bias. Again this Western alternative tradition is diverse, although it does tend to a "small is beautiful" position and in many cases some kind of communitarian living style. In Sulak's case the figure that he most refers to is E.F. Schumacher, well known as the author of *Small is Beautiful* (1979) and other works on what would now be called sustainable and ecological development (for example Schumacher 1973).

Yet Sulak does not fall exactly into any of these categories, although his thought shares many features with them. An attempt to locate him more accurately is not just an academic exercise, but will help substantially to clarify his critical social thought in its own unique configurations, ones with which not everyone is going to agree, but which do merit serious attention.

I would suggest that the label that fits Sulak best is "critical traditionalism." This is rather different from traditional conservatism, in which the past is glorified and change in the present is either denied, or undertaken along classical Right wing lines. Sulak, despite his stressing of the values of Buddhism and the civilities of traditional Asian lifestyles, could hardly be called a Rightist as his long career as an opponent of successive military governments, his twice being arraigned on lese-majeste charges and his general role as, to use a term he likes himself, a "gadfly" to anti-democratic regimes both sacred and secular. Critical traditionalism rather, I would suggest, describes a position in which while there is indeed a drawing on the past, history is treated critically, and while cultural traditions (in this case primarily Buddhism) are constantly invoked, they are done so as part of a critical methodology for the examination and evaluation of the present and its emergent values. Sulak thus takes history seriously, but as a resource from which lessons can be learnt as much from the mistakes of our ancestors, not as a mythical golden age.

Contained within Sulak's critical traditionalism are three other basic elements. The first of these is a form of tempered nationalism. Sulak is undoubtedly a Siamese nationalist, and his writings are full of apparent rejections of the West. This might be seen as a classical case of biting the hand that feeds (Sulak's tertiary education and his early career having been in Wales and London interspersed with travels on the Continent, and it was a number of Western nations that gave him asylum and support during his periods of exile from Thailand). A closer examination of his views however suggests that this is not the case. In fact Sulak's comments on the West should be seen from two points of view—his position that it has been Western colonialism and the imposition of inappropriate modernisation models that has violated the integrity of Asian societies (e.g. Sulak 1984), a position that puts him squarely in the wider stream of Asian anti or post colonial thinking; and the view, now widely shared in the West itself, that much of Western technology and economic expansion is one-sided, ecologically destructive and overrides humane values in the name of progress, development or globalisation. His views of the on the whole negative impact of the West must be seen in the wider context of his thought as a whole, and does not reflect some kind of knee-jerk or reactionary nationalism. As Sulak says quite clearly: "In fact, we must return to the essence of our Buddhist culture, with its spiritual and moral base, in order to wipe out the danger from modern cultural imperialism. However we must not make this issue to be nationalistic pride or patriotism at its worst element. In fact we wish to return to our Buddhist or any religious and cultural value in order to decrease lust for power and prestige, anger and hatred" (Sulak 1985: 91). So while Sulak is quite prepared to support the institution of the monarchy, even this, rooted as it is in Siamese history, depends on its adjusting and serving the lifestyle of the people (Sulak 1985: 101-2). It is not then Western science and technology in themselves that is the problem; it is their arrogant and universal application and the kind of philosophical rape that accompanies the imposition of hegemonic systems on local cultures. Sulak, as we have seen, is a strong supporter of the critical and prophetic strands of Judaism and Christianity which he also sees as emerging largely from the West, and so his position here is in fact very close to that of many of the West's internal critics, especially those like Matthew Fox (Fox 1990) or Thomas Merton (Merton 1989) who are also operating from a religious perspective, in those cases a Catholic one.

The second, and very much connected, element is Sulak's critique of capitalism which again, in common with a whole host of thinkers, he sees as the primary source of the greed and delusion that Buddhism struggles against. Although his thinking on economics is very underdeveloped and Sulak appears to have no systematic model of how the economy of a genuinely Buddhist society would actually work, he does suggest that "Capitalism, unfortunately is now at its worst. I see so much of the negative elements—above all, the desire to want what a person does not need. If we limit capitalism to mere free trade in a small society, I think Buddhism would tolerate that" (Sulak 1985: 102). His analysis does suggest that it is not possible to understand contemporary Southeast Asia without placing it in the context of the international economic order. This he suggests has two main components. The first is "The increasing penetration of the capitalist mode into the areas of social and economic life in the region. Not only does this characterise the tensions between countries as they compete for capital, but it is also characterised within each nation as access to wealth and power is rapidly centralised" (Sulak 1985: 133). The second, very prophetic words as they were written more than a decade before the Asian currency crisis began in 1997, suggests that "Accompanying this penetration have been the effects of the world crisis in exchanges and commodities. As wealth and power are accumulated by some groups, the absolute conditions of poverty and misery have worsened for the majority" (Sulak 1985: 133). This in turn has encouraged militarisation and the violation of human rights throughout the region (Sulak 1985: 137) and has promoted anti-human "development":

> "Human values must be taken into account in assessing development plans. The ascendancy of market values, and the primacy accorded technology as a social barometer, have devalued the worth of individuals, rendered irrelevant the quality of their lives, and stunted their creativity. Plans which set aside these values fly in the face of a fundamental problem. They are anti-human, developmentally counterproductive, and tend to produce an elite group with interests divorced from the mass of the people" (Sulak 1985: 170).

The "think-big" strategy of capitalism is incompatible with human-centred development, and that, ultimately, is its major failing.

The third plank in Sulak's critical traditionalism is, as was briefly suggested above, his location within a tradition of "radical communitarianism" with roots leading back to Gandhi, Schumacher, Emerson, many of the European anarchist thinkers, to utopian thinking and to the rich but largely unstudied phenomenon of Asian non-communist socialism and the many expressions that it has taken in communes, social movements and creative social thinking. What is distinctive about Sulak's approach is its attempt to build such a practice (expressed in this case through the foundation of the Wongsanit Ashram) and an underlying theory based on Buddhism. it is in this context to that Sulak has built links to the very different Buddhist lineage of the Dalai Lama (who contributed the foreword to Sulak's book *Seeds of Peace* and to the now internationally very well known Vietnamese Buddhist monk, peace activist and founder of a leading meditation centre Thich Nhat Hanh (who contributed the preface to the same book). Interestingly both these highly significant figures in the Buddhist world and its increasing internationalisation have been developing ideas parallel to or in some cases more or less identical with those of Sulak (e.g. Thich 1991, Dalai Lama 1996). A certain convergence of social thinking appears to be taking place in the discourse of engaged Buddhism. The result is an interesting model that proposes a non-Marxist "socialism" based on ideas of sharing, non-greed and what, borrowing ideas from Latin American liberation theology (especially the concept of conscientisation), Sulak calls "development for liberation" (Sulak 1977). Progressive ideas of social/political liberation and coming out from colonial and economic domination are in Sulak's thought blended with Buddhist notions of liberation. It is really in the interfacing of these two usually unrelated ideas of liberation that the originality of his work lies.

Sulak consequently stands in an interesting and sometimes tangential relationship to other movements and tendencies in recent Asian social thought. He can certainly be located centrally within the suddenly burgeoning "spirituality and development" movement that has been growing rapidly amongst NGOs in both South and Southeast Asia and the networks that sustain and in some cases actually constitute them (for example the Alliance for a Responsible and United World with its Asia-Pacific headquarters in Bangalore). But at the same time, although he can clearly be identified as a "postcolonial" thinker, he has never formally associated himself with academic postcolonialism, especially its South Asian varieties, whether through lack of acquaintance with its literature, or because of its secular bias (and its origins in a nevertheless basically Hindu environment). His own critique of colonialism is based less on an analysis of its direct economic and political impact than on its spiritual and cultural dimensions, something which stands in some continuity with the much more theorised work of the Indian social psychologist Ashis Nandy, who however also persists in a much more secularised approach to the psychically damaging effects of domination. It is in the particular—triangulation of his views on development, ethics, and Buddhist epistemology that the distinctiveness of Sulak's thought lies.

Fundamental to this theoretical and liberatory project I suggest is Sulak's critique of the philosophical basis of Western science—and its (mis)application to Asian societies—and by implication of the Western social sciences. His own critiques of the work of the Dutch anthropologist Niels Mulder (Sulak 1985: 97) and of the Ian Buruma, the journalist and all-purpose Asianist (Sulak 1991b; 174-5), both of whom have approvingly cited Sulak in their own writings, illustrates the ways in which he feels that even well-intentioned foreigners have largely misunderstood Southeast Asian and certainly Thai society and culture. While Sulak's dismissive comments could certainly be contested (and they do raise the classical question of the degree to which cross-cultural communication is possible), they do illustrate well how analysts not grasping or sharing the inner cosmology of a culture can indeed easily produce misleading accounts while nevertheless adhering to standard social science methodology.

Where does all this point to? I would suggest in several directions. One of these must be the theoretical refining of the notion of a Buddhist social ethics. To a great extent this is precisely the issue that is being taken up by "Engaged Buddhism." Sulak himself asserts rather than theorises the links between Buddhist values and humane development, where he seems to think that the "elective affinity" that he detects constitutes a demonstrable relationship. Without this link being made explicit however, his work, while morally powerful, lacks rigour. There is little evidence that Sulak has acquainted himself very deeply with the substantial body of work in critical social theory, or with the actual detailed and often empirical work of the liberation theologians that he makes passing reference to in many places in his writings. In this respect his work has not advanced substantially beyond the kind of critical development thinking that was already occurring (some of it, especially that emerging from Sri Lanka, also with a Buddhist basis) in Asia in the 1970s (e.g. UNESCO/UNADI 1977). In particular whereas he clearly has strong affinities for Christianity (and much of his ecumenical development work has been done with Christians), he almost entirely ignores the work going on in Southeast Asia amongst critical and progressive Muslim thinkers on social and economic issues, and the broader Muslim critiques of Western science and its ecological, spiritual and philosophical consequences (for example Nasr 1993).

Others have taken up these challenges however, challenges certainly thrown out by Sulak even if not fully pursued by him. In the context of the question of the universal applicability of the concept of human rights or understandings of human freedom from oppression for example Buddhist philosophers have raised that very question from their own faith perspective (e.g. Mabbett 1998) and Thai thinkers have raised similar questions in relation to the history of their own society (Thanet 1998), or have sought in Buddhism solutions to the specific social problems of Thailand (Suwanna 1999). While arguing for a universal Bill of Rights, Sulak neither makes it clear how this might differ from or be more rooted in specific (and not exclusively Western) cultural values than the existing Universal Declaration of Human Rights, nor does he actually engage at all with the thorny question of human rights abuses in his neighbouring Buddhist countries Cambodia and Burma, or of the problems of labour under rapid industrialisation encouraged but weakly monitored by the state itself, whether in its military or democratic guises (e.g. Somboon 1997). Indeed for all its very positive stresses on problems of youth, the rural sector and inter-religious dialogue, Sulak is weakest when it comes to political economy, both in terms of the actual inroads of capitalist style modernity on Thai and other Southeast Asian societies, and of alternative systems to put in its place. A crucial theoretical problem for any progressive model of development is how to achieve poverty alleviation without creating consumerism and materialism in its place. While Sulak's theory of the values-based society hints at solutions to this, the actual steps involved are never spelt out. And certainly these silences are important in an overall evaluation of Sulak's work.

An Alternative Social Theory?

Sulak Sivaraksa has emerged as a major figure in engaged Buddhism, but is still largely ignored by mainstream Asian and international social science. The main reason for this I think is his strong commitment to Buddhism (something of an embarrassment to secular social scientists still wedded to a Weberian separation of fact and value) and the implications for this as a critique of the philosophical basis of the positivist varieties of Western science. Whereas thinkers in other nominally Buddhist societies have moved in quite different directions much more congenial to the expectations of metropolitan social science (Japan's embracing of postmodernism for example), Sulak has rejected those possibilities in favour of what appears to be a "pre-modern" return to fundamental Buddhist values. Such a view should be evaluated with caution however, because in common with thinkers such as Gandhi, Sulak's "premodernity" is actually a critique of modernity itself and of the particular process of modernisation that has been its agent in Southeast Asia, and because some progressive Buddhist thinkers might argue that Buddhism itself, with its decentred view of the self, its concepts of agency and causality, and its deconstructionist methodology, is in fact and has always been "postmodern." In fact Sulak's thought perhaps suggests, although he does not explicitly make the suggestion, that this whole typically Western idea of the periodisation of history should itself be abandoned as it serves very little purpose except to keep academics employed.

The essence of Sulak's thinking then lies firstly in its diagnosis of the crisis of Asian modernity, and of its latest expression, "development," and of the spiritual and epistemological roots of this in the erosion of traditional (read Buddhist) values and the wholesale and uncritical adoption of not only Western science, but more significantly its positivist and secular philosophical assumptions. Secondly, it lies in his creation of numerous small social movements as the vehicles for his ideas, a very important step since it can certainly be argued that it is in such movements that practical rather than purely theoretical knowledge is generated and where the viability of alternatives can be tested without inflicting them on the whole of society. In his thought the boundaries between critique, methodology and practice are dissolved, something that both demonstrates the old Marxian idea of praxis (the unity of theory and practice), and aligns him with the work of more self-consciously postcolonial social theorists such as the Maori scholar Linda Tuhiwai Smith in her attempts to "decolonize methodology" (Smith 1999). Thirdly of course it resides in his attempt to articulate a Buddhist vision of society and to trace some at least of the implications of such a vision for social arrangements. Interestingly while in the social sciences generally the "cultural turn" has taken scholars away from society towards culture, in his later work Sulak has been moving from a culturalist approach to one far more concerned with the actual social implications of his Buddhist alternative position.

Sulak's thought then places him squarely within what is by some now being called "the politics of meaning"—a view of social, political and economic processes which places humane values first, stresses the spiritual sources of meaning, is highly critical of the materialism and consumerism resulting from conventional development models and sees the role of indigenous intellectuals as giving voice to such values rather than serving the status quo or the distorting hegemony of the mainstream (i.e. effectively Western) social sciences. As Thongchai Winichakuk points out that "Thai people, scholars or not, have always been warned not to *tamkon farang* ("tag along behind the Westerners"). For them Thainess, Thailand, Thai people, Thai studies, or whatever Thai is something the *farang* can approach but never reach with the utmost intimacy that Thai people can" (Thongchai 1997: 7). Sulak clearly fits within this category as regards his views on foreign scholar's attempts to understand Thailand, while simultaneously both avoiding any kind of narrow nationalism and promoting the universality of his vision of Buddhism ("Buddhism with a small 'b'" Sulak 1992: 62ff). Although in his English language publications he rarely cites any of his contemporary Thai "Buddhist radicals" (to use Thongchai's term) who also see Thai identity in crisis because of the inroads of Western culture (for example the authors collected in Sa-nga 1981 or Pracha 1983) he does have much in common with an important stream of indigenous Thai thought, although by no means a universally shared one amongst either Thai intellectuals whether on the Right or on the secular Left, or by all members of the Sangha, some of whom believe that Buddhism is well equipped with the means to manage Western science and need not succumb to its philosophical onslaughts. Rather he tends to refer to an older generation of critics of Thai Buddhism—Puey Ungphakorn in particular who Sulak clearly sees as some kind of mentor, and Buddhadasa Bhikku (and which also includes figures such as the Venerable Phoothirak and Boonsanong Punyothayana, many of whom, like Sulak, were of Sino-Thai origin, an interesting social location for some of the most prominent critics of Thai culture and religion). It is indeed because of his "progressive nationalism'' (Buruma 1991: 39) that Sulak rejects the name "Thailand", a hybrid Anglicised word, in favour of Siam, since the stripping of the name of a nation and its replacement with a name invented by a group of militarists signals for him the very kind of psychic violation that his work is designed to oppose and symbolised by the peasant garb and cloth shoulder-bag that have for some years been his trademark mode of dress.

Finally, at the core of Sulak's thought lies a paradox, one that perhaps helps to explain some of the features of his ideas and their form of expression. His work contains the potentiality of a radical critique of the philosophical presuppositions of Western epistemology and the science and social sciences that have emerged from it at least as the mainstream of the Western tradition. But at the heart of Buddhism is the idea that reality cannot be grasped with concepts but must be experienced and can be experienced by the diligent following of the appropriate spiritual methodology. The slippery interface in his work between Buddhism and "development" (a notion embodying all the Western worship of science, technology, progress and materialism) results in part at least from the attempt to grasp the conceptual with the non-conceptual and vice versa. While there may be ways to seek for a direction beyond this dilemma, Sulak's work wittingly and in some cases unwittingly poses the problem in its starkest form and formulates some key issues which both the social sciences and development studies will have to face if they are to find a route out of their current methodological and moral impasse.

Part Four

Religion and Popular Culture

11

Religion, Popular Culture and Cultural Communication in Contemporary Asia

In our rapidly globalising world problems of identity have once again come to the forefront of discussions in the social sciences. When it was possible to assume fairly stable nation-states, each one possessing its own language and culture (or plurality of cultures in multi-ethnic states), identity was tied largely to those nation-states or to some sub-division of them—an ethnic or religious minority in most cases. Insofar as this stability of identity has ever actually existed (for it has been challenged repeatedly by colonial expansion and decolonisation, by migrations of peoples and by patterns of international contact and integration brought about by trade), it is now fundamentally challenged by globalisation.

Globalisation is not only an economic process—the increasing integration of national economies into a world system—but also a cultural and sociological one. Systemic integration of economies for example (especially where those economies are now mainly capitalist ones) promotes consumerism, often of identical or very similar products across national borders, it strongly encourages the interpenetration of entertainment cultures (musics and film being the most prominent examples), promotes travel, often with the intention of engaging in internationalised forms of consumption (shopping, food and entertainment in particular) and of cultural consumption (of art, museums, architecture and heritage sites for instance) and particularly through the power of globalised media (operating through satellite broadcasting, cable and the internet) increasingly erodes the boundaries between discrete cultures, whether those cultures be national or ethnic ones. Under these conditions, the question of identity becomes problematic because the traditional boundaries of identity have become weaker and fuzzy, especially in the realm of culture. While I may have a passport issued by one particular state and as such have a specific "political" identity, my cultural identity is increasingly likely to be made up of elements from many cultures. I may well in a single day have a European breakfast, a Chinese lunch and a Thai dinner, listen to J-pop from Japan, Canto-pop from Hong Kong, and Taiwanese contemporary music on the radio while eating the first, hear jazz CDs being played as background music in my local coffee house and round up the evening with a Korean movie with Japanese subtitles borrowed from my local suburban Tokyo video rental shop. Such complex patterns of cultural borrowing are now commonplace, especially at the level of popular culture. Japanese *manga* (comics) can now be bought virtually anywhere in Thailand in translated editions and Japanese TV animations have penetrated markets from Malaysia eastwards, Taiwanese pop music is very popular in Singapore and Hong Kong, Shanghai discos play Cantonese music from Hong Kong and Singaporean ones play local, Taiwanese, Hong Kong, Western and Japanese music, and so on in endless combinations. This is now well known and has attracted a substantial amount of attention and literature. But the question here is, what does this increasing sharing of popular culture do to identity, especially for youth who are growing up in this environment of hybridity and cultural mixing? Does it futher fragment identities already separated by history, ethnicity and religions, or does it in fact provide the vehicle through which a new form of pan-Asian identity might be coming into being?

There have been of course attempts to define an Asian identity, a search perhaps made more urgent by the emergence of the European Union as a new form of political/economic/cultural entity without exact precedent in world civilisational history. Does, or could, something similar exist in East Asia or Southeast Asia? A number of prominent figures have indeed argued for there being an Asian identity, with Lee Kuan Yew, the former Prime Minister of Singapore for instance promoting a version based on an attempt to define common cultural values, in Singapore termed "Asian values," largely based on a modern interpretation of Confucianism, an idea that has been taken up by other commentators (e.g. Sheridan 1999). Such ideas have also shown up in surprisingly different practical contexts too, in advertising for example where attempts to find the "Asian face" or common symbolic codes that make advertising across national boundaries possible have been made, or perhaps more seriously, in the field of human rights, where scholars have again searched for cultural values that make it possible to define such rights in Asian contexts without doing violence to those cultures and their specific religious and cultural traditions (Bauer and Bell 1999). All of these moves indeed fall into the bigger context of what has become known as the "culture and development" approach to social transformation, in which it is recognised that a purely economistic analysis of human development problems (including pressing issues of poverty, social justice, gender relations and environment) is inadequate, and a cultural understanding of such processes is in fact necessary (Dove 1988; Schech and Haggis 2000).

There are in fact two questions here—the first being of the actual levels of contact and integration between contemporary Asian cultures, and especially popular cultures, and the second being the issue of whether, through such culture contact, a common identity could in fact be forged, even if it does not yet exist. Here we have to recognise that there are different strata of comparison. Lee Kuan Yew for example sees a common identity residing in what he and his followers called "Asian values"—a set of common assumptions about society and the world and a set of ethics deriving from these relating to such everyday issues as hard work, thrift, honesty, the stability of the family, and so forth that are actually an updated version of Confucianism shorn of some of its worst sexist and feudal dimensions, and believed, by its supporters, to be common to all East Asian societies, especially those of the so-called "Kanji zone" where the written languages are composed of (or largely of) Chinese characters. This definition of Asian values (on which Singapore at one time and briefly attempted to create a "national ideology"—see Clammer 1993a) would of course exclude South Asia, much of Southeast Asia and many minority peoples dwelling in the Kanji zone, even if it could be established that most East Asians do in fact subscribe to these values. Other attempts at various times have been made on the basis of religion (a "Buddhist zone" as distinct from the Islamic or Christian zones of much of Southeast Asia) or of "race" and the supposed genetic unity of the majority of the East Asian peoples. There are problems obviously with either of these two approaches, and a more promising perspective is through the medium of culture, not the traditional "high cultures" of the various countries involved which clearly differ substantially despite their commonalities, but the emerging hybrid popular cultures of the urban young.

Speaking of Southeast Asia, the Malaysian journalist and cultural commentator Karim Raslan, argues that there is indeed a common identity in that part of Asia, shaped by the overlapping histories of what are now the separate nation-states of the region, but which shared the experience of colonialism, decolonisation and the increasing penetration of modern globalised forms of capitalism, and which is expressed today in the common themes of its art (Karim 2002) as well as in membership of ASEAN at the political level. The situation in Northeast Asia is slightly different as there is no common political community yet in existence comparable even to ASEAN, and certainly not to the EU which with a couple of exceptions shares a common currency and borderless travel within the community. Old historical tensions and in particular those between Japan and China and Japan and Korea are not fully resolved; and very different political systems still exist leading in turn to rather different relationships to international economic forces. I think then that we can safely argue that while there is certainly as yet no common culture or identity in Northeast Asia, globalisation or regionalisation has brought with it forms of popular culture and consumer culture that are increasingly in conversation with each other and which are linked more and more by flows of influence, contacts between artists, writers, musicians and other generators of popular culture (understood here as forms of culture consumed, utilised and reproduced on an everyday basis by average people in terms of socio-economic status and education and which form their points of reference in conversation, socialisation and fashion), tourism and travel and cultural influence, borrowing and copying. All these processes are framed by new forms of global capitalism that are as much concerned with the dissemination of culture and cultural products in many media (film, television, CDs, videos, Internet, DVDs, music, fashion, foods, dance, club cultures, and complex combinations of these) as they are with "things" or services in a more traditional sense, a phenomenon that the British sociologists John Urry and Scott Lash have called "the economy of signs and space" (Lash and Urry 1991). So now we must turn to an examination of the actual processes of these flows and their effects on identity amongst those (mostly the relatively young) who habitually consume these cultural artefacts.

Cultural Flows and Shared Cultures in East Asia

It used to be assumed by many commentators on cultural globalisation that flows of influence were essentially from the West to the East. If this was ever true, and to some extent it was during the period of high colonialism, it is certainly no longer so, and some would argue that the flow has been in fact reversed. The films of the so-called Fifth Generation of Chinese movie directors (such as Zhang Yimou and Chen Kaige) frequently win the accolades at major international film festivals, Japanese *anime* or full length animated movies (especially those of Miyazaki Hayao) are now highly popular in the West, Japanese comics have spread worldwide, and so have Hong Kong and some Taiwanese films and a great deal of their popular music. Similar statements can be made for food cultures with sushi, Korean foods and of course Chinese cuisine having penetrated the eating habits of people just about everywhere, fashion, and, as we have seen, religion, with Japanese "New Religions" having gone international as have some Chinese-origin religious movements. Asian architects now build internationally and a substantial number of Asian actors/actresses and of course musicians have made themselves international reputations.

With cultural movements in both directions there are resistances, accommodations, assimilation and transformation and synthesis. The Japanese musician Kaneko Aska for example lives in Hawai'i, records in Japan and blends Indian, Arab and Chinese motifs into her compositions and performances, as does the more famous composer Ryuchi Sakamoto in his internationally obtainable CDs. But what is even more interesting for our purposes is not the question of East-West flows or vice versa, but the intra-Asian flows that are now a prominent part of the East Asian cultural environment. In fact we have already indicated many of these—the spread of Japanese popular music, comics and *anime* to much of the region, the cultural borrowing and adaptation that characterises the fashion industry, shared food cultures, film and television content, regional tourism, educational contacts, religion and the increased learning of each other's language, which leads not only to cultural sharing, but to active contacts and often residence. The very large numbers of Chinese students studying in Japanese universities and language schools has its counterparts in the number of young Koreans and Taiwanese who do the same, the substantial number of Japanese studying in Chinese universities and the popularity of both Chinese and Korean as optional languages studied in Japanese colleges.

Japan has been especially well studied in this regard and a large literature now exists documenting the spread of Japanese mass culture to other parts of Asia (for example Ching 1996, Wee 1997, Ben-Ari and Clammer 2000). Some aspects of Chinese culture, especially contemporary films have been similarly documented (e.g. Chow 1995) and the widespread penetration of Hong Kong popular culture, especially film and music has also been examined, including the ways in which it impacts Japan, seen by many as the single biggest cultural exporter (for example Edagawa 1997). With the appearance of videos and DVD, the internet, satellite TV broadcasting, increasing regional volumes of travel and the lowering of barriers to the import of culture (in Korea for example where an increasing range of Japanese cultural products are now beginning to appear) intra-regional cultural borrowing has become the norm. And of course there is one factor that encompasses all these specific examples—that the process is driven essentially by the rise of Asian capitalisms which not only promotes the consumption of culture as one of the main devices for its own expansion, but also dissolves the boundaries between East and West or between individual Asian societies, not to the extent of complete homogenetity, but certainly to an increasing degree. Globalisation and regionalisation are framed by economic forces and we must be aware of this in any discussion of culture, including its religious aspects.

So if we know what is happening, what are its effects? These are less clear, but very important. Does cultural sharing erode cultures in a negative way and simply replace them with a common consumer culture, or is the process in fact more complex and involves resistances, negotiations, hybrid forms, adaptations and even rejection? I think that we can assume the latter, and if so, we need to pursue two lines of thought—the first being to map some of the effects of cultural sharing in East Asia, and the other is to think ahead. If such sharing is occurring, as I think that we can agree that it is, can we direct it and channel it in the most socially positive directions? This is a major challenge, but hopefully we can move towards some useful ideas on this subject.

How then does cultural sharing effect identity? In brief at a number of levels and through a variety of mechanisms. It can of course operate at the macro-level, at the level of economic practices and patterns and of political processes for example. The shift of an economy from the production of things to the production of images brings with it a corresponding shift in behaviour. Shopping may replace subsistence activities, bought entertainment (at a cinema, theatre, dance hall, club) may supplant family or individually produced forms of diversion, and more and more of the work force are likely to be found in the provision of services or the production of cultural products than in traditional areas such as heavy industry, and with this comes a change in gender relations and female participation in the workforce, which in turn effects family structures and relationships. At the political level governments may resist, encourage or welcome certain kinds of foreign or domestic cultural products. Korea has until recently excluded most forms of Japanese popular culture, which Hong Kong has not. Singapore closely monitors and indeed censors foreign cultural imports, not only for their moral and political content, but also in terms of language with Mandarin being favoured over Chinese regional languages in the case of imports of film, music, videos and operas from the Chinese speaking world, in line with its "Speak Mandarin" campaign aimed not only at creating more linguistic unity amongst its majority ethnic group, but also because Mandarin is highly functional in doing business with the People's Republic of China. Economics and politics thus shape and are shaped by culture.

But there are other levels too, and perhaps the most important is that culture shapes subjectivities. One's world view, cosmology, sense of reality and sense of self are to a great extent culturally shaped. This being so, what kinds of cultural products one consumes becomes extremely significant. The British sociologist Anthony Giddens for example has argued that it is exactly these kinds of cultural shifts, fuelled and directed by new forms of flexible capitalism, that have brought about the most significant changes in self-identity in the modern world, and that these shifts in turn have other consequences, such as that people increasingly migrate from what he calls "emancipatory politics" concerned with freedom and a struggle for rights, to "lifestyle politics" in which they are mostly concerned with individual, privatised matters, and not with the collective interests of the wider society (Giddens 1991). Cultural consumption then is not just a private matter—it has social consequences. And many of these are potentially negative—withdrawal into private worlds or fixation on consuming for example—if the culture is not both critical and reflexive about its own trends and characteristics and concerned with public goods as much as private ones. For popular culture to be community-enhancing it clearly needs to contain appropriate values for that goal, and to be critical of social practices that work against humanisation, empowerment and increasing levels of social equality and observation of basic human rights. A potential danger of any social policy regarding culture is of course the question of "who decides?" and many governments have not always been very successful in defining cultural policies that promote positive social transformation rather than conservatism. The real actors here are not governments in fact but the two groups of the producers and the consumers of popular culture: the artists and their audiences. Although art in its broadest sense (including all serious cultural production) is often seen as an individualistic activity, in fact it arises from within communities of meaning and in turn helps to create them (something which sociologists of the arts have long known (for example Duvignaud 1967/1972).

The responsibility for the appearance of the kind of culture that helps to shape positive identities (in ethical, aesthetic, creative and socially responsible forms) lies then on the one hand with those who produce culture—not only composers and designers, musicians etc., but also the corporate forces and media enterprises that create artistes, manufacture and market their productions and so determine to a great extent how taste is shaped, and on the other with the consumer of culture. Individual decisions about what to consume have enormous cumulative impact and the passive consumer is doing a disservice to society by failing to exercise a critical function in relation to what she or he buys, reads, watches, or listens to. Since of course producers have to adjust their production to the demands of consumers, those consumers are not powerless but exercise a major role in determining the direction of a society's cultural identity, and with it their own. The challenge here is to determine how a (relatively) common cultural identity can be formed in East Asia, and secondly, how once this has been done, how will it articulate with the political and economic spheres and influence them in positive directions?

Many scholars in the region see the upsurge of interest in flows of popular culture in the region as a result of what the Japanese sociologist Koichi Iwabuchi calls "Japan's return to Asia"—the fact that much of contemporary Japanese culture is concerned with asserting its Asianness after decades of seeing the rest of Asia as culturally distant or inferior and Europe or North America as being the significant cultural Others, and that objectively it is Japanese popular culture that has had the biggest impact on the rest of East Asia. At the same time, as Japan has been reasserting its Asianness, other Asian nations have become, largely as a result of their growing economies, confident, assertive, and keen to promote their own Asianness. As this has happened, cultural sharing within the region has increased and whereas in the past "Asia" was more of a geographical concept, it has now become a substantial cultural one, linked together not only by traditional values, but more dynamically by overlapping and mutually consumed popular cultures. Their rapidly developing economic power has given rise to what some call "vernacular modernity" or "indigenized modernity"—new ways of being in the world based on the confidence of being serious actors on the international stage economically and politically, and as being creators and exporters of culture, not just recipients. Under the regime of globalisation or transnationalism, East Asian societies are increasingly sharing qualities, products, tastes and styles produced amongst themselves, as well as consuming and also adapting and then sometimes re-exporting what were originally Western cultural artifacts (Tobin 1992).

This new cultural sharing is importantly different from older attempts to find cultural similarities between the East Asian societies. As Iwabuchi puts it, "Unlike conservative Asian values discourses, the emerging resonance felt among young people in East Asia is not based upon exclusive views of primordial cultural traditions, because popular culture unavoidably embodies heterogeneous origins and routes of cultural mixing. The image of Asian youth, at least in marketing terms, might be defined as one of consuming hybrid youth who have material power and passion for consuming fashionable cultural products and who do not care about the origin of these consumer items or media products. Nevertheless, preferred cultural products are not without East Asian flavor, as those are re-worked in Asian context by hybridizing various latest fads. Affluent Asian youth are keen to consume things which are inescapably global and East Asian at the same time" (Iwabuchi 2000: 2). And as he goes on to point out, that whereas in the past East Asian nations would have tended to face the West as assimilators of mainly American popular culture, now they are facing each other, leading to fascinating new patterns of absorption, modification, hybridisation and re-export.

But we also have to recognise that these apparent commonalities have not eroded objective economic differences or local nationalist discourses. There are certainly many in Japan for example, including the influential governor of Tokyo, Ishihara Shintaro, who sees Japan as embodying a new and modern Asian civilisation. Such views often continue to mask feelings of economic or cultural superiority, views which however may well be undermined by the populist nature of mass culture which because of its non-elitist nature is inherently democratic and much less ethnocentric than some versions of "high" or traditional culture. Nevertheless, the potential dangers of new forms of cultural imperialism emerging under the guise of commonalities needs to be recognised, precisely so it can be combatted. It must also be asked to what extent many areas of Asian popular culture really are indigenous. Although throughout the region TV content is now largely local, in the music industry styles of presentation, costume, the underlying technology and even the music itself frequently are based on Western models and little that is "authentically Asian" may appear. We have again to remind ourselves that much popular culture is only "popular" in the sense that it is mass culture: it is in fact a commercialised consumer culture, often very materialistic in its orientation, rather than an expression of genuine indigenous yearnings.

This situation is not unique to East Asia. Most analysts of popular culture are aware of its ambiguities, that it represents cooption as much as it does resistance, that it is as much tied to the advertising industries and their homogenising tendencies as it is to expression of individuality or freedom. This essential ambiguity and the unevenness of cultural flows we need to keep in mind when asking ourselves about the ways in which popular culture might be used to create commonalities beyond those currently experienced in the region today, and which might potentially become a socially transformative force.

Popular Culture and Social Transformation in East Asia

Let us then summarise the argument up to this point. The question of whether there is a common Asian identity has exercised many minds, and in the past such a search tended to be focused on attempts to identify common values, ethno-linguistic continuities, historical parallels or even mystical links embodied in religion or forms of "Asian spirituality." Such attempts, never very successful and sometimes the basis for colonial or pan-nationalistic endeavours, have been largely supplanted by a focus on the increasingly shared nature of popular cultures within East Asia, a sharing that erodes traditional boundaries and is tending to create a new configuration or what anthropologists used to call a "culture area" in East and Southeast Asia. That this is empirically so can be shown by many examples, but a deeper question is whether this sharing as yet embodies a new identity? At some levels it clearly does—to share culture is to share a common vocabulary of images, ideas, styles, tastes and to discover that subjectivities, previously separated by political and geographical boundaries, are now drawing closer together. But at the same time we must also recognise that most of this popular culture is commercially driven and may embody values that are not necessarily socially positive (depending of course on one's point of view) and that political and economic differences still remain as powerful forces that frame and limit the possibilities of the emergence of a common culture, even if this is desirable. Many would indeed argue that what makes East Asia such a vibrant region culturally are precisely the "creative differences" that it contains, and which need to be approached not with a desire to homogenise, but through dialogue, mutual learning and sharing of different points of view—a process that actually leads to much deeper levels of mutual appreciation and understanding than sameness. As the German Jewish philosopher Martin Buber and many who have followed him have argued, you discover yourself in the face of the other, not in the mirror that simply reflects your own image (e.g. Otnes 1997). The question then becomes that of how to build a common identity that respects historical, ecological and cultural differences while seeking a common unity of purpose beneath them, and then how to transfer such an identity from the realm of culture into the political, economic and social arenas where it can have transformative and humanising powers.

C.I. Itty, in a book devoted to the place of youth in Asia (Itty 1984) suggests that there are a number of ways in which the emerging generation can contribute to the humanisation and development of society, which he summarises as conscientisation (building awareness, especially of problems of significant social issues and creating public opinion); motivating people to organise themselves to address these pressing issues; acting as pressure groups to influence the centres of power to undertake structural changes; acting as watchdogs of society to alert people to emerging or existing social problems; initiators of community development projects; as advocates of social reforms; as serving the needy; and as promoters of cultural values and standards amongst their peers (Itty 1984, 26-7). He was correct I think, but in 1984 he and his fellow contributors were still talking primarily in the context of the creative participation of youth in national development. In an age of globalisation this is now only partly true, since the key becomes creative participation in international development as well, given the intimate interconnections between societies. The concept of citizenship has itself shifted, or should shift, from primarily identification with a single national entity, to a much wider global responsibility (ecological issues for example as well as cultural ones, now cross international boundaries). Many of the other questions that were being asked in the 1980s however still remain valid, in particular those of the political vision of younger Asians and what Koson Srisang in the same book calls the "ethical yearnings" of contemporary Asian youth (1984: 45). He is correct: cultural issues have to be constantly related to not only the economic forces that we have already discussed, but also to politics, and the key question then becomes, what kind of society do Asian youth want to build, and what are the mechanisms, including cultural ones, that would enable those goals to be reached? The issue in our immediate context is how popular culture, rather than becoming an individualised escape from social reality and without stifling its vitality and creativity, might become a vehicle for social transformation. Part of the answer lies in Koson's second point—that youth is a period of intense idealism, an idealism often smothered by the educational system, political pressures and cooption by the economic system and consumer society. There is in principle no contradiction between ethical values and popular culture—it can as much promote them as undermine them if its producers and consumers desire it to do so. Another part of the answer lies in education for creativity. Much of the educational system of East Asia, regardless of the individual society, tends to stress technical skills related in a direct and obvious way to the economy (it is noteworthy that in many universities in the region, business majors represent the majority of students). Cultural training, while theoretically valued by society is actually given a very secondary place, and anyone who has tried to make a career in music, painting, creative writing, theatre, dance or the other creative arts has probably experienced this (it again being technical and applied arts such as industrial design, fashion and interior design that lead to respectable careers). If, however, more younger people enter the creative arts and society actually supports such activities and their connection to the development process is made clearer, then culture moves back to the central place in a society's scale of values from which it has been displaced by economics. When people talk of social transformation or "development" they most often mean economic development. In fact no society, however affluent or equal (and the two rarely go together) is worth living in unless it is ecologically sustainable, has a high level of social justice and is culturally vibrant. Cultural creativity is not restricted to any one group, and youth are perhaps closer to the sources of creativity and imagination than any other age group, and so participation in a popular culture informed by values becomes a political and socially transformative act.

Identity itself is never a fixed "thing," but an on-going negotiation or conversation with the surrounding reality. Nevertheless the psychology of identity seems to require that we also seek boundaries—fairly stable categories within which a sense of self can be nurtured, particularly if "they can be seen as a point of contact rather than a point of separation" (IHJ 2001: 85). In attempting to find a new understanding of what they call "cultural globalisation," Joseph Chan and Eric Ma propose the concept of what they call "transculturation"—a process where by modernity itself is diffused internationally, and simultaneously "cultural boundaries are always in a state of flux, subject to forces within and without" (Chan and Ma 2002: 4) in which the diffusionist assumptions of early modernisation and Westernisation theories are replaced by a much more complex model of actual cultural encounters with all their ambiguities and fluidities. Here the operational categories become those of cultural appropriation and recreation, deterritorialisation, transborder imagination, hybridised modernity and new forms of self-identity, which may take the form of embracing and enjoying these new globalised possibilities, or make take the form of individual or collective retreat into a "cocoon" where anxiety about these forces can be kept a bay by creating a sense of security, or by various strategies of indigenisation, localism or autarky. One force that stands against the potential disintegration of identities in the face of globalisation is in fact the recognition of a common cultural goal. If we can agree that a certain level of common culture can be achieved, and that this is the basis for dialogue between existing nation-states and societies, then this in itself provides a "project" around which a new identity can be built. For most of us in fact have more than one "identity," just as we perform more than one role. It is perfectly possible to be a citizen of one particular country and simultaneously to be a global or regional one, constantly moving between these levels as the context demands. It is this flexibility and ability to synthesise levels that is the challenge. If this were simply a political project it would be difficult, but it is made easier for us by the fact that it is now largely a cultural one, and culture, while consumed locally, may be a product of much larger globalising forces. This cultural project is made easier too by the relative ease with which "transborder imaginations" can be constructed in contemporary East Asia (Ma 2001), and paradoxically by the very logic of international media capitalism. As Leo Ching phrases it "This sociological definition of culture (media, fashion, entertainment, etc.), precisely because of its filiation to technological production which in itself is never nation-specific, points not to the ownership of cultural production (as national culturalists would have imagined) but to its accessibility within the circuit of capitalist commodification and accumulation. In other words, unlike the indigenous culture that is invented within the symbolic boundary of the nation, technoculture is always already potentially transnational" (Ching 1996: 191).

Popular culture in contemporary East Asia must then be seen in the framework of and as an expression of globalisation, contextualised in ever shifting political and economic frameworks and technological innovation. Identity in this situation is fluid and negotiable. For example insofar as identity is tied to language, the multilingual nature of much Asian popular culture (Hong Kong youths listening to Japanese pop music, Japanese ones to Taiwanese and so on) that identity is changed by exposure to the cultures carried by the various languages used. Private identities intersect with public worlds through place and space (where am I located?), through networks (who am I connected to, where are they and what influences are reaching me via these networks?) and memory (my place in a continuity, real or imagined that links me to the past and to other members of a group with whom I identify and about which I construct narratives of belonging). Larger structural circumstances enfold particular local or individual identities (globalisation and its changing economic forces being a prime example). The challenge in the contemporary world becomes that of successfully negotiating these levels, of finding ways to mediate between the global and the local and shared cultural interests are undoubtedly one of the ways in which this may be done. "Cultural citizenship" as much as older style political citizenship then becomes a concept that we must work to develop—membership in a wider cultural sphere that transcends and in many ways makes irrelevant political identity and national boundaries (for a formal discussion of many of these issues see Preston 1997), but which provides a new basis for political and social action and involvement, and for new forms of identity, belonging and community, many of them through religion, itself a neglected aspect of popular culture.

The concepts of nation, community, and belonging then all have to be reconfigured in this globalised cultural context, and even the notion of culture itself has undergone radical revisions from a static and essentialist idea of fixed identity, to a dynamic and fluid one characterised by negotiation not ascription, and by fluidity and hybridity rather than fixed categories of meaning. We cannot escape history, but we can to some extent redefine where we want it, and the contemporary social and economic forces now shaping it, to take us. This is the emerging task of those who will inherit this future and whose cultural versatility and sharing of an increasingly common culture across the region creates an unprecedented opportunity to find dialogue in differences and indeed to dissolve those differences not into a single homogeneous sameness, but into a new form of culture that creates a common language amongst the separated political communities of the past. This is possible when there is genuine equality between the societies and economies of the region and when there is a vision of shared values, common goals, and mutually communicating imaginaries that seek to find common meanings in the future despite the separations of the past.

Bibliography

Abelmann, N. 1993. "Minjung Theory and Practice," pp. 139-165 in *Cultural Nationalism in East Asia*, ed. H. Befu. Berkeley: University of California Institute of East Asian Studies.

Ackerman, S.E. and Raymond L.M. Lee 1990. Heaven in Transition: Non-Muslim Religious Innovation and Ethnic Identity in Malaysia. Kuala Lumpur: Forum.

Akbar S. Ahmed and Hastings Donnan, eds. 1994. *Islam, Globalization and Postmodernity*. London and New York: Routledge.

Alatas, Syed Farid, ed. 2000. "Alternative Discourses in the Social Sciences in Asia," Special Number of the *Southeast Asian Journal of Social Science* 28(1).

Amado, Jorge. 1989. *Tent of Miracles*, Translated from Portuguese by Barbara Shelby. London: Collins Harvill.

Ames, R.T., W. Dissanayake and T.P. Kasulis, eds. 1994. *Self as Person in Asian Theory and Practice*, Albany: State University of New York Press.

Amstutz, G. 1997. *Interpreting Amida: History and Orientalism in the Study of Pure Land Buddhism*, Albany: State University of New York Press.

Anaclecti, O. 1996. "Research into Local Cultures: Implications for Participatory Development," pp. 69-72 in *Development and Social Diversity*, ed. D. Eade. Oxford: Oxfam.

Anderson, B. 1991. *Imagined Communities: Reflections on the Origins and Spread of Nationalism*. London:Verso.

Ang, I. 1992. "Dismantling 'Cultural Studies'," *Cultural Studies* 6(3): 311-21.

Ang, I. 1998. "Eurocentric Reluctance: Notes for a Cultural Studies of the New Europe," pp. 87-108 in *Trajectories: Inter-Asia Cultural Studies*, ed. K.H. Chen. London: Routledge.

Appadurai, A. 1996. *Modernity at Large: Cultural Dimensions of Globalization*, Minneapolis: University of Minnesota Press.

Arndt, H.W. and H. Hill, eds. 1999. *Southeast Asia's Economic Crisis: Origins, Lessons and the Way Forward*. Singapore: Institute of Southeast Asian Studies.

Asad, T. 1996. "Comments on Conversion," pp. 263-273 in *Conversion to Modernities: The Globalization of Christianity*, ed. Peter van der Veer. New York and London: Routledge.

Augé, M. 1999. *An Anthropology for Contemporaneous Worlds*. Stanford: Stanford University Press.

Bachnik, J.M. and C.J. Quinn, eds. 1994. *Situated Meaning: Inside and Outside in Japanese Self, Society and Language*. Princeton: Princeton University Press.

Baker, H.D.R. 1979. *Chinese Family and Kinship*. London: Macmillan.

Balagangadhara, S.N. 1994. *The Heathen in His Blindness: Asia, the West and the Dynamics of Religion*. Leiden: E.J. Brill.

Banerji, D., ed. 1985. *Marxian Theory and the Third World*. New Delhi and Beverley Hills: Sage.

Barglow, R. 1994. *The Crisis of the Self in the Age of Information*. London: Routledge.

Barthes, R. 1970. *L'empire des Signes*. Paris: Flammarion.

Batchelor, S. 1998. "The Other Enlightenment Project: Buddhism, Agnosticism and Postmodernity," pp. 113-127 in *Faith and Praxis in a Postmodern Age*, ed. U. King. London: Cassell.

Baudrillard, J. 1983. *In the Shadow of the Silent Majorities, Or, The End of the Social*. New York: Semiotext (E).

Baudrillard, J. 1988. *America*. London: Verso.

Bauer, J.R. and D.A. Bell, eds. 1999. *The East Asian Challenge for Human Rights*. Cambridge: Cambridge University Press.

Bauman, Z. 1989. *Modernity and the Holocaust*. Cambridge: Polity Press.

Bauman, Z. 1995. *Life in Fragments: Essays in Postmodern Morality*. Oxford: Blackwell.

Bauman, Z. 2000. *Liquid Modernity*. Cambridge: Polity Press.

Befu, H. 1998. *Globalization of Japan: Its Implications for the Globalization Model*. Kyoto: International Research Center for Japanese Studies.

Behdad, A. 1994. *Belated Travels: Orientalism in the Age of Colonial Dissolution*. Cork: Cork University Press.

Bello, W., S. Cunningham and Li Kheng Poh. 1998. *A Siamese Tragedy: Development and Disintegration in Modern Thailand*. London: Zed Books, Oakland, CA: Food First and Bangkok: White Lotus.

Ben-Ari, E. and J. Clammer, eds. 2000. *Japan in Singapore: Cultural Occurances and Cultural Flows*. London: Curzon Press.

Benjamin, G. 1976. "The cultural logic of Singapore's 'multiracialism'," pp. 115-133 in *Singapore: Society in Transition*, ed. R. Hassan. Kuala Lumpur: Oxford University Press.

Berger, P. 1979. *Facing Up to Modernity*. Harmondsworth: Penguin Books.

Berman, M. 1990. *Coming to Our Senses: Body and Spirit in the hidden History of the West*. New York: Bantem.

Berry, C. 1996. "Sexual DisOrientations: homosexual rights, East Asian films and postmodern postnationalism," pp. 157-182 in *In Pursuit of Contemporary East Asian Culture*, eds. Xiaobing Tang and S. Snyder. Boulder: Westview Press.

Berry, Philippa and Andrew Wernick, eds. 1992. *Shadow of Spirit: Postmodernism and Religion*. London and New York: Routledge.

Beyer, Peter. 1997. *Religion and Globalization*. London and Thousand Oaks: Sage.

Bhabha, H. 1994. *The Location of Culture*. London: Routledge.

Bocking, B. 1994. "Of Priests, Protests and Protestant Buddhists: The Case of Soka Gakkai International," pp. 117-132 in *Japanese New Religions in the West*, eds. Clarke, P.B. and J. Somers. Folkestone: Japan Library.

Breen, J. 1996. "Accommodating the Alien: Okuni Takamasa and the Religion of the Lord of Heaven," pp. 179-197 in *Religion in Japan*, eds. P.F. Kornicki and I.J. McMullin. Cambridge: Cambridge University Press.

Broadbent, J. 1998. *Environmental Politics in Japn: Networks of Power and Project*. Cambridge: Cambridge University Press.

Brown, D. 1993. "The Corporatist Management of Ethnicity in Contemporary Singapore," pp. 16-33 in *Singapore Changes Guard: Social, Political and Economic Changes in the 1990s*, ed. G. Rodan. Melbourne: Longman Cheshire; New York: St. Martin's Press.

Bruun, Ole and Arne Kalland, eds. 1995. *Asian Perceptions of Nature*. Richmond: Curzon Press.

Buruma, I. 1991. *God's Dust: An Asian Journey*. London: Vintage.

Butr-Indr, S. 1979. *The Social Philosophy of Buddhism*. Bangkok: Mahamakut Buddhist University Press.

Callicott, J. Baird and Roger T. Ames, eds. 1989. *Nature in Asian Traditions of Thought: Essays in Environmental Philosophy*. New York: State University of New York Press.

Camilleri, Joseph A. and Chandra Muzaffar, eds. 1998. *Globalisation: The Perspectives and Experiences of the Religious Traditions of Asia Pacific*. Petaling Jaya: International Movement for a Just World.

Capra, F. 1983. *The Turning Point: Science, Society and the Rising Culture*. London: Flamingo.

Capra, F. 1988. *The Tao of Physics: An Exploration of the Parallels between Modern Physics and Eastern Mysticism*. London: Flamingo.

Carrier, J., ed. 1995. *Occidentalism: Images of the West*. Oxford: Clarendon Press.

Chakrabarty, D. 1992. "Postcoloniality and the Artifice of History: Who Speaks for the Indian Past?" *Representations* (Winter) 37.

Chan, H.C. 1975. "Politics in an Administrative State: Where has the Politics Gone?" pp. 1-17 in *Trends in Singapore*, ed. Seah Chee Meow. Singapore: Singapore University Press for the Institute of Southeast Asian Studies.

Chan, J.M. and E. Ma. 2002. "Transculturating Modernity: A Reinterpretation of Cultural Globalization," pp. 3-18 in *In Search of Boundaries: Communication, Nation-States and Cultural Identities*, eds. J.M. Chan and B.T. McIntyre. Westport CT and London: Ablex.

Chan, S.Y. 1988. *A Study of Nichiren Shoshu in Singapore. Unpublished Academic Exercise*. Department of Sociology, National University of Singapore.

Chaudhuri, K.N. 1990. *Asia Before Europe*. Cambridge: Cambridge University Press.

Cheater, A.P. 1989. *Social Anthropology: An Alternative Introduction*. London: Unwin Hyman.

Chee, H.L. and C.K. Chan, eds. 1984. *Designer Genes*. Petaling Jaya: Insan.

Chen Kuan-Hsing. 1998. "Introduction: The Decolonization Question," pp. 1-53 in *Trajectories: Inter-Asia Cultural Studies*, ed. K.H. Chen. London: Routledge.

Chen, K.H., ed. 1998. *Trajectories: Inter-Asia Cultural Studies*. London: Routledge.

Chew, E.C.T. and E. Lee, eds. 1991. *A History of Singapore*. Singapore: Oxford University Press.

Chiang, C. 1994. "Female migrants in Singapore: Towards a Strategy of Pragmatism and Coping," pp. 238-263 in *Women and Chinese Patriarchy: Submission, Servitude and Escape*, eds. M. Jaschok and S. Miers. Hong Kong University Press and London: Zed Books.

Ching, L. 1994. "Imaginings in the Empire of the Sun: Japanese Mass Culture in Asia," *Boundary* 2(21): 198-219.

Ching, L. 1996. "Imaginings in the Empires of the Sun: Japanese Mass Culture in Asia," pp. 169-194 in *Contemporary Japan and Popular Culture*, ed. J.W. Treat. Richmond: Curzon Press.

Chng, N., ed. 1977. *Questioning Development in S.E. Asia*. Singapore: Select Books.

Chow, R. 1995. *Primitive Passions: Visuality, Sexuality, Ethnography and Contemporary Chinese Cinema*. New York Columbia University Press.

Chow, R. 1998. *Ethics After Idealism: Theory-Culture-Ethnicity-Reading*. Bloomington: Indiana University Press.

Chun, A. 1996. "Discourses of Identity in the Changing Spaces of Public Culture in Taiwan, Hong Kong and Singapore," *Theory, Culture and Society* 13(1).

Clammer, John. 1975a. "Colonialism and the perception of tradition in Fiji," pp. 199-222 in *Anthropology and the Colonial Encounter*, ed. T. Asad. New York: Humanities Press.

Clammer, John. 1975b. "Overseas-Chinese Assimilation and Resinification: A Malaysian Case Study," *Southeast Asian Journal of Social Science* 3(2).

Clammer, John, ed. 1983. *Studies in Chinese Folk Religion in Singapore and Malaysia*. Singapore: Contributions to Southeast Asian Ethnography 2.

Clammer, John. 1984. "Secularization and Religious Change in Contemporary Asia," *Southeast Asian Journal of Social Science* 12(1): 50-58.

Clammer, John. 1985. *Anthropology and Political Economy: Theoretical and Asian Studies*. London: Macmillan.

Clammer, John. 1988. "Singapore's Buddhists Chant a Modern Mantra," *Far Eastern Economic Review* 29 (December): 26-28.

Clammer, John. 1991. *The Sociology of Singapore Religion*. Singapore: Chopmen Publishers.

Clammer, John. 1993a. "Deconstructing Values: The Establishment of a National Ideology and its Implications for Singapore's Political Future," pp. 34-51 in *Singapore Changes Guard: Social, Political and Economic Directions in the 1990s*, ed. G. Rodan. Melbourne: Longman Cheshire and New York: St. Martin's Press.

Clammer, John. 1993b. "Le mythe de la race et de la Chine ancienne parrni les Chinois d'outre mer: memoire, historic, ethnicite," *STRATES* 5-7. Paris: CNRS.

Clammer, John. 1995. *Difference and Modernity: Social Theory and Contemporary Japanese Society*. London and New York: Kegan Paul International.

Clammer, John. 1997a. "Sustaining Otherness: Self, Nature and Ancestralism Amongst Japanese Christians," *Japan Forum* 9(2): 177-194.

Clammer, John. 1997b. *Contemporary Urban Japan: A Sociology of Consumption*. Oxford: Blackwell.

Clammer, John. 2000a. "In, But not of, the World? Japan, Globalization and the 'End of History'," pp. 147-167 in *Demystifying Globalization*, eds. Colin Hay and David Marsh. London: Macmillan.

Clammer, John. 2000b. "The Global and the Local: Gender, Class and the Internationalisation of Consumption in a Tokyo Neighbourhood," pp. 249-283 in *Consumption and Material Culture in Contemporary Japan*, eds. M. Ashkenazi and J. Clammer. London: Kegan Paul International.

Clammer, John. 2000c. "The Happiness-Making Machine: Soka Gakkai and the Japanese Cultural Presence in Singapore," pp. 175-193 in *Japan in Singapore: Cultural Occurances and Cultural Flows*, eds. E. Ben-Ari and J. Clammer. Richmond: Curzon Press.

Clammer, John. 2000d. "Cultural Studies/Asian Studies: Alternatives, Intersections and Contradictions in Asian Social Science," *Southeast Asian Journal of Social Science* 28(1): 47-65.

Clammer, John. 2000e. "Received Dreams: Consumer Capitalism, Social Process and the Management of the Emotions in Contemporary Japan," pp. 203-223 in *Globalization and Social Change in Contemporary Japan*, eds. J.S. Eades, T. Gill and H. Befu. Melbourne: Trans Pacific Press.

Clammer, John. 2001a. "The Dilemmas of the Oversocialized Intellectuals: The Universities and the Political and Institutional Dynamics of Knowledge in Postcolonial Singapore," *Inter-Asia Cultural Studies* 2(2).

Clammer, John. 2001b. "The Categories of Knowledge in the Annee Sociologique," *Etudes Durkheimiennes* 6.

Clammer, John. 2001c. *Japan and its Others: Globalization, Difference and the Critique of Modernity*. Melbourne: Trans Pacific Press.

Clammer, John. 2002. "Beyond the Cognitive Paradigm: Majority Knowledges and Local Discourses in a Non-Western Donor Society," pp. 43-63 in *Participating in Development: Approaches to Indigenous Knowledge*, eds. P. Sillitoe, A. Bicker and J. Pottier. London: Routledge.

Clammer, John. 2005. "Beyond Power: Alternative Conceptions of Being and the (Asian) Reconstitution of Social Theory," *Asian Journal of Social Science* 33(1): 62-76.

Clarke, P.B. 1994. "Japanese 'Old,' 'New' and 'New New' Religious Movements in Brazil," pp. 150-161 in *Japanese New Religions in the West*, eds. Clarke, P.B. and J. Somers. Folkestone: Japan Library.

Clarke, P.B. and J. Somers, eds. 1994. *Japanese New Religions in the West*. Folkestone: Japan Library.

Clecak, P. 1983. *America's Quest for the Ideal Self.* New York: Oxford University Press.

Clifford, J. and G. Marcus, eds. 1996. *Writing Culture*. Berkeley: University of California Press.

Cohen, A.P. 1994. *Self-Consciousness: An Alternative Anthropology of Identity*. London: Routledge.

Croll, E. 1995. *Changing Identities of Chinese Women*. Hong Kong: Hong Kong University Press and London: Zed Press.

Dalai Lama (Tenzin Gyatso). 1996. *Beyond Dogma: The Challenge of the Modern World*. New Delhi: Rupa.

Dale, P. 1995. *The Myth of Japanese—Uniqueness*. London: Routledge.

Dallmayr, Fred. 2002. *Dialogue Among Civilizations: Some Exemplary Voices*. New York and Basingstoke: Palgrave Macmillan.

Davis, W. 1992. *Dojo: Magic and Exorcism in Modern Japan*. Stanford: Stanford University Press.

Davis, W. 1998. "Religion and National Identity in Modern and Postmodern Japan," pp. 169-185 in *Religion, Modernity and Postmodernity*, ed. P. Heelas. Oxford: Blackwell.

De Bary T. and Tu Weiming, eds. 1998. *Confucianism and Human Rights*. New York: Columbia University Press.

Deguchi, A. 1999. *Tanjyou no jeneorojii* [Genealogy of Birth]. Tokyo: Sekaisho Seminar.

Derrett, E. 1987. "Signs along a Better Way: The Methods of Evangelization of a Japanese New Religion in Brazil and Thailand," pp. 95-112 in *The New Evangelists: Recruitment, Methods and Aims of New Religious Movements*, ed. P. Clarke. London: Ethnographica.

Dirlik, A. 1996. "Looking Backward in the Age of Global Capital: Thoughts on History in Third World Cultural Criticism," pp. 183-215 in *In Pursuit of Contemporary East Asian Culture*, eds. Xiaobing Tang and S. Snyder. Boulder: Westview Press.

Dirlik, Arif and Xudong Zhang, eds. 2000. *Postmodernism and China*. Durham NC. and London: Duke University Press.

Doi, Takeo 1973. *The Anatomy of Dependence*. Tokyo: Kodansha International.

Dove, M.R., ed. 1988. *The Real and Imagined Role of Culture in Development*. Honolulu: University of Hawaii Press.

Dumont, L. 1980. *Homo Hierarchicus: The Caste System and its Implications*. Chicago: University of Chicago Press.

Dumont, L. 1985. "A Modified View of Our Origins: the Christian Beginnings of Modern Individualism," pp. 93-122 in *The Category of the Person*, ed. M. Carrithers, S. Collins and S. Lukes. Cambridge: Cambridge University Press.

Dumont, L. 1986. *Essays in Individualism: Modern Ideology in Anthropological Perspective*. Chicago: University of Chicago Press.

Dumoulin, H. 1994. *Understanding Buddhism: Key Themes*. New York and Tokyo: Weatherhill.

Dussel, Enrique. 1996. *The Underside of Modernity*. Atlantic Heights NJ: Humanities Press.

Duvignaud, J. 1967. *Sociologie de l'Art. Paris:* Presses Universitaires de France. English edition translated by Timothy Wilson The Sociology of Art, London: Paladin, 1972.

Eades, J.S., T. Gill and H. Befu, eds. 2000. *Globalization and Social Change in Contemporary Japan.* Melbourne: Trans Pacific Press.

Easthope, A. 1992. *From Literary to Cultural Studies*. London: Routledge.

Edagawa, K. 1997. "Honkon bunka wa Tokyo no atama wo tobikoeta" [Hong Kong popular culture ahead of Tokyo], *Ushio* August: 132-139.

Esteva, G. 1992. "Development," in *The Development Dictionary: A Guide to Knowledge and Power*, ed. W. Sachs. London: Zed Books.

Esteva, G. and M.S. Prakash. 1998. *Grassroots Post-Modernism: Remaking the Soil of Cultures*. London: Zed Books.

Fanon, F. 1967. *Black Skin, White Masks*. New York: Grove Weidenfield.

Fanon, F. 1967. *The Wretched of the Earth*. Harmondsworth: Penguin.

Featherstone, S. Lash and R. Robertson. London: Sage.

Featherstone, M. and Lash, S. 1997. "Globalization, Modernity and the Spatialization of Social Theory: An Introduction," pp. 1-24 in *Global Modernities*, eds. M. Featherstone, Mike. 1997. *Undoing Culture: Globalization, Postmodernity and Identity*. London and Thousand Oaks: Sage.

Fei, H.T. 1981. *Toward a People's Anthropology*. Beijing: New World Press.

Fekete, John, ed. 1987. *Life After Postmodernism: Essays on Value and Culture*. New York: St. Martin's Press.

Fox, M. 1990. *Creation Spirituality: Liberating Gifts for the Peoples of the Earth*. San Francisco: HarperSanFrancisco.

Frank, A.G. 1998. *ReOrient: Global Economy in the Asian Age*. Berkeley: University of California Press.

Friedman, J. 1996. *Cultural Identity and Global Process*. London: Sage.

Friedman, J. 1997. "Global System, Globalization and the Parameters of Modernity," pp. 69-90 in *Global Modernities*, eds. M. Featherstone, S. Lash and R. Robertson. London: Sage.

Fuchs, Martin. 2004. "Articulating the World: Social Movements, the Self-transcendence of Society and the Question of Culture," pp. 37-56 in *Creative Social Research: Rethinking Themes and Methods*, ed. Ananta Kumar Giri. Lanham and Oxford: Lexington Books.

Fujimura-Fanselow, K. and A. Kameda, eds. 1995. *Japanese Women: New Feminist Perspectives on the Past,* present and Future. New York: Feminist Press at the City University of New York.

Fujita, K. and R.C. Hill, eds. 1993. *Japanese Cities in the World Economy*. Philadelphia: Temple University Press.

Fujita, S. 1998. *Kamisama Hotokesama: Gendai Shukyo no Kogengaku*. Tokyo: Aspect Publishing.

Gans, E. 1985. *The End of Culture: Towards a Generative Anthropology*. Berkeley: University of California Press.

Garon, S. and M. Mochizuki. 1993. "Negotiating Social Contracts," pp. 145-166 in *Postwar Japan as History*, ed. A. Gordon. Berkeley: University of California Press.

Geertz, Clifford. 1988. *Works and Lives: The Anthropologist as Author*. Stanford: Stanford University Press.

Gellner, E. 1983. *Nations and Nationalism*. Oxford: Basil Blackwell.

Ghosh, Devleena and Stephen Muecke. 2004. "Commerce and Culture in the Pre-colonial Indian Ocean," pp. 13-30 in *Rogue Flows: Trans-Asian Cultural Traffic*, eds. Koichi Iwabuchi, Stephen Muecke and Mandy Thomas. Hong Kong: Hong Kong University Press.

Giddens, Anthony. 1983. *Central Problems in Social Theory: Action, Structure and Contradiction in Social Analysis*. London: Macmillan.

Giddens, Anthony. 1990. *The Consequences of Modernity*. Cambridge: Polity.

Giddens, Anthony. 1991. *Modernity and Self-Identity: Self and Society in the Late Modern Age*. Stanford: Stanford University Press.

Gluck, C. 1985. Japan's Modern Myths: Ideology in the Late Meiji Period. Princeton: Princeton University Press.

Goh, Robbie B.H. 2004. "The Culture of Asian Diasporas: Intergating/Interrogating (im)migration, Habitus, Textuality," pp. 1-13 in *Asian Diasporas: Cultures, Identities, Representations*, eds. Robbie B.H. Goh and Shawn Wong. Hong Kong: Hong Kong University Press.

Goldstein, J. 1994. *Insight Meditation: The Practice of Freedom*. Boston: Shambhala.

Goodman, D.G. and M. Miyazawa. 1995. *Jews in the Japanese Mind: The History and Uses of a Cultural Stereotype*. New York: Free Press.

Goody, J. 1996. *The East in the West*. Cambridge: Cambridge University Press.

Gordon, A., ed. 1993. *Postwar Japan as History*. Berkeley: University of California Press.

Greider, W. 1997. *One World, Ready or Not: The Manic Logic of Global Capitalism*. New York: Simon and Schuster.

Greider, W. 1998. *One World, Ready or Not: The Manic Logic of Global Capitalism*. Harmondsworth: Penguin Books.

Hall, Catherine, ed. 2000. *Cultures of Empire: A Reader*. New York: Routledge.

Hall, D.L. and R.T. Ames. 1998. *Thinking from the Han: Self, Truth and Transcendence in Chinese and Western Culture*. Albany: State University of New York Press.

Hamaguchi, E. 1982. *Kanjinshugi no Shakai: Nihon* [Japan: The Interpersonalistic Society]. Tokyo: Toyo Keizai Shinposha.

Hamilton, Annette. 2004. "The Moving Zones of China: Flows of Rite and Power in Southeast Asia," pp. 31-52 in *Rogue Flows: Trans-Asian Cultural Traffic*, eds. Koichi Iwabuchi, Stephen Muecke and Mandy Thomas. Hong Kong: Hong Kong University Press.

Hamm, Bernd and Russell Smandych eds, 2005. *Cultural Imperialism: Essays on the Political Economy of Cultural Domination*. Peterborough Ontario, Broadview Press.

Hamrin, T. 2001. "Tenrikyo in Singapore: Re-representing the Japanese Presence," pp. 194-215 in *Japan in Singapore: Cultural Occurances and Cultural Flows*, eds. E. Ben-Ari and J. Clammer. Richmond: Curzon Press.

Hardacre, H. 1988. *Kurozumiko and the New Religions of Japan*. Princeton: Princeton University Press.

Hardacre, H. 2003. "After Aum: Religion and Civil Society," pp. ??? in *The State of Civil Society in Japan*, eds. S. Pharr and F. Schwartz. Cambridge and New York: Cambridge University Press.

Haynes, J. 1993. *Religion in Third World Politics*. Buckingham: Open University Press.

Heelas, Paul. ed. 1998. *Religion, Modernity and Postmodernity*. Oxford: Blackwell.

Hefner, R.W., ed. 1993. *Conversion to Christianity: Historical and Anthropological Perspectives on a Great Transformation*. Berkeley: University of California Press.

Hefner, Robert W. 1998. "Secularization and Citizenship in Muslim Indonesia," pp. 147-68 in *Religion, Modernity and Postmodernity*, ed. Paul Heelas. Oxford: Blackwell.

Heine, S. 1995. "Ie-ism ('sacred familialism') and the Discourse of Postmodernism in Relation to Nativism/Nationalism/Nihonism," pp. 25-53 in *Japan in Traditional and Postmodern Perspectives*, eds. Charles W-H. Fu and S. Heine. Albany: State University of New York Press.

Heng, G. and J. Devan. 1991. "State Fatherhood: the Politics of Nationalism, Sexuality and Race in Singapore," pp. 114-135 in *Nationalisms and Sexualities*, eds. A. Parker, *et al*. New York: Routledge.

Hetherington, Kevin. 1998. *Expressions of Identity: Space, Performance, Politics*. London and Thousand Oaks: Sage.

Hexham, Irving and Karla Poewe. 1997. *New Religions as Global Cultures*. Boulder: Westview Press.

Hinsch, B. 1990. *Passions of the Cut Sleeve: The Male Homosexual Tradition in China*. Berkeley: University of California Press.

Hobsbawn, E, and T. Ranger, eds. 1992. *The Invention of Tradition*. Cambridge: Cambridge University Press.

Honolulu: University of Hawai'i Press.

Hoston, G. 1986. *Marxism and the Crisis of Development in Prewar Japan*. Princeton: Princeton University Press.

Hsieh, J. 1978. "The Chinese Community in Singapore: the Internal Structure and its Basic Constituents," pp. 184-226 in *Studies ASEAN Sociology: Urban Society and Social Change*, ed. P.S.J. Chen. Singapore: Chopmen Publishers.

Hsu, Francis L.K. (1975). *Under the Ancestors' Shadow*. Stanford: Stanford University Press.

Hu, Y. 1996. "Writing Erratic Desire: Sexual Politics in Contemporary Chinese Fiction," pp. 49-68 in *In Pursuit of Contemporary East Asian Culture*, eds. Xiaobing Tang and S. Snyder. Boulder: Westview Press.

Ichikawa, H. 1991. *Seishin Toshite no Shintai*. Tokyo: Keisou Shobo.

Ichikawa, H. and J. Clammer, eds. 2002. *Revisiting Civil Society: Interfacing Development, Business and the International Order*. Tokyo: Sophia University Institute of Comparative Culture.

Iida, Y. 2002. *Rethinking Identitv in Modern Japan: Nationalism as Aesthetics*. London and New York: Routledge.

Ikeda, S. 1996. "The History of the Capitalist World-System vs. the History of East-Southeast Asia," *Review* 19 (1): 49-78.

International House of Japan. 2001. Beyond "Development": Searching for a New Vision: The Role of Youth in the 21st Century. Tokyo: International House of Japan and the Japan Foundation Asia Center.

International Shinto Association. 1995. Shinto and Japanese Culture. Tokyo: International Shinto Association.

Ishida, H. 1992. *Social Mobility in Contemporary Japan*. London: Macmillan.

Isin, E. and P. Wood. 1999. *Citizenship and Identity*. London: Sage. Itaca Press.

Itty, I.C. 1984. "Development Goals and Values," pp. 15-28 in *Searching for Asian Paradigms: Contribution of Youth to the Promotion of Social Goals and Cultural Values in the Development Process*, ed. I.C. Itty. Bangkok: Asian Cultural Forum on Development.

Iwabuchi, K. 2000. "Popular Culture, East Asian Modernities and Japan's Desire for the Transnational". Paper presented at the Inter-Asia Cultural Studies Conference, Fukuoka, December.

Iwamura, A.E. ed. 1996. *Re-Imagining Japanese Women.* Berkeley: University of California Press.

Iwane, K. 1993. Atarashi shakai undo no yobanseki seikatsu kurabu-dairnin [The Quarter Century of the New Social Movement: The Seikatsu Club and the Proxy Movement]. Tokyo: Kyodo Tosho Kabushiki Kaisha.

Japan Times, June 15, 2002 "Defence Agency Deals Democracy a Blow," p. 18.

Jaschok, M. 1984. "On the lives of women unwed by choice in pre-Communist China," *Republican China* 10(1).

Jaschok, M. and S. Miers, eds. 1994. *Women and Chinese Patriarchy: Submission, Servitude and Escape*. London: Zed books and Hong Kong: Hong Kong University Press.

Jasper, James, M. 1997. *The Art of Moral Protest: Culture, Biography and Creativity in Social Movements*. Chicago and London: Chicago University Press.

Jenner, W.J.F. 1994. *The Tyranny of History: The Roots of China's Crisis.* Harmondsworth: Penguin Books.

Jomo, K.S., ed. 1993. *Islamic Economic Alternatives: Critical Perspectives and New Directions*. Kuala Lumpur: Ikraq.

Jordan, Glenn and Chris Weedon, eds. 1995. *Cultural Politics: Class, Gender, Race and the Postmodern World.* Oxford: Blackwell.

Kahn, Joel S., ed. 1998. *Southeast Asian Identities: Culture and the Politics of Representation in Indonesia, Malaysia, Singapore and Thailand.* Singapore: Institute of Southeast Asian Studies.

Kammayer, K.C.W., G. Ritzer and N.R. Yetman. 1990. *Sociology: Experiencing Changing Societies*. Boston: Allyn and Bacon.

Karim, W.J. 1996. "Anthropology Without Tears: How a 'Local' Sees the 'Local' and the 'Global'," pp. 115-138 in *The Future of Anthropological Knowledge*, ed. H.L. Moore. London: Routledge.

Karim, Wazir Jahan. 1995. *'Male' and 'Female' in Developing Southeast Asia*. Oxford: Berg.

Kasulis, T.P., R.T. Ames and W. Dissanayake, eds. 1993. *Self as Body in Asian Theory and Practice*. Albany: State University of New York Press.

Kato, Norihiro. 1997. Haisengoron. Tokyo: Kodansha.

Kawada, M. 1993. *The Origins of Ethnography in Japan*. London: Kegan Paul International.

Kearney, R. 1992. *Visions of Europe*. Dublin: Wolfhound Press.

Kelly, D. and A. Reid, eds. 1998. *Asian Freedoms: The Idea of Freedom in East and Southeast Asia*. Cambridge: Cambridge University Press.

Kelly, W. 1995. "Finding a place in metropolitan Japan," pp. XXX in *Postwar Japan as History*, ed. A. Gordon. Berkeley: University of California Press.

Kiely, R. and P. Marfleet, eds. 1998. *Globalization and the Third World*. London: Routledge.

King, Ursula, ed. 1998. *Faith and Praxis in a Postmodern Age*. London and New York: Cassell.

Kisala, R. 1999. *Prophets of Peace: Pacifism and Cultural Identify in Japan's New Religions*. Honolulu: University of Hawai'i Press.

Kleinman, Arthur. 1988. *The Illness Narratives: Suffering, Healing and the Human Condition*. New York: Basic Books.

Koh, C.C. 1994. "Implementing Government Policy for the Protection of Women and Girls in Singapore 1948-66 Recollections of a Social Worker," pp. 122-140 in *Women and Patriarchy: Submission, Servitude and Escape*, eds. M. Jaschok and S. Miers. Hong Kong: Hong Kong University Press and London: Zed Books.

Kondo, D. 1990. *Crafting Selves: Power, Gender and Discourses of Identity in a Japanese Workplace*. Chicago: University of Chicago Press.

Koson Srisang. 1984. "Ethics and Politics: Youth in National Development," pp. 43-53 *Searching for Asian Perspectives: Contribution of Youth to the Promotion of Social Goals and Cultural Values in the Development Process*, ed. I.C. Itty. Bangkok: Asian Cultural Forum on Development.

Kulananda. 1997. *Western Buddhism*. London: HarperCollins.

Kumarappa, J.C. 1984. *Economy of Permanence: A Quest for Social Order*. Varanasi: Sarva Seva Sangh Prakashan.

Kusno, A. 2000. *Beyond the Postcolonial: Architecture, Urban Space and Political Culture in Indonesia*. New York: Routledge.

Kymlicka, W. 1995. *Multicultural Citizenship: A Liberal Theory of Minority Rights*. Oxford: Clarendon Press.

Kymlicka, W. and W. Norman, eds. 2000. *Citizenship in Diverse Societies*. Oxford: Oxford University Press.

LaFleur, W.R. 1974. "Saigyo and the Buddhist Value of Nature," *History of Religion* 13: 93-128, 227-148.

Lambeck, Michael. 1993. *Knowledge and Practice in Mayotte: Local Discourses of Islam, Sorcery and Spirit Possession*. Toronto and London: University of Toronto Press.

Lash, S. and J. Urry. 1994. *Economies of Signs and Space*. London: Sage.

Law, Jane Marie, ed. 1995. *Religious Reflections on the Human Body*. Bloomington: Indiana University Press.

LeBlanc, R. 1999. *Bicycle Citizens: The Political World of the Japanese Housewife*. Berkeley: University of California Press.

Lee, K.Y. 1983. "The education of women and pattern of procreation," Singapore: Regional Institute of Higher Education and Development, *Bulletin* (August).

Lewis, M.W. and K.E. Wigen. 1997. *The Myth of Continents: A Critique of Metageography*. Berkeley: University of California Press.

Lii, Ding-Tzann.(1998. "A Colonized Empire: Reflections on the Expansion of Hong Kong films in Asian countries," pp. 122-141 in *Trajectories: Inter-Asia Cultural Studies*, ed. K.H. Chen. London: Routledge.

Lim, S.T. 1992. "The Confucian Tradition and Its Future in Singapore: Historical, Cultural and Educational Perspectives," pp. 204-240 in *Asian Traditions and Modernization: Perspectives from Singapore*, ed. M.C. Yong. Singapore: Times Academic Press.

Lu, M. 1983. *Confucianism: Its Relevance to Modern Society*. Singapore: Federal Publications.

Ma, E. 2002. "Mapping Transborder Imaginations," pp. 249-263 in *In Search of Boundaries: Communication, Nation-States and Cultural Identities*, eds. J.M. Chan and B.T. McIntyre. Westport CT and London: Ablex.

Mabbett, I. 1998. "Buddhism and Freedom," pp. 19-36 in *Asian Freedoms: The Idea of Freedom in East and Southeast Asia*, eds. D. Kelly and A. Reid. Cambridge: Cambridge University Press.

Mak, L.F. 1992. "Convergence and Divergence: Traditional Voluntary Associations in Singapore," pp. 31-55 in *Asian Traditions and Modernization: Perspectives from Singapore*, ed. M.C. Yong. Singapore: Times Academic Press.

Mannoni, O. 1990. *Prospero and Caliban: The Psychology of Colonialism*. Ann Arbor: University of Michigan Press.

Manoochehri, Abbas. 2005. "Enrique Dussel and Ali Shari'ati on Cultural Imperialism," pp. 290-300 in *Cultural Imperialism: Essays on the Political Economy of Cultural Domination*, eds. Bernd Hamm and Russell Smandych. Peterborough Ontario: Broadview Press.

Marcus, G.E. and M.M.L. Fischer. 1986. *Anthropology as Cultural Critique*. Chicago: University of Chicago Press.

Marfleet, Phil. 1998. "Globalization and Religious Activism," pp. 185-215 in *Globalization and the Third World*, eds. Ray Kiely and Phil Marfleet. London and New York: Routledge.

Martin, David. 1978. *A General Theory of Secularization*. New York: Harper Colophon.

Matsui, Midori. 1998. "The Implicit Return: Kobayashi Hideo's Failure to Achieve Modernism and the Problems Concerning his Ideological Conversion (tenko)," pp. 91-103 in *Literary Intercrossings: East Asia and the West*, eds. M. Lee and A.D. Syrokomla-Stefanowska. Sydney: Wild Peony.

Matsumoto, K. 1991. *The Rise of the Japanese Corporate System*. London and New York: Kegan Paul International.

McFarland, N.H. 1967. *The Rush Hour of the Gods: A Study of new Religious Movements in Japan*. New York: Macmillan.

McGrane, B. 1989. *Beyond Anthropology: Society and the Other*. New York: Columbia University Press.

McVeigh, B.J. 2004. *Nationalism of Japan: Managing and Mystifying Identity*. Lanham and Oxford: Rowman and Littlefield.

Melton, J.G. 1994. "New Japanese Religions in the United States," pp. 33-53 in *Japanese New Religions in the West*, eds. Clarke, P.B. and J. Somers. Folkestone: Japan Library.

Merton, T. 1989. *Conjectures of a Guilty Bystander*. New York: Doubleday.

Meyer, J.W. 1980. "The World Polity and the Authority of the Nation-State," pp. 203-225 in *Studies of the Modern World System*, ed. A. Bergeson. New York: Academic Press.

Meyer, Thomas. 2001. *Identity Mania: Fundamentalism and the Politicization of Cultural Differences*. London and New York: Zed Books.

Milner, A. 1997. *The Invention of Politics in Colonial Malaya*. Cambridge: Cambridge University Press.

Miyoshi, M. and H.D. Harootunian, eds. 1989. *Postmodernism and Japan*. Durham NC: Duke University Press.

Miyoshi, M. and H.D. Harootunian, eds. 1993. *Japan in the World*. Durham, N.C.: Duke University Press.

Monbiot, G. 2003. *The Age of Consent*. London: Flamingo.

Moore, Henrietta L., ed. 2000. *Anthropological Theory Today*. Cambridge: Polity Press.

Mori, H. 1993. Korewa PKO: Kenbou to kokusaikyoryoku o kangaeru 50 wa [This is PKO: 50 stories about the constitution and international cooperation]. Tokyo: Iwanami Junior Sinsyo.

Morin, E. 1987. *Penser l'Europe*. Paris: UGE.

Morris, B. 1991. *Western Conceptions of the Individual*. Oxford: Berg.

Morris-Suzuki, T. 1998. "Unquiet Graves: Kato Norihiro and the Politics of Mourning," *Japanese Studies* 18 (1): 21-30.

Mouer, R. and Y. Sugimoto. 1986. *Images of Japanese Society*. London: Kegan Paul International.

Mulder, N. 1979. *Everyday Life in Thailand: An Interpretation*. Bangkok: Editions Duang Kamol.

Mulder, N. 1996. *Inside Southeast Asia: Religion, Everyday Life, Cultural Change*. Kuala Lumpur and Amsterdam: The Pepin Press.

Mullins, M.R. 1998. *Christianity Made in Japan: A Study of Indigenous Movements*. Honolulu: University of Hawai'i Press.

Munck, R. and D.O'Hearn, eds. 1999. *Critical Development Theory*. London: Zed Books.

Muto, I. 1998. "Alliance of Hope and the Challenges of Global Democracy," pp. 346-59 in *Trajectories: Inter-Asia Cultural Studies*, ed. Chen Kuan-Hsing. London: Routledge.

Najita, T. and H.D. Harootunian. 1998. "Japan's Revolt Against the West," pp. 247-272 in *Modern Japanese Thought*, ed. B.T. Wakabayashi. Cambridge: Cambridge University Press.

Nandy, A. 1983. *The Intimate Enemy: Loss and Recovery of Self Under Colonialism*. Bombay: Oxford University Press.

Nandy, A. 1998. "A New Cosmopolitanism: Toward a Dialogue of Asian Civilizations," pp. 142-149 in *Trajectories: Inter-Asia Cultural Studies*, ed. K.H. Chen. London: Routledge.

Naqvi, S.N.H. 1981. *Ethics and Economics: An Islamic Synthesis*. Leicester: The Islamic Foundation.

Nasr, Seyyed Hossein. 1993. The Need for a Sacred Science. Richmond: Curzon Press.

Odin, S. 1995. "Derrida and the decentered universe of Ch'an/Zen Buddhism," pp. 1-24 in *Japan in Traditional and Postmodern Perspectives*, eds. C. W-H. Fu and S. Heine. Albany: State University of New York University Press.

Okusho, K. 1972. *Kyuseishu no Shutsugen to Chijo Tengoku*. Tokyo: Kasumigaseki Shobo.

Ommundsen, Wenche. 2004. "Cultural Citizenship in Diaspora: A study of the Chinese in Australia," pp. 76-94 in *Asian Diasporas: Cultures, Identities, Representations,* eds. Robbie B.H. Goh and Shawn Wong. Hong Kong: Hong Kong University Press.

Ong Aihwa. 2000. "Clash of Civilizations or Asian Liberalism? An Anthropology of the State and Citizenship," pp. 48-72 in *Anthropological Theory Today*, ed. H.L. Moore. Cambridge; Polity.

Ong, A. 1996. "Anthropology, China and Modernities: the Geopolitics of Cultural Knowledge," pp. 60-92 in *The Future of Anthropological Knowledge*, ed. H.L. Moore. London: Routledge.

Ota, Yoshinobu. 2002. "Culture and Anthropology in the Ethnographic Present," pp. 61-80 in *Anthropology Beyond Culture*, eds. Richard Fox, G. and Barbara S. King. Oxford and New York: Berg.

Otnes, P. 1997. *Other-Wise*. Oslo; Scandinavian University Press.

Overing, *Joanna and Alan Passes*, eds. 2000. The Anthropology of Love and Anger: The Aesthetics of Conviviality in Native Amazonia. London and New York: Routledge.

Ozawa, C. 2001. "Beyond the Body/Mind? Japanese Contemporary Thinkers on Alternative Sociologies of the Body", *Body and Society* 6(8): 21-38.

Pensri Kanchanomai. 1989. "Religions and Japanese Modernization," pp. 1-41 in *Thai Perceptions of Japanese Modernization*, ed. Kunio Yoshihara. Kuala Lumpur: Falcon Press and Kyoto: Centre for Southeast Asian Studies.

Pharr, S. and F. Schwartz. eds. 2003. *The State of Civil Society in Japan*. Cambridge and New York: Cambridge University Press.

Pieris, A. 1992. *An Asian Theology of Liberation*. Maryknoll, NY: Orbis Books.

Piyasilo, Ven. 1988. *Nichiren: The New Buddhism of Modem Japan*. Petaling Jaya: The Friends of Buddhism Malaysia.

Pollack, D. 1986. *The Fracture of Meaning: Japan's Synthesis of China from the Eighth through the Eighteenth Centuries*. Princeton: Princeton University Press.

Pollmann, J. 1996. "A Different Road to God: The Protestant Experience of Conversion in the Sixteenth Century," pp. 47-64 in *Conversion to Modernities: The Globalization of Christianity*, ed. Peter van der Veer. New York and London: Routledge,.

Posey, Darrell. 2002. "Upsetting the Sacred Balance: Can the Study of Indigenous Knowledge Reflect Cosmic Connectedness?" pp. 24-42 in Participating in Development: Approaches to Indigenous Knowledge, eds. Paul Sillitoe, Alan Bicker and Johan Pottier. London and New York: Routledge.

Pracha pasannathammo, Phra. 1983. "Than phutthathat kap kanpatiwat watthannatham" [Buddhadassa Bhikku and cultural revolution], *Pacharaysan* 10(1): 51-81.

Prakash, Gyan. 1995. *After Colonialism: Imperial Histories and Postcolonial Displacements*. Princeton: Princeton University Press.

Preston, P.W. 1997. *Political/Cultural Identity: Citizens and Nations in a Global Era*. London: Sage.

Pye, M. 1994. "National and International Identity in a Japanese Religion," pp. 77-88 in *Japanese New Religions in the West*, eds. Clarke, P.B. and J. Somers. Folkestone: Japan Library.

Queen, C.S. and S.B. King, eds. 1996. *Engaged Buddhism: Buddhist Liberation Movements in Asia*. Albany: State University of New York Press.

Racelis, M. 1998. "Christianity, the State and Civil Society in the Philippines," pp. 163-177 in *Religion, Politics and Society in South and Southeast Asia*, eds. N.N. Vohra and J.N. Dixit. Delhi: Konark Publications.

Rao, V.K.R.V. 1970. The Gandhian Alternative to Western Socialism. Bombay: Bharatiya Vidya Bhavan.

Raslan, Karim. 2002. *Journeys Through Southeast Asia*. Singapore and Kuala Lumpur: Times Books International.

Reader, I. 1991. *Religion in Contemporary Japan*. Honolulu: University of Hawaii Press.

Ritzer, C. 1996. *The McDonaldization of Society: An Investigation into the Changing Character of Contemporary Social Life*. Thousand Oaks, CA: Pine Forge Press.

Robertson, R. 1989. "Globalization, Politics and Religion," pp. 10-23 in *The Changing Face of Religion*, eds. James A. Beckford and Thomas Luckmann. Beverly Hills: Sage.

Robertson, R. 1992. *Globalization: Social Theory and Global Culture*. London: Sage.

Rohlen, T.P. 1979. *For Harmony and Strength: Japanese White Collar Organization in Anthropological Perspective*. Berkeley: University of California Press.

Rosenberger, N. 1993. "Japanese Young Women and Elite Global Identities: Constructions and Contradictions". Paper Presented to the American Anthropological Association, Washington D.C., November.

Sachs, W., ed. 1995. *The Development Dictionary: A Guide to Knowledge and Power*. London: Zed Books.

Said, E. 1978. *Orientalism*. London: Routledge and Kegan Paul.

Said, E. 1993. *Culture and Imperialism*. London: Chatto and Windus.

Sakai, N. 1989. "Modernity and its Critique: the Problem of Universalism and Particularism," pp. 93-122 in *Postmodernism and Japan*, eds. M. Miyoshi and H.D. Harootunian. Durham, NC: Duke University Press.

Salaff, J.W. 1988. *State and Family in Sinapore*. Itham: Cornell University Press.

Saliba, J.A. 1995. *Perspectives on New Religious Movements*. London: Geoffrey Chapman.

Sassen, S. 1990. *The Global City*. Princeton: Princeton University Press.

Sa-nga Luchaphattthanaphorn, ed. 1981. Wikrittakan Ekkalakthai [The Crisis of Thai Identity]. Bangkok: Pacharaysan.

Saunders, E.D. 1972. *Buddhism in Japan*. Rutland, Vt., Tuttle.

Schech, S. and J. Harris. 2000. *Culture and Development: A Critical Introduction*. Oxford: Blackwell.

Schech, Susanne and Jane Haggis. 2000. *Culture and Development*. Oxford: Blackwell.

Schumacher, E.F. 1973. "Buddhist Economics," pp. 231-239 in *Toward a Steady-State Economy*, ed. H.E. Daly. San Francisco: W.H. Freeman and Company.

Schumacher, E.F. 1979. *Small is Beautiful: A Study of Economics as if People Mattered*. London: Abacus.

Schuurman, P.J., ed. 1996. *Beyond the Impasse: New Directions in Development Theory*. London: Zed Books.

Schwartz, F. and S. Pharr, eds. 2003. *The State of Civil Society in Japan*. Cambridge and New York: Cambridge University Press.

Scott, James C. 1985. *Weapons of the Weak: Everyday Forms of Peasant Resistance*. New Haven and London: Yale University Press.

Seagrave, S. 1996. *Lords of the Rim*. London: Corgi Books.

Seidensticker, E. 1983. *Low City, High City: Tokyo from Edo to the Earthquake*. New York: Knopf.

Seider, V.J. 1994. *Recovering the Self*. London; Routledge.

Shamsul, A.B. 1999. "Consuming Anthropology: The Social Sciences and Nation-Formation in Malaysia," pp. 133-157 in *Consuming Ethnicity and Nationalism: Asian Experiences*, ed. K. Yoshino. Richmond: Curzon Press.

Sheridan, G. 1999. *Asian Values, Western Dreams: Understanding the New Asia*. St Leonards NSW: Allen and Unwin.

Shimoda, M. 1994. *Japan's 'Guest Workers': Issues and Public Policies*. Tokyo: University of Tokyo Press.

Shohat, E. and R. Stam. 1994. *Unthinking Eurocentrism; Multiculturalism and the Media*. London: Routledge.

Sivaraksa, S. 1992. *Seeds of Peace: A Buddhist Vision for Renewing Society*. Berkeley: Parallax Press.

Sivaraksa, S. *et al.* eds. 1991. *Searching for Asian Cultural Integrity*. Bangkok: Sanit Pracha Dhamma Trust.

Smith, L.T. 1999. *Decolonizing Methodologies: Research and Indigenous Peoples*. London: Zed books, Dunedin: University of Otago Press.

Smith, Linda Tuhiwai. 1999. *Decolonizing Methodologies: Research and Indigenous Peoples*. London: Zed Books and Dunedin: University of Otago Press.

Solinger, D.J. 1999. *Contesting Citizenship in Urban China: Peasant Migrants, the State and the Logic of the Market*. Berkeley: University of California Press.

Somboon Siriprachai. 1997. "Inconsistencies and Inequalities in Thai Industrialization," pp. 183-205 in *Social Change in Southeast Asia*, eds. J. Dragsbaek Schmidt, J. Hersh and N. Fold. Harlow: Longman.

Somboon Suksamran. 1977. *Political Buddhism in Southeast Asia: The Role of the Sangha in the Modernization of Thailand*. London: C. Hurst.

Soysal, Y. 1994. *The Limits of Citizenship*. Chicago: Chicago University Press.

Spivak, G.C. 1990. *The Postcolonial Critic*. New York: Routledge.

Srivastava, R.K., ed. 1998. *Vital Connections: Self, Society, God: Perspectives on Swadhyaya*. New York and Tokyo: Weatherhill.

Stanley, T.A. 1988. "Japan as a Model for Economic Development: the Example of Singapore," pp. 232-244 in *Japan and the World*, eds. G.L. Bernstein and H. Fukui. London: Macmillan Press.

Starr, A. 2000. *Naming the Enemy: Anti-Corporate Movements Confront Globalization*. London: Zed Books.

Steven, R. 1983. *Classes in Contemporary Japan*. Cambridge: Cambridge University Press.

Stevenson, N., ed. 2000. *Culture and Citizenship*. London: Sage.

Stone, J.I. 2003. "Nichiren's Activist Heirs: Soka Gakkai, Rissho Koseikai, Nipponzan Myohoji," pp. 63-94 in *Action Dharma: New Studies in Engaged Buddhism*, eds. C. Queen, C. Prebish and D. Keown. London: RoutledgeCurzon.

Straits Times (Singapore) (1987) August 8.

Sugimoto, Y. 1999. "Making Sense of Nihonjinron," *Thesis Eleven* 57: 81-96.

Sugirtharajah, R.S., ed. 1998. *The Postcolonial Bible*. Sheffield: Sheffield Academic Press.

Sulak Sivaraksa. 1977. "Religion and Development," pp. 11-18 in *Questioning Development in Southeast Asia*, ed. N. Chng. Singapore: Select Books.

Sulak, Sivaraksa. 1979. *Siam in Crisis*. Bangkok: Asian Cultural Forum on Development.

Sulak, Sivaraksa. 1984. "Culture and Development in Southeast Asia," pp. 29-42 in *Searching for Asian Paradigms*, ed. C.I. Itty. Bangkok: Asian Cultural Forum on Development.

Sulak, Sivaraksa. 1985. *Siamese Resurgence: A Thai Buddhist Voice on Asia and a World of Change*. Bangkok: Asian Cultural Forum on Development.

Sulak, Sivaraksa. 1991a. "The Crisis of Siamese Identity," pp. 13-26 in *Santi Pracha Dhamma Institute, Searching for Asian Cultural Integrity*. Bangkok: Sathirakoses-Nagapradipa Foundation.

Sulak, Sivaraksa. 1991b. "Non-violence vs. Revolutionary Change," pp. 166-215 in *Searching for Asian Cultural Integrity*. Bangkok: Sathirakuses-Nagapradipa Foundation.

Sulak, Sivaraksa. 1992. *Seeds of Peace: A Buddhist Vision for Renewing Society*. Berkeley: Parallax Press.

Sulak, Sivaraksa. 1998. *Loyalty Demands Dissent: Autobiography of an Engaged Buddhist*. Berkeley: Parallax Press.

Suwanna Satha-Anand. 1999. "Looking to Buddhism to Turn Back Prostitution in Thailand," pp. 193-211 in *The East Asian Challenge for Human Rights*, eds. J.R. Bauer and D.A. Bell. Cambridge: Cambridge University Press.

Tamney, J.B. n.d. "An Analysis of the Decline of Allegiance to Chinese Religion," pp. 12-24 in *Analysis of an Asian Society-Singapore*, eds. Riaz Hassan and J.B. Tamney. Singapore: Department of Sociology, University of Singapore.

Tarrow, S. 1996. *Power in Movement: Social Movements, Collective Action and Politics*. Cambridge: Cambridge University Press.

Tenzin Gyatso (The Dalai Lama). 2000. *Ancient Wisdom. Modern World: Ethics for the New Millennium*. London: Abacus.

Thanet Aphornsuvan. 1998. "Slavery and Freedom: Freedom in the Making of Modern Siam," pp. 161-186 in *Asian Freedoms: The Idea of Freedom in East and Southeast Asia*, eds. D. Kelly and A. Reid. Cambridge: Cambridge University Press.

Thich Nhat Hanh. 1991. *Peace in Every Step: The Path of Mindfulness in Everyday Life*. London: Rider.

Thomas, Nicholas. 1994. *Colonialism's Culture: Anthropology, Travel and Government*. Cambridge: Polity Press.

Thomsen, H. 1963. The New Religions of Japan. Tokyo: Charles E. Tuttle.

Thongchai, Winichakul. 1997. *Siam Mapped: A History of the Geo-Body of a Nation*. Honolulu: University of Hawai'i Press.

Thornsen, H. 1963. *The New Religions of Japan*. Rutland, Vt. and Tokyo: Charles E. Tuttle.

Tobin, J.J., ed. 1992. *Remade in Japan: Everyday Life and Consumer Taste in a Changing Society*. New Haven: Yale University Press.

Tomlinson, John. 2000. *Globalization and Culture*. Cambridge: Polity Press.

Topley, M. 1954. "Chinese Women's Vegetarian Houses in Singapore," *Journal of the Malayan Branch of the Royal Asiatic Society* 27(1).

Topley, M. 1975. "Marriage Resistance in Rural Kwangtung," pp. 94-124 in *Women in Chinese Society*, eds. M. Wolf and R. Witke. Stanford: Stanford University Press.

Toynbee, A. and D. Ikeda. 1989. Choose Life: A Dialogue. Oxford: Oxford University Press.

Tripathy, Biyot K. 2005. "Redefining Cultural Imperialism and the Dynamics of Culture Contacts," pp. 300-316 in *Cultural Imperialism: Essays on the Political Economy of Cultural Domination*, eds. Bernd Hamm and Russell Smandych. Peterborough Ontario: Broadview Press.

Turner, B.S. 1994. *Orientalism, Postmodernism and Globalization*. London: Routledge.

Ueno, C. 1999. "The Politics of Memory: Nation, Individual and Self," *History and Memory* 2 (2): 129-152.

UNESCO/UNADI. 1977. Asian Rethinking on Development. New Delhi: Abhinav Publications.

Upham, F. 1987. *Law and Social Change in Postwar Japan*. Cambridge, MA and London: Harvard University Press.

Van Breman, J. and A. Shimizu, eds. 1999. *Anthropology and Colonialism in Asia and Oceania*. Richmond: Curzon Press.

Van der Mehden, F.R. 1968. *Religion and Nationalism in Southeast Asia*. Madison: University of Wisconsin Press.

Van der Veer, P., ed. 1996. *Conversion to Modernities: The Globalization of Christianity*. New York and London: Routledge.

Vaughan-Lee, L. 1993. *The Bond With the Beloved*. Inverness, Cal.: The Golden Sufi Center.

Viswanathan, G. 1998. *Outside the Fold: Conversion, Modernity and Belief.* Princeton: Princeton University Press.

Vlastos, S., ed. 1993. *Mirror of Modernity: Invented Traditions in Modern Japan.* Berkeley: University of California Press.

Vohra, N.N. and J.N. Dixit, eds. 1998. *Religion, Politics and Society in South and Southeast Asia.* New Delhi: Konark Publishers.

Wakabayashi, B.T., ed. 1998. *Modern Japanese Thought.* Cambridge: Cambridge University Press.

Ward, B. 1965. "Varieties of the Conscious Model: the Fishermen of South," pp. 113-137 in *The Relevance of Models for Social Anthropology,* ed. M. Banton. London: Tavistock.

Warren, J.F. 1994. *Ah Ku and Karayuki-san: Prostitution and Singapore Society.* Singapore: Oxford University Press.

Watson, J.L. and E.S. Rauski, eds. 1988. *Death in Late Imperial and Modern China.* Berkeley. University of California Press.

Watson, J.L., ed. 1998. Golden Arches East: McDonald's in East Asia. Palo Alto, CA: Stanford University Press.

Watson, R. 1991. "Wives, Concubines and Maids: Servitude and Kinship in the Hong Kong Region 1900-1940," pp. 231-255 in *Marriage and Inequality in Chinese Society,* eds. R.S. Watson and P.B., Ebrey. Berkeley: University of California Press.

Watson, R.S. and P.B. Ebrey, eds. 1991. *Marriage and Inequality in Chinese Society.* Berkeley: University of California Press.

Wee, C.J.W. 1997. "Buying Japan: Singapore, Japan and East Asian Modernity". *Journal of Pacific-Asia,* 4, 21-46.

Weiner, M., ed. 1997. *Japan's Minorities: The Illusion of Homogeneity.* London and New York: Routledge.

Weller, R.P. 1999. *Alternative Civilities: Democracy and Culture in China and Taiwan.* Boulder, Colorado: Westview Press.

Wexler, Philip. 1990. "Citizenship in the Semiotic Society," pp. 164-175 in *Theories of Modernity and Postmodernity,* ed. Bryan S. Turner. London and Newbury Park: Sage.

Whang Soon-Hee. 2002. W Hai Saka no Nekyoa to Zsan: 2002 nen nikan warrudokapu o megute [Enthusiasm and Inheritance of the World Cup: About the 2002 Japan-Korean World Cup]. Tokyo: Sekashiso Seminar.

Wignaraja, P., ed. 1993. *New Social Movements in the South.* London: Zed Books.

Williams, P. and L. Chrisman, eds. 1993. *Colonial Discourse and Post-Colonial Theory.* Hemel Hempstead: Harvester Wheatsheaf.

Wilson, B. 1982. *Religion in Sociological Perspective.* New York: Oxford University Press.

Wolf, M. 1994. *A Thrice Told Tale: Feminism, Postmodernism and Ethnographic Responsibility*. Stanford: Stanford University Press.

Yoneyama, L. 1999. *Hiroshima Traces: Time, Space and the Dialectics of Memory*. Berkeley: University of California Press.

Yoo, David K., ed. 1999. *New Spiritual Homes: Religion and Asian Americans*. Honolulu: University of Hawai'i Press.

Yoshihara, Kunio, ed. 1989. *Thai Perceptions of Japanese Modernization*. Kyoto: Centre for Southeast Studies and Kuala Lumpur: Falcon Press.

Yoshino, K. 1992. *Cultural Nationalism in Contemporary Japan*. London; Routledge.

Yoshino, K. 1997. *Bunka Nashonarizumu no Shakaigaku* [*The Sociology of Cultural Nationalism*]. Nagoya: Nagoya Daigaku Shuppankai.

Yuasa, Y. 1987. *The Body: Towards an Eastern Mind-Body Theory*. Albany: State University of New York Press.

Yuasa, Y. 1993. *The Body, Self-Cultivation and Ki-Energy*. Albany: State University of New York Press.

Zito, A. and T.E. Barlow, eds. 1994. *Body, Subject and Power in China*. Chicago: Chicago University Press.

Zohar, D. 1990. *The Quantum Self*. London: Flamingo.

Index

Creative Multiverse: New Explorations in Transformative Learning and Research

There is an epochal challenge of learning from multiple experiments in self and social transformations now. *Creative Multiverse* seeks to explore and present different pathways of transformations in societies and histories around the world. It builds upon engagements in learning in different disciplines of life and academy and seeks to create a transdisciplinary space of research, dialogues and transformations.

A Series from Shipra Publications, Delhi
Email: info@shiprapublications.com

Editor: Ananta Kumar Giri,
Madras Institute of Development Studies, Chennai, India.
Email: aumkrishna@yahoo.com; Website: www.mids.ac.in/ananta.htm

International Editorial Advisory Board